W9-APL-433

Florida Butterfly Gardening

Marc C. Minno and Maria Minno

Illustrations by Diane Pierce

Foreword by Thomas C. Emmel

University Press of Florida

GAINESVILLE TALLAHASSEE TAMPA BOCA RATON PENSACOLA ORLANDO MIAMI JACKSONVILLE

# Florida Butterfly Gardening

A Complete Guide to Attracting, Identifying, and Enjoying Butterflies of the Lower South

Gulf Fritillaries visiting Carolina Aster flowers

Copyright 1999 by the Board Regents of the State of Florida
Printed in Hong Kong through Asia Pacific Offset, Inc., on acid-free paper
All rights reserved

07  06  05  04  03  02      7  6  5  4  3  2

Library of Congress Cataloging-in-Publication Data
Minno, Marc C.
Florida butterfly gardening: a complete guide to attracting, identifying, and
enjoying butterflies of the lower South / Marc C. Minno and Maria Minno;
illustrations by Diane Pierce; foreword by Thomas C. Emmel.
p. cm.
Includes bibliographical references (p.   ) and index.
ISBN 0-8130-1665-7 (cl.: alk. paper)
1. Butterfly gardening—Florida. I. Minno, Maria. II. Title.
QL544.6.M55   1999
638'.5789—dc21   99-12040

The University Press of Florida is the scholarly publishing agency for the
State University System of Florida, comprising Florida A & M University,
Florida Atlantic University, Florida International University, Florida State
University, University of Central Florida, University of Florida, University
of North Florida, University of South Florida, and University of West
Florida.

University Press of Florida
15 Northwest 15th Street
Gainesville, FL 32611
http://www.upf.com

In loving memory of Alain George Minno

There was a child went forth every day,
And the first object he looked upon and received with
wonder or pity or love or dread, that object
he became,
And that object became a part of him for the day or a certain
part of the day . . . or for many years or stretching
cycles of years.
The early lilacs became part of this child,
And grass and white and red morningglories, and white
and red clover, and the song of the phoebe-bird . . .
—Walt Whitman, *Leaves of Grass*

For my two fathers—
I'm so lucky to have both!
—Maria

# Contents

# Foreword

Our natural childhood fascination with butterflies and other creatures of the world of nature has grown in recent years to encompass many adult pursuits as well. Among these, butterfly gardening has become an exceptionally popular avocation. A plethora of books on butterfly gardening have appeared, and nurseries across the country now stock plants for both butterfly nectar sources (to attract the adults) and butterfly food plants (to increase the number of butterflies breeding in the backyard or in public landscaping areas such as parks).

What we have long lacked is a book devoted specifically to Florida and the Southeast, where butterfly gardening can take place twelve months a year. The subtropical climate of our state allows a wonderful abundance of butterfly species to flourish. A great many of their preferred nectar sources and host plants make attractive additions to the Florida or southeastern garden. The opening of new attractions such as Butterfly World at Coconut Creek in south Florida and Wings of Wonder at Cypress Gardens in central Florida have caused a burgeoning interest in butterfly gardening among tens of thousands of Florida's residents annually—yet they lack a good manual on how to create their own butterfly garden.

Now Marc and Maria Minno have written a beautifully illustrated book that will fill this gap. With this book anyone can make a successful butterfly garden and attract these beautiful creatures to year-round profusion. More than seventy of Florida's most common butterflies and a dozen of the more interesting moth species are authoritatively covered in the text and are illustrated with beautiful photographs, including color plates of caterpillars, pupae, and host plants. Additional color plates painted by Diane Pierce depict not only nectar plants for the adults, but food plants for the larvae as well. Her experience as an avid butterfly gardener for more than ten years is reflected in the delicate detail that she incorporates in her evocative work.

Truly, this is a book to use and to treasure. One can browse in it for a few minutes before heading to the nursery and selecting some plants to start a garden. Or one can spend hours going through it, devouring each delicious morsel of information on the butterflies that you want to attract to your Florida garden. Careful planning with this book will make anyone a successful butterfly gardener and will greatly enrich the lives not only of the gardener and his or her family, but all the friends and relatives who will come to see the memorable display of living butterflies and their intimate associates among the plants.

Authoritative and thorough, comprehensive and yet easily readable, *Florida Butterfly Gardening* conveys with exceptional effectiveness the excitement and thrills that lie ahead of you as you begin gardening for butterflies.

Thomas C. Emmel
*Director, Division of Lepidoptera Research*
*University of Florida*

# *Acknowledgments*

We very much appreciate the help of Timothy Adams (Dunedin), Mary Barfield (Miami), Henry Block (Miami), Janice Broda (Vero Beach), Jana Campbell (Hollywood), Becky Centoducati (Miami), R. Clark (Kissimmee), Harry Dalvine (Tampa); R. G. Dickinson (Hollywood), Alana Edwards (Delray Beach), G. B. Edwards (Florida Department of Agriculture and Consumer Services), Judy Ensley (Hollywood), Heather Federkeil (Hollywood), Deborah Grimes (Lutz), Roger Hammer (Dade County Parks), Thomas Hecker (Missouri Botanical Garden), Claire Herzog (Sarasota), Richard Hesterberg (Wings of Wonder Butterfly Conservatory), Anna Johnston (Fort Lauderdale), Palmer Kinser (Palatka), Catherine LaBrie (Sarasota), Sharon LaPlante (Odessa), Claudia Larson (Micanopy), Patricia Leffingwell (Melbourne), Steven Lenberger (Naples), J. Lutz (Davie), Valeri McHugh (Plantation), Judy Morris (Sarasota), Regina Muchmore (Tampa), Thomas Neal (Gainesville), Patti and Milt Putnam (Gainesville), Jeffrey R. Slotten (Gainesville), Thomas Tomlinson (Palm City), Lois Weber (Palm Harbor), Nancy West (Bradenton), and Ruth Wing (Seminole). Their gardening advice, butterfly information, plants, and caterpillars contributed in many ways to the production of this book. Some of the nature study activities were suggested by Dr. Peter Feinsinger. Many thanks also go to Jim Tuttle of Troy, Michigan, for allowing us to use his photo of the Hummingbird Clearwing caterpillar. Milt Putnam of Gainesville generously donated several of his butterfly garden slides as well. All other photographs are by Marc and Maria Minno. This book would not have been possible without the help of Kenneth J. Scott, Lynn Werts, Gillian Hillis, and Larry Leshan of the University Press of Florida.

# Introduction

What is your vision of a beautiful garden? Is it a peaceable kingdom of tropical flowers and exotic animals? Imagine a yard alive with colorful butterflies frolicking among red, yellow, blue, and white flowers. This could be your yard, no matter if you live in the heart of Miami or far from the bustling city. Not all flowers are attractive to butterflies, nor do their caterpillars eat the leaves of just any plant. In order to bring butterflies to your yard, you must know which kinds of plants to grow. Developing a butterfly garden is a way of relieving stress, meeting other people, and enriching the landscape in order to make your yard, neighborhood, and community a better place to live.

Why do Americans spend so much time, money, and labor growing grass? Short-cut grass surrounding the home was a rarity before the development of varieties suitable for lawns (all non-native species) and of mowing machinery. In the South, yards were often swept dirt enlivened by kitchen or border gardens. At the beginning of the twentieth century, lawns in upper-class neighborhoods and on golf courses helped to create a new landscape aesthetic. Through educational programs and advertising from the emerging lawn care industry, Americans began to view lawns as a symbol of wealth and domestic values (Jenkins 1994). The new aesthetic took hold in a big way. Few Americans today would view their home as complete without a large grassy yard. In 1991 there were some 45 million lawns covering 30 million acres of the United States. The lawn care industry generates many billions of dollars annually. But this mad scramble to have good looking grass isn't necessarily healthy for people. More than 70 million pounds of chemical fertilizers, herbicides, and pesticides are applied to lawns each year in the United States. That's a tremendous amount of water, air, and soil pollution! Also, exhaust from lawn mowers is a significant source of air pollution.

In a sense, some of us have been brainwashed into thinking that large grassy lawns are the only way that yards can be landscaped. However, new and environmentally sound aesthetics are beginning to take hold. Butterfly gardening is environmentally friendly, adds more value to your home than a simple grass lawn, and brings beautiful butterflies to live amidst a bounty of flowers at your doorstep!

Butterfly gardening is not only for the homeowner. Schools throughout Florida and the Southeast are planting and maintaining butterfly gardens. Teachers generally agree that hands-on experience is the best approach for learning. Lessons on plant-insect interactions, predation, pollination, dispersal, population dynamics, life cycles, and other ecological interactions among organisms, or between organisms and their environment, can be applied directly on the school grounds (Feinsinger and Minno 1990). Later in this book, you will find hands-on activities that can be carried out with butterflies.

Butterfly gardening also serves a therapeutic function (Morris and Herzog 1995). Growing plants and butterflies is helping many patients recovering from injuries to relearn living skills and rebuild self-confidence and independence. Residents of nursing homes and other facilities for the elderly receive joy and satisfaction from caring for butterfly gardens and watching the seasonal changes of the plants or the metamorphosis of the butterflies. Similarly, day care centers with butterfly gardens give children a chance to explore and inquire about our natural world.

A butterfly garden may be as ephemeral as a pot of parsley on the patio, as elegant as a border of mixed perennials, or as elaborate as an entire yard. Various styles such as natural gardening, wildlife gardening, square foot gardening, organic gardening, and xeric landscaping can be applied to the butterfly garden. This guide will open a window on the secret lives of butterflies, and more! At the beginning of the book you will find information on butterfly biology, behavior, and identification. The middle section gives detailed natural history accounts and color photos of more than sixty butterflies and a dozen moths commonly found in our gardens. Next follows a few easy steps toward creating and caring for your garden. At the end of the book are activities for students, a checklist of Florida butterflies, and a resource guide for books, magazines, public gardens, and sources of plants and equipment. Gentle reader, proceed with caution through the following chapters. They may change your life!

# Understanding Butterflies

Spicebush Swallowtails frolicking around a Sweet Bay.

## Butterfly Evolution

Butterflies are day-flying insects that have four wings, scales, and clubbed antennae. Together with moths they compose the group Lepidoptera, or scale-winged insects. The closest living relatives of butterflies and moths are the caddisflies (Trichoptera or hair-winged insects). These are somewhat similar in appearance to the Lepidoptera, but caddisflies have larvae that are aquatic and the wings are covered with short hairs. Caddisflies have chewing type mouthparts, but the jaws are very reduced in size, and the adults feed mostly on liquids.

Fossil lepidopterans are quite rare. The oldest known are tiny moths that lived from 100 to 130 million years ago, during the time of the dinosaurs. The oldest butterfly fossils are much younger, at about 48 million years old, which is long after the dinosaurs had passed into extinction. When flowering plants diversified profusely near the end of the Cretaceous Period, the Lepidoptera did likewise.

Butterflies and moths are closely dependent upon flowering plants for food. Now over 190,000 species of moths and 15,000 species of butterflies are known throughout the world. Many others remain to be discovered. In Florida, it's doubtful that any new butterflies will be found, but new moths are discovered on a regular basis.

Butterflies are derived from moths, but which group? There are about a hundred different families of moths. Some day-flying moths have evolved butterfly-like characteristics, such as clubbed antennae and colorful wings, but they are only distant butterfly relatives. Of the moths, it appears that the Hedylidae, small tropical moths related to inchworms (Geometridae), are the closest living cousins of the butterflies.

Differentiating butterflies from moths can sometimes be confusing, but with a little practice and some keen observation even difficult species become easy. Generally butterflies are day-active insects with clubbed antennae and colorful wings. At rest the wings are usually held pressed together over the back. Most moths are active at night. The antennae are either feathery or slender throughout (even at the tip), and the wings are held at the sides while at rest. Moths often have more hairlike scales on the body than butterflies, and some look fuzzy or furry.

## Butterfly Form and Function

Adult butterflies and other insects are composed of three body regions: the head (the sensory and feeding section), the thorax (the locomotion section), and the abdomen (the digestion and reproduction section). Each body region is further made up of segments. Butterflies and moths are covered with tiny scales, not only on the wings, but on the body, antennae, and legs as well. Without scales, the body is plain brown or black. The exterior of the body is made of hard plates. In order to allow for movement and growth, a flexible membrane connects the plates. This outer layer or exoskeleton is not made of cells, but is a mixture of chitin (a carbohydrate) and proteins. A thin layer of wax on the outside of the exoskeleton helps prevent water loss.

### Head

The segments of the butterfly head are fused into a hard capsule. There are two large compound eyes on each side of the head. The compound eyes are composed of hundreds of six-sided individual simple eyes (ommatidia). These are dark and opaque on most swallowtails, skippers, hairstreaks, and blues but are clear with small dark spots or stripes on other butterflies. No one knows exactly what butterfly vision is like, but most seem to see very well. They are easily able to detect movement, such as the sweep of a hand.

Insect eyes are sensitive to a different range of color than human eyes. They are able to distinguish colors into the ultraviolet range, but often cannot see red light. Thus, yellow or red porch lights attract fewer moths and other insects than white lights. Swallowtails, sulphurs, and heliconians, however, are readily attracted to red flowers.

### Antennae

At the top of the head is a pair of long antennae. Each antenna has numerous segments. Those near the tip are enlarged, forming a club. Except for part of the club, the antennae are covered by scales that often form checkered black and white patterns. The surface of the antenna has tiny sensory hairs, pegs, and pits that help the butterfly find host plants, flowers, and mates.

1. The face of a Fiery Skipper.

### Palpi

At the lower part of the head near the mouth is a pair of three-segmented, brushlike sensory structures called palpi. The size and orientation of the palpi vary from species to species. In most species they curve upward, covering the face. The Snout Butterflies (family Libytheidae) have enormously long palpi that project forward like a beak.

### Proboscis

Between the palpi lies the flexible proboscis, or "tongue," of the butterfly. The proboscis is made up of two parts, each of which has a groove along the inner side. When the adult emerges from the chrysalis, the two separate parts of the proboscis can often be seen. However, as the butterfly quickly begins to coil and uncoil the proboscis, the two halves permanently fuse together into a kind of drinking straw. Unlike a straw, however, the proboscis has muscles, nerves, and air tubes down its length. Blood forced into the proboscis extends it. Muscles enable the proboscis to move during feeding. There are tiny sensory pegs on the outside of the proboscis, especially near the tip, that help the butterfly find and taste the nectar in flowers. Zebra Longwings use these structures to help gather pollen, a source of protein.

### Thorax

The thorax is the thick, middle part of the body, where the legs and wings are attached. This region is made up of three fused segments. The first segment (the prothorax) is smaller than the other two and has a pair of legs on the underside. The middle segment (the mesothorax) bears the forewings and the middle legs. The last part (the metathorax) has the hindwings and the hind legs. There are two breathing holes (spiracles) on each side of the thorax, between segments 1 and 2 and segments 2 and 3.

### Legs

The legs are composed of several sections. From body to toe the leg sections are called the coxa, trochanter, femur, tibia, and tarsus. The coxa connects the leg to the body. The trochanter is a small segment that forms a movable joint with the coxa. The opposite end of the trochanter is firmly fixed to the femur. The femur and tibia are the longest parts of the leg. The last section, the tarsus, has five segments.

Most leg movement occurs between the trochanter and coxa and between the femur and tibia. The tibia often has rows of spines and one or two pairs of enlarged spines called spurs. The tarsus also has spines, sensory structures, and a pair of claws at the tip. Butterflies sometimes use some of the smaller spines on the tarsus to pierce or scratch the leaves of plants. Females taste plants with receptors on the tarsus to find out if they are the proper host plant. Other receptors allow both sexes to taste and feed. Touching a bit of paper towel soaked in dilute honey to the tarsus of a captive butterfly often causes the proboscis to uncurl.

The forelegs are usually smaller than the others. Skippers, swallowtails, and some moths have a small extension on the foretibia (the epiphysis) that they use to clean their antennae. The forelegs of female blues and hairstreaks are much smaller than those of the males. Both sexes of brushfooted butterflies have tiny, brushlike forelegs.

### Abdomen

The abdomen is the slender, hind part of the butterfly's body. It is composed of ten segments. Segments 1 through 7 have a spiracle for breathing on each side. Segments 9 and 10 are modified for mating, egg laying, and excretion. Males have a pair of claspers (valvae) on segment 9 that grab the tip of the female's abdomen during mating. Females have two reproductive openings, one used for mating and another for laying eggs.

## Wings

The wings are a double layer of waxpaper-like sheets with hollow, tubular veins between. The veins in the wings follow a basic pattern found in all winged insects. The pattern varies among families of insects but is relatively constant within a family. Most butterflies have a subcostal and five radial veins near the leading edge of the forewings. There are also three medial and two cubital veins toward the middle of the outer margin, and one or two anal veins near the hind margin of the wings. The veins form a closed polygon, the cell, with spokes radiating out to the margin at regular intervals. The hindwing pattern is similar. The veins are a source of support and strength in the fragile wing.

## Scales and Colors

Attached to the wings and body are multitudes of scales. Each scale was formed from a single cell. Scales vary greatly in shape according to species and location on the body. Mostly they are broad and flat throughout their length with a short basal attachment. On the wings they overlap like shingles. Scales do not grow after the adult is formed. Once they are lost, they cannot be replaced. The scales are rather loosely attached in some butterflies such as hairstreaks, and handling those butterflies is likely to leave quantities of scales on your fingers. In others, especially those that are poisonous to birds, the scales are more firmly attached and do not dislodge easily. Color patterns formed by the scales are important to the adults for recognizing the opposite sex. Some scales are modified for the dispersal of scents (pheromones) used to communicate between the sexes. Scales also have a thermoregulation function. They serve as heat collectors that help to warm the butterfly on cool mornings. Some scales near the body are hair-like and probably help the body retain heat.

The colors that we see on butterfly wings are derived in several different ways. Only rarely is the wing membrane colored. The color patterns of butterflies are due to the scales. Scales usually contain pigments, and groups of similarly colored scales form the wing patterns. Colors may also be derived by the blending of differently colored scales in a single patch. For instance,

the spring form of the Checkered White has greenish streaks along the veins. Upon closer inspection with a lens, however, one can see that the streaks are really a mixture of black scales and yellow scales that blend to a shade of green when viewed from farther away.

The iridescent colors of some butterflies, particularly hairstreaks and blues, are not derived from pigments but from the refraction of light. The iridescent scales have ridges and other features that break up white light into its component colors. Most of the colors are absorbed by melanin in the scales—except for the reflected light. All iridescent colors and nearly all blues and greens are structural colors. The color of a brilliant blue butterfly will change to violet or black if your viewing angle changes. Due to the lack of light-absorbing pigments, colorless scales appear as white because all of the light is reflected. Sometimes the scales of certain patches are greatly reduced in size or fall off soon after the adult emerges. The result is transparent or translucent spots or patches on the wings. Many skippers and some moths have this type of pattern.

Butterfly wings may also have color patterns that most people cannot see. These patterns show up in the ultraviolet range of the color spectrum. Butterflies and many other insects see well into the ultraviolet range, but human vision usually stops at violet. The hidden patterns can be viewed by using special photography techniques. A butterfly that appears to be yellow to us may be dark (UV absorbing) or iridescent (UV reflecting) to other butterflies. Many flowers as well have hidden patterns that help guide insect visitors to the nectar.

## Pheromones

Some species have androconial scales that help release pheromones during courtship. Pheromones are scents that act as hormones. These modified scales may be in distinctive patches or in small bundles (hair pencils), and may have fine fringes that increase surface area. Androconial scales can be seen on the outer border of the Cloudless Sulphur, as a small button near the edge of the forewing in hairstreaks, or as a line through the middle of the forewing in many branded skippers such as the Whirlabout. The broadwinged skippers frequently have the androconial scales in a linear patch along the forewing, which is covered by a narrow flap of the wing. Glandular tissue on the wings below the scales produce the pheromones.

Male milkweed butterflies have a small black pouch near the middle of the hindwing. This gland produces the pheromone chemicals. The males also have a pair of short hair pencils at the tip of the abdomen. Usually the hair pencils are withdrawn into the body and are not visible. Before courting a female, the male bends the abdomen upward, while the wings are folded over the back, and inserts the hair pencils into the pouches. This coats the hairlike scales with scent. During courtship the male fans out the hair pencils to disseminate the scent. The pheromone induces changes in the female's behavior and allows the male to couple with her.

Some skippers, such as Checkered Skippers, have tufts of hairlike scales on the hind tibia that aid in disseminating pheromones during courtship. These hair pencils can be inserted into a glandular pouch formed between the thorax and the abdomen to receive the scent.

## On the Insides of Butterflies

Inside an adult butterfly, the nervous system controls many body functions. In contrast to the spinal cord of vertebrates, the nervous system is organized around a nerve cord running the length of the body along the butterfly's belly. The brain, especially the optic lobes that control the eyes, is the largest element of the nervous system. Additional enlargements of the nervous system in the head (ganglia) control the mouthparts and digestion. Two ganglia in the thorax and four in the abdomen govern these parts. Nerves branch off the ganglia and nerve cord, running to the muscles and organs throughout the body. Some major hormonal glands are closely associated with the brain.

### Digestion

The digestive system begins at the tip of the proboscis where fluids are taken into the body. In order to suck nectar from a flower, strong muscles in the head stretch the first part of the esophagus. As the food enters the head, salivary glands add enzymes that begin digestion. The food passes through the thorax via the narrow esophagus and is stored in a sac (the crop) in the abdomen. From the crop, the food is moved into the midgut, where most digestion and absorption take place, then to the hindgut. Water balance is controlled by the hindgut. An organ that rids the body of nitrogen wastes and excess salts (the Malpighian tubules) dumps uric acid into the gut to be expelled with the feces. Since their diet is mostly water, adult butterflies pass feces in liquid form as droplets expelled at the tip of the abdomen.

Fat bodies store substances absorbed by the gut. A fat body is a compact mass of cells enclosed in a membranous sheath. Fats and carbohydrates stored in fat bodies are converted into sugar for energy. The fat body is also the site of much protein production and is a store of nitrogen compounds used in proteins.

### Respiration

Butterflies do not have lungs. Instead, air passes through small holes (spiracles) in the sides of the body and enters a system of fine, interconnected tubes (trachea) and sacs. There are two pairs of spiracles on the thorax and seven on the abdomen. The spiracles have a guard of hairs to keep out dirt and parasites. Just inside the spiracle opening, there is a gate that can be closed. Closing the spiracles during periods of low activity, when oxygen demand is slight, helps to prevent water loss. Air is moved in and out of the tracheal system through contractions of the abdomen and the systematic closure of spiracles. There is a directed flow of air through the body. The trachea deliver air to all parts of the body, especially the muscles, and even into the wings.

### Circulation

The blood and circulatory system of butterflies is very different from ours. Since air is brought into the body through the tracheal system, the blood (hemolymph) does not need to carry oxygen. The blood circulates food, hormones, and other materials throughout the body. Butterfly blood is a clear, greenish, or yellowish fluid that contains several different types of cells. The blood flows through channels and chambers around the body tissues, rather than through a closed vascular system such as ours. The heart is a narrow tube with small holes at intervals. It extends the length of the body along the back, but makes a curious loop in the thorax. Expansion and contraction of the abdomen and small pumps in the thorax help to move the blood through the body as well as the major wing veins, legs, antennae, proboscis, and palpi.

## Reproduction

The reproductive systems of male and female butter-flies are located in their abdomens. Males have a relatively simple reproductive system. Follicle cells in the testes produce the sperm. The testes are fused together and may be whitish, yellow, or red in color. The testes and a pair of accessory glands that produce fluid containing nutrients and other materials are connected to the ejaculatory duct. The mating tube (aedaegus) at the end of the ejaculatory duct penetrates the female during copulation. Appendages on the tip of the abdomen, especially a pair of claspers, are used to hold on to the female during mating.

Follicle cells inside an ovariole of the female butterfly give rise to the eggs. Butterflies have eight ovarioles, and some species can lay hundreds of eggs in just a few hours. The eggs pass one at a time from the ovarioles into a larger tube, the oviduct. As an egg moves down the oviduct, it is fertilized by sperm stored in the spermatheca. Later the egg passes the opening of an accessory gland that applies glue, and perhaps nutrients, to the outside of the shell. When the female finds a host plant, the egg, guided by a pair of short appendages at the tip of the abdomen (ovipositor), is glued bottom side down to the leaf.

The female also has another reproductive opening that is used only for mating. During copulation, the male injects fluids and sperm into a sac (bursa copulatrix) in the female. Some of the fluids solidify into a tough white body with a narrow neck called a spermatophore. After mating, sperm migrate from the spermatophore to another part of the female's reproductive system, the spermatheca. The spermatophore is then digested within the bursa copulatrix, and the nutrients are absorbed.

### Eggs

Butterfly eggs have an outer shell (chorion) that is secreted by the follicle cells in the ovarioles. The outer shell is very porous to allow for respiration. Several larger pores at the top of the egg allow for the sperm to enter. The eggs of butterflies are usually sculpted, with polygonal patterns reflecting the form of the follicle cells in the ovary, or they may have ribs or ridges. Each group of butterflies has eggs of characteristic size, shape, and pattern.

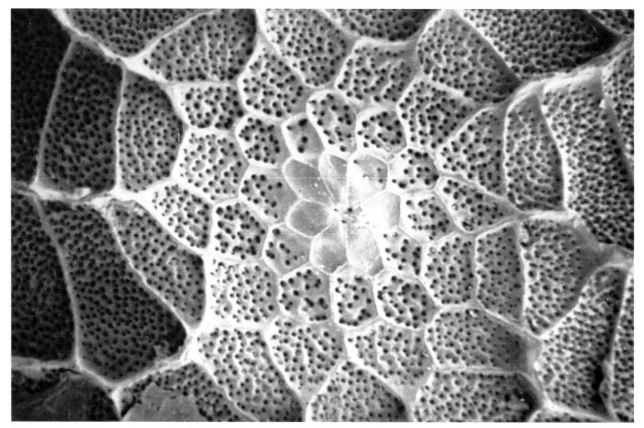

2. Scanning electron micrograph of the top of a Common Checkered Skipper egg.

A

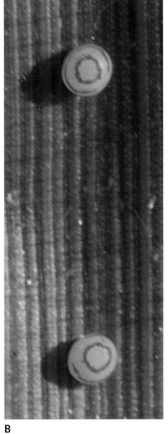

B

C

D

E

F

G

3. Butterfly eggs.

A: Twin Spot Skipper;

B: Delaware Skipper;

C: Zebra Swallowtail;

D: Atala;

E: Tawny Emperor;

F: Pearl Crescent;

G: Carolina Satyr.

## Caterpillars

Like butterfly adults, caterpillars have three body sections. The head is a hard capsule with the mouth on the lower side. A very short antenna and usually six eyes occur on each side of the head near the mouth. Two powerful jaws move from side to side inside the mouth. The cutting surface of the jaws is especially hard and is often formed into teeth or blades for snipping leaves into small pieces. Other mouthparts include an upper flap (labrum) and a lower lip (labium) that help to manipulate the food. The labium has two pairs of sensory palpi as well as the opening of the silk glands (spinneret).

The next three segments of the caterpillar comprise the thorax. The body segmentation of butterfly larvae is not always clear due to extra folds of the outer covering (cuticle). The cuticle of the thorax and abdomen is flexible to allow for growth. The first segment of the larval thorax may have a hardened plate on top called the prothoracic shield. Swallowtail caterpillars have an eversible defensive gland that opens just in front of the prothoracic shield. Brushfooted butterflies and skippers have a different gland, whose function is not known for certain, on the underside of the prothorax. There is a pair of relatively large spiracles on the side of the prothorax. Each thoracic segment of the larva bears a pair of segmented legs that will eventually become the adult legs.

The hind part of the caterpillar is the abdomen. It is made up of ten segments. Segments 1 through 8 each have a pair of spiracles. The last pair is usually larger than the others because it must supply oxygen to the entire rear end of the body. Segments 3 through 6 and segment 10 have pairs of fleshy legs called prolegs. Series of tiny hooks at the tips of the prolegs allow the caterpillar to hold firmly to the substrate. Sawfly larvae (order Hymenoptera) closely resemble the caterpillars of moths and butterflies, but these have six to eight pairs of prolegs. Some moth caterpillars such as inchworms and loopers have only two or three pairs of prolegs and move about in a characteristic looping fashion.

The caterpillars of blues and hairstreaks sometimes have special ant-attracting glands on the top of segments 7 and 8. Giant Skippers and many Branded Skippers produce wax from glands on the undersurface of the abdomen, usually segments 7 and 8, just prior to pupation.

The exterior of butterfly and moth caterpillars is covered by hairs (setae). The hairs may be very short or long and distributed uniformly or in bundles. Their shape is usually a simple shaft tapering to a point, but some species have feathery, flattened, or clubbed setae. The caterpillar may also have simple spines (horns), branching spines (scoli), or fleshly filaments (tubercles) extending from the body. The larval stages of each group of butterflies have a characteristic shape and ornamentation.

The internal anatomy of caterpillars is similar to the adults. The Canna Skipper is a good species to study because the cuticle is transparent. The pulsating heart can be seen along the back. Some individuals have two whitish bodies, one on each side of the heart, about two-thirds of the way down the body along the back. These are the male testes. The tracheal system can be seen as a mass of small tubes clustered at the spiracles. Unlike in the adult, the midgut occupies a large percentage of the body. Other structures that can be viewed are fat bodies and Malpighian tubules.

## Chrysalides

The pupal stage of a butterfly is often called a chrysalis, a word derived from the Greek, meaning gold-colored pupa. Unlike beetles and some other insect groups, the appendages are tightly glued to the pupa rather than being freely movable. The head, thorax, and abdomen can be seen on the chrysalis, as well as the eyes, antennae, forelegs, middle legs, proboscis, and forewings. The hind legs and hind wings are mostly hidden from view. In addition to these structures, the head may have one or two points or horns, and the dorsum (top) of the body may have points, flanges, or spines on the mesothorax and abdomen. The hindlegs of the caterpillar become fused into a new structure, the cremaster of the pupa. Hooks on the cremaster anchor the chrysalis to the substrate. Spiracles on the thorax and abdomen allow the chrysalis to breathe.

## The Life Cycle

Lepidopterans pass through several very different stages as they grow. This process is called metamorphosis. Some insects have a simplified or incomplete life cycle that lacks a pupal stage. The life cycle of butterflies and moths proceeds from the egg to the larval, pupal, and

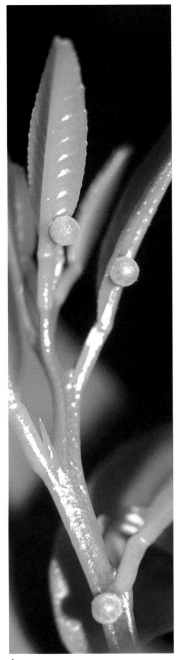

A

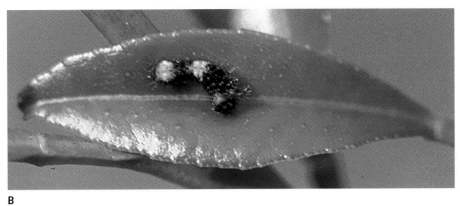

B

C

D

4. The Giant Swallowtail
life cycle.

A: Eggs;

B: first-stage larva;

C. third-stage larva;

D: last-stage larva;

E: pupa;

F: adult.

E

F

finally to the adult stage. They have complete metamorphosis.

The butterfly life cycle begins when a female lays an egg on a host plant. The egg usually hatches in three to five days, but some species may require two weeks or more. The eggs of certain hairstreaks that have only one generation a year, do not hatch until the following spring, some nine or ten months after being laid. These larvae actually develop at a normal rate but do not leave the egg until spring. Butterfly eggs change color or develop a reddish ring as they mature. The dark head of the larva is often visible at the top of the egg before the caterpillar emerges.

To emerge, the young caterpillar chews a hole in the top of the egg and crawls out of the opening. Some species consume the remainder of the egg shell before wandering off. Very young caterpillars require tender leaves, flowers, or developing seed pods to eat. Caterpillars are mostly concerned with eating and escaping from predators.

The droppings of caterpillars are dry pellets (frass). Skipper caterpillars have a special hand-shaped structure on the rear end that helps to propel the frass away from the host plant, sometimes for several feet. When skippers are raised in containers, ricocheting frass is a common sound!

If well fed, the body quickly expands in size until the exoskeleton has stretched to its limit. Then the caterpillar must shed the old cuticle (molt) and form a larger "skin." The caterpillar first lays down a mat of silk and firmly embeds the hooks of the prolegs into this substrate. Part of the old cuticle is digested and absorbed, and a new exoskeleton is formed. The larva swallows air to enlarge itself. At the appropriate time, the cuticle splits along the back of the thorax and the larva wriggles out of the old skin. The first part of the foregut, hindgut, and trachea remain attached to the old cuticle and are also shed at each molt. In a few hours, the new cuticle hardens and the hungry caterpillar crawls away. The entire process takes a day or two. Molting and metamorphosis are controlled by hormones that respond to stretch receptors and other stimuli.

There are typically five larval stages. At each molt, the size, color, and ornamentation of the caterpillar changes. The easiest way to judge which stage a particular caterpillar has reached is by examining the head capsule. Although the body length may double within a stage, the head stays the same size. The head capsule is shed separately from the cuticle, except at the final molt.

## Pupation

The caterpillar reaches full size in two to four weeks, sometimes longer. When mature, the caterpillar stops eating, discharges all the food in the gut, and crawls away from the food plant to find a place to pupate. The larva may wander a considerable distance. Once a site is chosen, the caterpillar lays down a mat of silk with the attachments needed to support the pupa. Most butterfly chrysalides are supported by the cremaster at the tail end and by a silk thread about the middle of the body. Some groups are attached only by the cremaster.

After the supports have been prepared, the caterpillar settles for a time and begins to look a bit lumpy. The lower surface of the larva faces the substrate. At the critical moment, the cuticle splits along special lines of weakness on the back of the thorax and is wriggled into a clump at the tail end. The pupa then lifts the rear end out of the larval skin, while supported by the silk girdle, and hooks the cremaster into a small pad of silk. With a few violent struggles, the larval skin falls to the ground, and the pupa gradually changes shape and hardens into the final chrysalis form.

This process is much the same in the groups that lack the silken girdle. These caterpillars attach the hooks of the last pair of prolegs to the silk pad and hang head downward. The caterpillar assumes a "J" shape at first, but straightens when the time to shed the larval skin approaches. As the larval skin is wriggled toward the tail end, the pupa pinches it between two of the abdominal segments. This prevents the pupa from falling. Then the rear end is withdrawn from the larval skin. Once the cremaster hooks are firmly embedded in the silk pad, the abdominal segments let go, and the larval skin is cast to the ground.

The pupal stage may last a few weeks, months, or even years. If there are no delays in development, the adult may emerge in about ten days. Although the chrysalis may appear to be resting, tremendous changes are taking place as the larval tissues are broken down and transformed into adult structures.

## Adult Emergence

Just before the adult is ready to emerge (eclose), the chrysalis clears and reveals the upper surface of the miniature forewings. Usually, emergence is timed to occur during the early morning. To help break out of the pupa, the adult enlarges itself with air sucked into the tracheal system and the crop. As the adult pushes forward, the pupal cuticle splits along certain lines of weakness. The butterfly clambers out of the chrysalis shell and settles down to expand the wings. Blood is quickly forced into the veins, stretching and straightening the wings. The pupa was unable to excrete metabolic wastes, but now the adult squirts out this fluid (meconium), which may be brown, reddish, or green in color. After a few hours, the wings harden, and the butterfly flies away.

## Butterfly Lifespans

Most adult butterflies live from a few days to several weeks in the wild. Zebra butterflies may live for several months. Overwintering Monarchs are especially long-lived, lasting eight months or more. The perfect wings of a freshly emerged butterfly quickly lose scales and become tattered around the edges as the adults go about their lives. The wings of an aged butterfly appear rubbed, torn, or chipped. The delicate tails are often the first part of the wings to go. Predators such as birds and lizards may grab the wings. Lucky butterflies get away, but some carry V-shaped notches from lizard or bird bites or suffer the loss of portions of the wings. Eyespots on the wings help to direct predatory attacks away from the vulnerable body. Although butterflies have four wings, we've seen individuals that are still able to fly with only the first pair intact.

## Butterfly Seasons

During their brief adult lives, butterflies must find mates and host plants on which to lay eggs. Florida butterflies usually have several generations or broods each year. A brood takes at least four to six weeks to complete. Some species such as the Gulf Fritillary may have six or seven broods per year, others three or four, and a few have only one generation. The winter months synchronize the timing of the generations. The peak seasons for butterflies are spring, early summer, and especially fall. The number of adults declines greatly from November through February, but there are always at least a few butterflies to be found flying about on sunny days, even after periods of below-freezing weather.

Spring is the time when the first butterflies of the year begin to appear. Species that overwintered in the pupal stage, such as swallowtails, the Cabbage White, and the Gray Hairstreak, are the first new butterflies to emerge. In northern Florida, swallowtails may appear as early as the latter part of January. March is the peak of the spring season, and by April the first generation has passed.

Mid-April to the end of June marks the early summer appearance of some lycaenids such as the Banded Hairstreak and the Striped Hairstreak. These butterflies have only one generation, and the adults are only present for a few weeks each year. The second generation of swallowtails and other butterflies emerges during this period as well.

Late summer and fall, from the latter part of August through mid-October, is the season of greatest abundance and species diversity for Florida butterflies. Not only do resident species reach their peak numbers at this time, but many migrating butterflies such as the Cloudless Sulphur, Common Buckeye, Monarch, and Long-Tailed Skipper fly southward into Florida by the millions.

## Overwintering

Florida butterflies have developed a variety of ways to diapause, or overwinter. Diapause is a period of suspended development due to seasons of cold, dry, or otherwise unfavorable conditions. Overwintering may take place during the egg stage (some hairstreaks), the young larval stage (Abbott's Wood Nymph), when larvae are partly grown (skippers), when larvae are mature (dusky wing skippers, Yucca Giant Skipper), the pupal stage (swallowtails, pierids, lycaenids), or the adult stage (pierids, nymphalids).

Temperate butterflies that overwinter during the adult stage such as the Question Mark, Red Admiral, and American Painted Lady hide in wood piles, hollow trees, or other sheltered places during the coldest months. They may venture out on warm days to sip water or juices from fermenting fruit. Tropical species

5. Seasonal variation in the Barred Sulphur.

tend to either have continuous generations or overwinter in the adult stage. The fall generations of the Barred Sulphur, Common Buckeye, Tropical Checkered Skipper, and others are reddish or brownish on the underside of the hindwings and look quite different from the summer generations. These species pass the winter in a reproductively suspended state. During cold periods they hide in dense vegetation. On warm days they seek out water or flowers. Others, such as the Long-Tailed Skipper, the Dorantes Skipper, and the Cloudless Sulphur breed all year in South Florida, although the generation time may be slowed considerably due to cool temperatures.

## Host Plants

Female butterflies choose to lay their eggs only on certain plants that the caterpillars will ultimately eat. Each species has only a narrow range of plants that are able to nourish the caterpillars, which is similar to the situation among humans. Of the world's 234,000 known species of plants, humans depend on just a few kinds (especially grasses) for food. Plants usually contain poisonous chemicals that protect them from herbivores. Butterflies have co-evolved with plants, and are able to detoxify poisons in their particular host species. The ability to detoxify is limited to specific chemicals, however. The caterpillar of a milkweed butterfly cannot switch to eating Passion-Flower. The plant chemistry is too different. Once a caterpillar begins to feed, it becomes programmed to that host species. Switching a Tailless Swallowtail larva from one species of *Aristolochia* to another may result in slower growth,

smaller size, or starvation. Some of the plants on which butterflies thrive are deadly poisonous or toxic to humans. Often they contain strong or pleasant fragrances. Never taste butterfly host plants unless you know they are safe to eat.

Some of the butterflies featured in this book are considered to be pests by farmers and cause extensive damage to crops in the Bean, Carrot, Citrus, Grass, and Mustard Families. For the butterfly gardener, however, the crops are planted in order to enjoy the butterflies, not the vegetables.

Butterfly host plants have interesting stories themselves. For instance, the story of the Passion-Flower started long ago. In 1610, Jacoma Bosio, an Italian monastic scholar, heard reports of a wonderful flower, the "*Flos Passionis,*" that grew in New Spain (Mexico). The parts of the flower were said to reveal the Passion of Jesus Christ. The Mexican friars who described the plant believed that it had been created by God as a sign that the native people of Mexico should be converted to Christianity. Bosio wrote an often quoted account of the plant, but there are several varying descriptions. By some accounts the plant had lobed leaves representing the hands of Jesus' persecutors, but Bosio remarked that the leaves were lance-shaped, referring to the spear that was thrust into the side of Jesus as he hung on the cross. Round spots on the underside of the leaves signified the thirty pieces of silver paid to Judas by the Romans. The ten sepals and petals were the Apostles (Peter and Judas being absent). The column of the flower was the pillar against which Christ was beaten, and the long, coiled tendrils were the whips. The ring of filaments was the crown of thorns. The petals were likened to the garments of Christ divided among the soldiers that carried out the Crucifixion. The three stigmas were the three nails used to fix Jesus to the cross. The five stamens were the five wounds on Jesus' hands, feet, and flank. Lastly, the young seed pod represented the sponge dipped in vinegar that was mockingly offered to quench Christ's thirst.

## Nectar Plants

Adult butterflies are dependent upon plants for energy and nutrients. In return they help to distribute pollen between plants. The long proboscis of a butterfly is able to reach the nectar in short as well as long flowers. Skippers such as the Whirlabout, Clouded Skipper, and Canna Skipper will often crawl into morning glories and other deep-throated flowers to reach the nectar. As with larval host plants, not all flowers are attractive to butterflies. Generally, plants in the Aster, Mint, Madder, and Vervain Families are some of the best butterfly attractors.

When seeking food, butterflies evaluate the shape, color, fragrance, and taste of flowers. The antennae, palpi, tarsi (feet), and proboscis all have sensory receptors that guide the adult to food. Hungry butterflies may visit just about any flower and even colored bits of plastic in the hope of finding food. They must compete with bees, flies, and other insects for the nectar.

Nectar contains not just sugar but also proteins and other chemicals. Male milkweed butterflies seek out flowers rich in pyrrolizidine alkaloids, which are used to produce their pheromones. Aster and Borage Family plants such as *Senecio, Eupatorium,* and *Heliotropium* species contain pyrrolizidine alkaloids in the leaves as well as in the nectar.

Flowers may secrete nectar only at certain times of the day. Weather, exposure, and soil moisture also affect the quantity and quality of the nectar. A plant that is very attractive in one area may be ignored among a different mixture of flowers. There are also regional preferences. Many butterfly gardening guides recommend nectar plants (Purple Cone Flower, Daisies, Black-Eyed Susans, Marigolds, Abelia, Gaillardia) that do not attract many butterflies in Florida. Tables 1 and 2 list some of the best native and exotic nectar plants for Florida butterflies.

6. Queen Butterfly eggs on a milkweed.

**Table 1. Native plants attractive to Florida butterflies (S = small, M = medium, and L = large)**

| Plant | Form | Color | Size |
|---|---|---|---|
| **Araliaceae (Aralia Family)** | | | |
| *Aralia spinosa* (Devil's Walkingstick) | Shrub | White | S, M, L |
| **Arecaceae (Palm Family)** | | | |
| *Sabal etonia* (Scrub Palmetto) | Shrub | White | S, M |
| *Serenoa repens* (Saw Palmetto) | Shrub | White | S, M |
| **Asclepiadaceae (Milkweed Family)** | | | |
| *Asclepias curtissii* (Curtiss' Milkweed | Herb | Greenish | S, M |
| *Asclepias humistrata* (Sandhill Milkweed) | Herb | Pink | S, M |
| *Asclepias tomentosa* (Velvet Leaf Milkweed) | Herb | Greenish | S, M |
| *Sarcostemma clausum* (White Vine) | Vine | White | M, L |
| **Asteraceae (Aster Family)** | | | |
| *Aster carolinianus* (Carolina Aster) | Sprawling Shrub | Purple | S, M, L |
| *Aster elliottii* (Elliott's Aster) | Tall Herb | Purple | S, M, L |
| *Balduina angustifolia* (Yellow Buttons) | Herb | Yellow | S, M |
| *Bidens alba* var. *radiata* (Spanish Needles) | Herb | White | S, M, L |
| *Carphephorus corymbosus* (Paint Brush) | Herb | Pink | S, M, L |
| *Carphephorus odoratissimus* (Vanilla Plant) | Herb | Purple | S, M |
| *Cirsium horridulum* (Thistle) | Herb | Purple, White | S, M, L |
| *Conoclinium coelestinium* (Mistflower) | Herb | Blue | S, M, L |
| *Elephantopus elatus* (Elephant's Foot) | Herb | Purple | S, M, L |
| *Garberia heterophylla* (Garberia) | Shrub | Pink | S, M, L |
| *Liatris* spp. (Prairie Feather) | Herb | Pink | S, M, L |
| *Melanthera nivea* (Cat Tongue) | Herb | White | S, M |
| *Polymnia uvedalia* (Bear's Foot) | Herb | Yellow | S, M |
| *Pterocaulon virgata* (Blackroot) | Herb | White | S |
| *Verbesina virginica* (Frostweed) | Tall Herb | White | S, M, L |
| *Vernonia gigantea* (Ironweed) | Tall Herb | Purple | S, M, L |
| **Avicenniaceae (Black Mangrove Family)** | | | |
| *Avicennia germinans* (Black Mangrove) | Small Tree | White | M |
| **Boraginaceae (Borage Family)** | | | |
| *Bourreria ovata* (Strongback) | Tree | White | M, L |
| *Cordia globosa* (Bloodberry) | Shrub | Greenish | S, M |
| *Heliotropium angiospermum* (Heliotrope) | Herb | White | S, M, L |
| **Chrysobalanceae (Coco Plum Family)** | | | |
| *Chrysobalanus icaco* (Coco Plum) | Shrub | White | M |
| *Licania michauxii* (Gopher Apple) | Trailing Shrub | White | S, M |
| **Convolvulaceae (Morning Glory Family)** | | | |
| *Ipomoea hederifolia* (Scarlet Morning Glory) | Vine | Orange-red | M, L |
| **Ericaceae (Heath Family)** | | | |
| *Lyonia ferruginea* (Rusty Lyonia) | Shrub | White | S, M |
| *Vaccinium arboreum* (Sparkleberry) | Shrub | White | S, M, L |
| *Vaccinium myrsinites* (Shiny Blueberry) | Shrub | White | S, M, L |
| **Euphorbiaceae (Spurge Family)** | | | |
| *Cnidoscolus stimulosus* (Tread Softly) | Herb | White | S, M |

| Plant | Form | Color | Size |
|---|---|---|---|
| **Fabaceae (Bean Family)** | | | |
| *Cercis canadensis* (Redbud) | Small Tree | Pink | S, M, L |
| *Dalea pinnata* (Summer Fairwell) | Herb | White | S, M, L |
| *Lysiloma latisiliquum* (Wild Tamarind) | Tree | White | S, M |
| *Pithecellobium keyense* (Blackbead) | Small Tree | White | S, M |
| **Haemodoraceae (Redroot Family)** | | | |
| *Lachnanthes caroliniana* (Redroot) | Herb | Yellow | S, M, L |
| **Lamiaceae (Mint Family)** | | | |
| *Conradina grandiflora* (Large Flowered Rosemary) | Shrub | Purple | S, M |
| *Piloblephis rigida* (Pennyroyal) | Low Shrub | Purple | S, M |
| *Salvia coccinea* (Tropical Sage) | Herb | Red | M, L |
| *Salvia lyrata* (Lyre-Leaved Sage) | Herb | Blue | M, L |
| **Onagraceae (Primrose Family)** | | | |
| *Ludwigia peruviana* (Primrose Willow) | Tall Herb | Yellow | S, M |
| **Polygonaceae (Buckwheat Family)** | | | |
| *Eriogonum tomentosum* (Wild Buckwheat) | Herb | White | S, M, L |
| *Polygonum hydropiperoides* (Mild Water Pepper) | Herb | White | S, M |
| **Pontederiaceae (Pickerelweed Family)** | | | |
| *Pontederia cordata* (Pickerelweed) | Herb | Blue | S, M, L |
| **Rosaceae (Rose Family)** | | | |
| *Prunus angustifolia* (Chickasaw Plum) | Small Tree | White | S, M, L |
| *Prunus serotina* (Wild Cherry) | Small Tree | White | S, M, L |
| *Prunus umbellata* (Hog Plum) | Small Tree | White | S, M, L |
| *Rubus cuneifolius* (Sand Blackberry) | Shrub | White | S, M, L |
| *Rubus trivialis* (Southern Dewberry) | Trailing Shrub | White | S, M, L |
| **Rubiaceae (Madder Family)** | | | |
| *Cephalanthus occidentalis* (Buttonbush) | Shrub | White | S, M, L |
| *Diodia teres* (Poor Joe) | Herb | White | S, M |
| *Hamelia patens* (Firebush) | Shrub | Orange | M, L |
| *Morinda royoc* (Cheese Shrub) | Sprawling Shrub | White | M, L |
| *Psychotria nervosa* (Wild Coffee) | Shrub | White | M, L |
| **Salicaceae (Willow Family)** | | | |
| *Salix caroliniana* (Carolina Willow) | Shrub/Small Tree | Yellow | S, M |
| **Scrophulariaceae (Figwort Family)** | | | |
| *Agalinis fasciculata* (False Foxglove) | Herb | Purple | S, M |
| *Agalinis purpurea* (False Foxglove) | Herb | Purple | S, M |
| *Capraria biflora* (Goatweed) | Herb | Purple | M, L |
| **Verbenaceae (Vervain Family)** | | | |
| *Glandularia tampensis* (Tampa Verbena) | Herb | Purple | S, M |
| *Lantana depressa* (Trailing Lantana) | Shrub | Yellow | S, M, L |
| *Lantana involucrata* (Wild Sage) | Shrub | White | S, M, L |
| *Phyla nodiflora* (Carpetweed) | Mat Plant | Pink | S, M |
| *Stachytarpheta jamaicensis* (Porterweed) | Herb | Blue | S, M, L |

**Table 2. Exotic and naturalized plants attractive to Florida butterflies (S = small, M = medium, L = large)**

| PLANT | FORM | COLOR | SIZE |
|---|---|---|---|
| **Acanthaceae (Acanthus Family)** | | | |
| *Odontonema stricta* (Firespike) | Shrub | Red | M, L |
| **Anacardiaceae (Cashew Family)** | | | |
| *Schinus terebinthifolius* (Brazilian Pepper) | Shrub/Small Tree | White | S, M, L |
| **Asteraceae (Aster Family)** | | | |
| *Senecio confusis* (Flame Vine) | Vine | Orange | S, M |
| *Taraxacum officinale* (Dandelion) | Herb | Yellow | S, M |
| *Tithonia diversifolia* (Mexican Sunflower) | Tall Herb | Orange | S, M, L |
| *Zinnia elegans* (Garden Zinnia) | Herb | Various | S, M |
| **Boraginaceae (Borage Family)** | | | |
| *Heliotropium amplexicaule* (Heliotrope) | Herb | Blue | S, M, L |
| **Caricaceae (Papaya Family)** | | | |
| *Carica papaya* (Papaya) | Shrub | Yellow | M, L |
| **Convolvulaceae (Morning Glory Family)** | | | |
| *Ipomoea cairica* (Bush Morning Glory) | Vine | Purple | S, M |
| *Ipomoea quamoclit* (Cypress Vine) | Vine | Red | M, L |
| **Fabaceae (Bean Family)** | | | |
| *Melilotus alba* (Sweet Clover) | Herb | White | S, M |
| **Lamiaceae (Mint Family)** | | | |
| *Hyptis mutabilis* (Common Bitter Mint) | Herb | Pale Blue | S, M, L |
| *Lamium amplexicaule* (Henbit) | Herb | Purple | S, M |
| **Loganiaceae (Logania Family)** | | | |
| *Buddleja davidii* (Butterfly Bush) | Shrub | Various | S, M, L |
| **Lythraceae (Loosestrife Family)** | | | |
| *Cuphea hyssopifolia* (False Heather) | Low Shrub | Purple, White | S, M, L |
| **Nyctaginaceae (Four-O-Clock Family)** | | | |
| *Bougainvillea glabra* (Bougainvillea) | Sprawling Shrub | Various | M, L |
| **Oleaceae (Olive Family)** | | | |
| *Ligustrum japonicum* (Japanese Privet) | Small Tree | White | S, M |
| *Ligustrum sinense* (Chinese Privet) | Shrub | White | S, M |
| **Polemoniaceae (Phlox Family)** | | | |
| *Phlox drummondii* (Annual Phlox) | Herb | Various | S, M, L |
| **Polygonaceae (Buckwheat Family)** | | | |
| *Antigonon leptopus* (Coral Vine) | Vine | Pink | M, L |

| Plant | Form | Color | Size |
|-------|------|-------|------|
| **Rosaceae (Rose Family)** | | | |
| *Eriobotrya japonica* (Loquat) | Small Tree | White | M, L |
| *Rhaphiolepis indica* 'Majestic Beauty' (Indian Hawthorn) | Small Tree | Pink | M, L |
| **Rubiaceae (Madder Family)** | | | |
| *Pentas lanceolata* (Pentas) | Herb | Various | S, M, L |
| **Rutaceae (Citrus Family)** | | | |
| *Murraya koenigii* (Curry Leaf Tree) | Tree | White | S, M |
| **Solanaceae (Nightshade Family)** | | | |
| *Cestrum diurum* (Day Jessamine) | Shrub | White | M, L |
| **Verbenaceae (Vervain Family)** | | | |
| *Clerodendrum speciosissium* (Glory Bower) | Shrub | Red | M, L |
| *Duranta repens* (Golden Dewdrop) | Shrub/Small Tree | Blue, White | M, L |
| *Glandularia pulchella* (Moss Verbena) | Herb | Various | S, M |
| *Lantana camara* (Lantana) | Shrub | Various | S, M, L |
| *Lantana montevidensis* (Purple Lantana) | Trailing Shrub | Purple | S, M, L |
| *Stachytarpheta mutabilis* (Pink Porterweed) | Herb | Pink | S, M, L |
| *Stachytarpheta urticifolia* (Nettleleaf Porterweed) | Herb | Blue | S, M, L |
| *Verbena bonariensis* (Roadside Verbena) | Herb | Blue | S, M, L |
| *Verbena brasiliensis* (Brazilian Verbena) | Herb | Blue | S, M, L |

# Butterfly Behavior

Cassius Blues investigating a larval host plant, Leadwort.

7. A pair of Common Buckeyes mate while a second male waits.

## Mating

Adult butterflies lead a life of leisure. Their primary concerns are eating, mating, laying eggs, sleeping, and escaping from predators. Males spend considerable time looking for mates. The meeting place may be a forest opening, a treetop, a patch of host plant, some flowers, or a slightly elevated spot in an open field. Species such as the Black Swallowtail use a patrolling strategy to locate a mate. The males fly around in areas where the females are likely to be present. Other butterflies such as the Tawny Emperor are perchers. The males perch on leaves and fly out to investigate passing butterflies, falling leaves, or other moving objects. Buckeye males perch on the ground in open areas and defend small territories. Battles ensue when another male flies into the territory. The males circle or flap against each another in an upward spiral. The victor, usually the original male, will return to claim the territory.

Males recognize the females by color and scent. If a male encounters a female of the same species, courtship behavior ensues. Occasionally we've seen overly excited males courting females of different species, such as when a male Palamedes Swallowtail pursues a female Spicebush Swallowtail. Most species have dance-like courtships, where the male hovers over the female, wafting pheromones in her direction. To the Monarch, courtship is less sophisticated. The male brutally forces the female to the ground, then vigorously attempts to mate. Very aggressive Monarchs will take down and try to mate with other males. We've even observed a Monarch trying to couple with a Red Admiral!

The females of some butterflies mate only once, but others mate multiple times. A receptive female will land and fold her wings over her back after a few minutes of courtship. The male lands behind, then crawls beside the female. He bends the tip of his abdomen to meet the female's reproductive opening, and grabs her firmly with the claspers. Thus attached, the pair face in opposite directions. If disturbed, the female usually flies with the male in tow, passively holding on with his wings shut. It takes several hours for the male to inseminate the female. Lucky males may mate with several to many females during their lifetimes.

The Zebra Longwing is unusual in having pupal mating. Males wait near the chrysalis of a female that is ready to hatch. Just as the female begins to emerge, there is a scramble, but one of the males pushes his abdomen into the chrysalis and couples with the female before she has pulled free of the pupal shell. They mate while she expands and dries her wings.

A female that has already mated will try to avoid a courting male by flying into vegetation or making a sudden dash. However, males can be very persistent and try to force the female to land. A pierid female that cannot escape a courting male will land, open her wings, and elevate her abdomen. This rejection pose tells the male not to persist, and he usually flies away.

## Egg Laying

Mated females spend much of their time looking for host plants on which to lay eggs. As opposed to males, which are rapid fliers, females flutter slowly close to the ground or around vegetation. Butterflies identify host plants by their appearance and chemistry. After close inspection, the female lands on the plant, tasting it with her feet. If the plant has the right chemistry, she quickly bends her abdomen downward, touching the tip to the plant, and deposits an egg. The bottom of each egg is coated with glue, and the egg adheres tightly to the leaf. Most species deposit their eggs on the undersides of young leaves. Tiger Swallowtails attach their eggs on the upper sides of mature leaves. Hairstreaks and blues lay eggs on flower buds, leaf buds, or twigs.

8. A female Queen Butterfly laying eggs on Velvet-Leaved Milkweed.

## Feeding

When feeding, butterflies hold on to flower petals with their legs, extend the proboscis, and push the tip into the base of the flower to reach the nectar. Swallowtails flutter their wings while feeding, but other species perch with their wings closed or partly open. At clusters of small flowers, the proboscis is moved quickly from one flower to another.

Butterflies frequently seek out nutrients other than nectar. Forest species such as satyrs, the Question Mark, the Red Admiral, and hackberrys are strongly attracted to fermenting fruit. Sapsuckers, a kind of woodpecker, peck rows of small holes in the bark of trees. In the spring, fermenting sap sometimes oozes from the holes, attracting multitudes of insects and butterflies. Brushfooted butterflies may visit fresh manure, urine, or rotting dead animals. Male swallowtails, sulphurs, broadwinged skippers, and blues will sip water from damp sand or mud containing concentrations of salt. This behavior is called mud-puddling or puddling. We've observed the Long-Tailed Skipper and Silver Spotted Skipper probing bird droppings with their proboscises while moistening the pellets with clear fluid squirted from the rear end. The Zebra butterfly is very unusual in that the females gather balls of pollen on the tips of their proboscises. The pollen is digested externally by regurgitated enzymes. The nutrients, especially proteins, are used to develop and enrich the eggs.

## Sleeping

Under cloudy conditions and at night, butterflies sleep perched on vegetation. They usually sleep singly, but some may form small aggregations on the tips of grass stems or on leaves. During the fall migration, Monarchs often congregate in temporary roosting clusters of up to hundreds of individuals. The large sulphur butterflies seek out yellow leaves on trees and shrubs on which to roost. Most butterflies fold the wings over the back, exposing the dull undersurfaces while sleeping. However, the Giant Swallowtail rests with the wings outstretched at the sides, and some dusky wing skippers hold the wings like moths. Although they are cold-blooded animals, butterflies can raise their body temperatures for flight on cool days by basking. Cold butterflies open the wings and expose the body to the sun to warm up. Moths shiver the wing muscles to raise their temperature for flight.

## Grooming

Butterflies try to be tidy animals. Their antennae must be kept clean in order to function properly. Skippers, swallowtails, and pierids use their forelegs to groom the antennae. Lycaenids and brushfooted butterflies, which have small or tiny forelegs, use their middle legs. Grooming simply involves lowering the antenna, crossing the leg over, and rubbing it down the shaft and club. The legs can do little to clean other parts of the body. Swallowtails sometimes become coated on the underside of the wings with pollen from Royal Poinciana and similar tropical trees in the Bean Family. The pollen grains of these plants stick together, aiding their dispersal.

9. Zebra Swallowtails puddling at wet sand.

## Flight Patterns

Each species of butterfly has a particular flying style. Skippers are fast and darting. The Zebra Longwing has a slow, fluttering flight pattern. When startled, even the slow species quicken the pace and fly upward. Butterflies also fly at a preferred height. Carolina Satyrs and buckeyes stay close to the ground. Hairstreaks like the tops of trees. Most butterflies fly from one to three meters above the ground.

## Migration

Adult butterflies are capable of flying considerable distances. During the fall, Monarchs may travel from southern Canada to central Mexico. But the Monarch is not the only long distance traveler in Florida. During late August, September, and early October, huge numbers of Cloudless Sulphurs, Long-Tailed Skippers, Common Buckeyes, Gulf Fritillaries, Clouded Skippers, and others fly into Florida from other parts of the eastern United States. These species cannot withstand freezing temperatures for very long and overwinter in southern Florida. The females lay eggs on larval host plants they encounter while moving south.

Also during the fall, large numbers of tropical butterflies from southern Florida such as the White Peacock, Orange-Barred Sulphur, Great Southern White, Dainty Sulphur, and Dorantes Skipper disperse northward. These species lay eggs as they expand their range, bolstering their populations, but most are killed in northern Florida by freezing temperatures during the winter. The Barred Sulphur, Little Sulphur, and Sleepy Orange move about in large numbers during the fall as well, but they are less directed in their dispersal. After an especially cold winter, some tropical butterflies may not appear in northern Florida until late August, September, or October. Coastal areas and river corridors are major dispersal lanes, perhaps because the butterflies become concentrated along these distinctive features.

## Larval Behavior

The major activities of caterpillars are eating and resting. Caterpillars usually eat the edges of leaves, but small Question Mark larvae chew holes near the middle of the leaf. A caterpillar begins walking first by moving up the rear segments, and lastly the head. When moving from one area to another, caterpillars move the head from side to side and lay down a trail of silk. Caterpillars generally do not like the sun and rest under leaves or in shelters. Some are reported to feed mostly at night.

# Danger and Defense

## Parasites

There are numerous ecological interactions between butterflies and other animals. Parasites are organisms that feed on other living things but do not kill the host. Tiny biting flies in the family Ceratopogonidae sometimes seek out butterfly and moth caterpillars and drink their blood, just as sandflies bite humans.

More commonly, butterflies are attacked by parasitoids. These organisms develop inside a host and eventually kill it. Mymarid and trichogrammatid wasps lay their eggs in those of butterflies. The wasps are so small that a dozen or so may hatch out of just one butterfly egg! Certain other wasps (especially Braconidae and Ichneumonidae) lay their eggs inside caterpillars. After the eggs hatch, the wasp larvae feed on the caterpillar's tissues. When mature, the wasp larvae bore out of the caterpillar and spin small cocoons nearby. The caterpillar may live for several days after the wasps have spun their cocoons, but it eventually dies. The wasp cocoons may be white, yellow, or brown, smooth and flat, or round and fuzzy. Some of the larger wasp species produce only one or two individuals per butterfly. Smaller species may produce dozens of wasps from one caterpillar. The wasp larvae often do not appear until the caterpillar is fully grown. A few kinds of wasps (Chalcididae, Pteromalidae, Eulophidae) pupate inside the caterpillar or chrysalis and exit through a small hole chewed in the side.

Butterfly caterpillars, especially swallowtails and skippers, are also attacked by flies in the family Tachinidae. The female fly glues a few eggs onto the skin of each larva she finds. The eggs are white and flat. After the maggots hatch in a few days, they burrow into the caterpillar and begin to feed. When full grown, the maggots leave the caterpillar, or perhaps the chrysalis, and pupate in the soil. Although they destroy many caterpillars, parasitoids serve useful roles in nature by regulating butterfly and moth populations.

10. Braconid wasp cocoons under a parasitized Clouded Skipper caterpillar.

## Diseases

A variety of disease organisms such as viruses, bacteria, fungi, and protozoa attack caterpillars. If you are raising butterflies indoors, the rearing equipment should be kept clean and dry. Provide ventilation in plastic containers by gluing pieces of fine screening over holes cut in the lids of at least one inch in diameter. High humidity or water in the containers will certainly lead to microbial disease problems. Paper towels placed in the bottom of the rearing container will help control excess moisture. The towels should be changed regularly. Wash the rearing containers with hot water and soap every few days.

Caterpillars are very susceptible to the bacterium *Bacillus thuringiensis,* commonly called Bt. Bt is sold as a "natural" insecticide. For obvious reasons, Bt and butterfly gardens do not mix. The protozoan *Ophrycystis elektroscirrha* is a microbe that attacks Monarchs. Spores of this single-celled animal are abundant around the ovipositor of an infected female. The spores stick to the outside of the eggs as they are laid. The larva becomes infected after hatching and consuming the egg shell. Caterpillars are weakened or killed by the protozoan. Another group of protozoans, the Microsporidia (*Nosema* spp.), also infects moths and perhaps butterflies. Some *Nosema* species are used as "natural" insecticides. Caterpillars sick with microbes will become sluggish and lose their appetite. Fluid may leak from the mouth or rear end. The cuticle may develop black patches. If disease problems occur in caterpillars you are raising, release or destroy the livestock and start again with new containers, or with equipment sterilized with a mild bleach solution.

## Predators

Predators may also attack any of the butterfly life stages. Like parasitoids, a predator destroys other organisms but feeds on many hosts, not just one. Ants are major predators of butterfly eggs and caterpillars. Plants such as *Cassia* species and Passion-Flower have special glands that produce nectar at the base of the leaves. Secretions from these extrafloral nectaries attract ants. The ants roam all over the plants and carry away any butterfly eggs or young caterpillars they find. The Imported Fire Ant (*Solenopsis invicta*) and tree ants (*Pseudomyrmex* spp.) frequently eat the immature stages of butterflies and moths. The predatory stink bug (*Euthyrhynchus floridanus,* family Pentatomidae) harpoons caterpillars and other insects with its beak. This bluish-black bug has red spots and is often found in gardens. Paper wasps (*Polistes* spp.) hunt caterpillars to feed their own larvae. There are several species in Florida ranging in size from small to large. The larva of one Florida butterfly, the Harvester (*Feniseca tarquinius*), has turned the tables from prey to predator. Its caterpillar is a carnivore that eats only wooly aphids!

Many sit-and-wait predators catch and eat adult butterflies, especially as they perch or visit flowers.

11. This Eastern Pondhawk dragonfly is eating a Great Southern White.

Mantids, the Wheel Bug (*Arilus cristatus*) and other assassin bugs (Reduviidae), ambush bugs (Phymatidae), crab spiders (*Misumenoides formosites* and *Misumenops celer* in the family Thomisidae), and the Green Lynx spider (*Peucetia viridans,* family Oxyopidae) are common predators of butterflies in Florida gardens. Web-spinning spiders such as the Banana or Golden Silk Spider (*Nephila clavipes*), the Golden Garden Spider (*Argiope aurantia*), the Banded Garden Spider (*Argiope trifasciata*), and the Silver Garden Spider (*Argiope argentata*) in the family Araneidae often set up shop near patches of flowers and catch butterflies.

Dragonflies are another predator group that may catch and eat adult butterflies, especially the Eastern Pondhawk (*Erythemis simplicicollis*). We've seen this medium-sized, green dragonfly eating butterflies ranging from crescents to swallowtails in size. Among the vertebrates, animals such as lizards, birds, and even mice eat butterflies. When the butterflies are asleep, bats and flying squirrels are like sharks in the night sky, preying on moths.

## Pesticides

Insecticides applied to lawns and agricultural fields are very harmful to butterflies and other wildlife. Urban areas in Florida are frequently sprayed with Malathion and other poisons during the summer to kill mosquitoes. Although spraying for mosquitoes is usually done at night, butterflies are still at risk, since the chemicals are dispersed as a very fine mist, and adults as well as immatures are exposed on vegetation. Laboratory experiments by Dr. Thomas C. Emmel and Peter Eliazar of the University of Florida determined that a single, tiny droplet of mosquito spray quickly killed butterflies as large as the Giant Swallowtail. Many mosquito ecologists feel that spraying for adult mosquitoes and deploying bug-zapper lights do very little to control mosquitoes but do great harm to many beneficial insects such as butterflies and moths. If your municipality or county has a mosquito control program, be sure to call and request that your yard not be sprayed. The butterflies will not be able to thank you enough!

## Protective Coloration

In a world full of dangers, butterflies have evolved a number of different defenses to keep from being eaten.

12. The false face pattern on the rear end of a Black Swallowtail caterpillar.

Coloration is their most important defense. While the upper-side patterns may be bright and conspicuous, the lower surfaces of the wings (those exposed during rest) have duller colors. Many butterflies are cryptically colored, meaning that they blend in with the background. Good examples of cryptic coloration are the leafwing butterflies, which resemble dead leaves, and the leaflike pupae of the Cloudless Sulphur. Some butterflies resemble inedible objects, such as young swallowtail caterpillars that mimic bird or lizard droppings.

Disruptive coloration is another type of crypsis. Stripes or patches of light and dark color break up the body outline of adults and larvae, helping them blend with the background. The wings of the Giant Swallowtail are boldly marked above with rows of yellow spots. At rest this butterfly holds the wings at the sides, displaying the upper pattern. In nature, however, the yellow spots on the brown background mix with the shadows and highlights of leaves, making the butterfly less noticeable. The caterpillar of the Giant Swallowtail also uses disruptive coloration, being dark brown with a pale patch in the middle and on the rear end.

Butterflies with false face patterns use yet another strategy for survival: frightening coloration. This defense involves startling potential predators by presenting the image of an animal that may bite back. The snakelike larvae of the Spicebush and Palamedes swallowtails are classic examples of frightening coloration. Also, eyespots on the wings of adult butterflies may frighten or confuse lizards and insectivorous birds.

Hairstreaks not only have eyespots at the tip of the hindwings but also slender tails that resemble antennae. Lycaenids usually perch with the true head facing downward, frequently rubbing their hindwings together. This position and movement deflect the predator's attention away from the true head and toward the false eyespots on the wings. If the predator does strike, a bit of wing is all the butterfly may lose.

Animals with poisons advertise their noxious properties with bright or contrasting patterns of red, yellow, orange, white, and black. Butterflies such as the Pipevine Swallowtail, the Florida Atala, pierids, milkweed butterflies, and heliconians use warning coloration to inform predators that they are not edible. Caterpillars of the milkweed butterflies or the Frangipani Sphinx (*Pseudosphinx tetrio*) also have warning coloration. Chemicals in their bodies taste bad or make birds throw up. The flight patterns of these butterflies are slow and fluttering. Young or naive birds may sample a few butterflies with warning coloration, but they quickly learn to avoid them after becoming sick. Butterfly poisons seem to be most effective on vertebrate predators, especially birds. We have seen mantids, spiders, and other invertebrate predators happily munching away on butterflies that are supposed to be chemically "protected."

Some edible butterflies have evolved color patterns similar to those of distasteful species. The female Black Swallowtail and the dark female form of the Tiger Swallowtail look very similar to the distasteful Pipevine Swallowtail. The Viceroy resembles the chemically protected Monarch, especially in the northern part of the state. This system of an edible species resembling a distasteful species is called Batesian mimicry.

## Protective Behavior

Butterfly caterpillars have a few defenses in addition to coloration. The larvae of skippers, some swallowtails, and hackberry butterflies hide in curled or folded leaf shelters between bouts of feeding. Brushfooted butterfly caterpillars often feed on leaves enclosed by silk webbing. If disturbed, caterpillars react by swinging the front of the body from side to side. Skipper larvae turn the head to the side and open and close the jaws.

Swallowtail caterpillars can defend themselves against some predators with their smelly osmeterium gland. Some lycaenids have glands on the top of abdominal segment 7 that produce honeydew and others that release an ant-attracting pheromone. The ants protect the larvae from parasitoids and predators and receive occasional rewards of honeydew for their trouble.

Butterfly pupae rely mostly on cryptic coloration for protection. A pupa may wriggle violently if disturbed early on. Skippers are able to move the abdomen in circles, but the brushfooted butterflies can only wiggle sideways. The pupa of the Great Purple Hairstreak squeaks if molested.

13. The defensive gland (osmeterium) of the Giant Swallowtail is scarlet red.

# Butterfly Distribution

Monarchs feeding on Scarlet Milkweed, a nectar plant and a favorite larval food.

## Florida's Past

Florida has not always appeared the way we see it today. The basement rocks that lie deep underground were part of Africa and South America hundreds of millions of years ago. Above these basement rocks is a thick layer of limestone formed at the bottom of a shallow sea. Florida's surficial sands and clays are materials eroded from the Appalachian Mountains.

Although the oldest terrestrial vertebrate fossils in Florida date to 25 million years ago, much of the peninsula has been inundated by the sea and then exposed many times in the past. South Florida and the Keys have been above sea level for only a relatively short time in a geological sense, perhaps only a few thousand years.

The butterflies that occur in Florida today came mostly from elsewhere. Many species invaded Florida from the southeastern continental region. Tropical species found their way to the extreme southern mainland and the Keys. Some of the butterfly immigrants have evolved into slightly different forms from their relatives just to the north or south. In modern times exotic butterflies have become established in Florida, hitchhiking in with plants, goods, and people.

## Butterfly Diversity

Tropical or subtropical areas of the earth, with moderate or high rainfall, typically enjoy a great abundance of butterfly species. The areas of greatest diversity in the world lie in eastern Peru and western Brazil. Hundreds of species can be found in a few acres of tropical rainforest at these sites. There are at least 160 different kinds of butterflies that have breeding populations in Florida. Many others have been found here only occasionally. Even tiny butterflies are sometimes capable of flying long distances.

In some ways, Florida's butterfly fauna is not very diverse. Compared to Central American or South America, we have relatively few species. Because the Florida peninsula is only one side away from being an island, the number of species coming from the southeast and west are limited. Emigrants from nearby tropical and subtropical areas must cross wide oceans. In other ways we do have a rich butterfly fauna. Florida is blessed with a variety of tropical species inhabiting the southern peninsula and temperate species to the north. In central Florida where these two groups meet, a relatively rich fauna of tropical and temperate species occurs.

Florida also has some kinds of butterflies that are found nowhere else. These endemics are mostly races (subspecies) that have developed different color patterns from their relatives due to the isolation of the Florida peninsula. A subspecies is a geographical variant of a species.

## Ice Age Events

During the Pleistocene Period (20,000 to 1 million years ago), glaciers covered large areas of the northern hemisphere. The enormous amount of water bound up in the ice lowered sea levels such that Florida was a much larger place than it is today. During warm periods, the glaciers melted and the oceans rose to higher than today's levels. At the peak of these events, Florida may have been but a series of islands straddling what is now the Lake Wales Ridge. Plants and animals on the islands were not able to breed with individuals outside of Florida, and some differentiated. Today, there are at least forty butterflies found only or mostly in Florida (table 3), making it one of the richest centers of unique species in North America. Sea levels are on the rise, but hopefully it will take thousands of years before south Florida again becomes submerged.

## Habitat

Habitat is the place or type of area where a plant or animal naturally or normally lives. There are about 2,500 species of plants that are native, or naturally occurring, in Florida. Another 1,500 or so non-indigenous species are naturalized (they grow and reproduce without cultivation). These numbers are small compared to the 25,000 species estimated to be cultivated in the state (Lippincott 1996). We are able to grow numerous plants from tropical and temperate areas throughout the world in our gardens.

Plants with similar adaptations to environmental conditions tend to be found together. These associations are called communities. Some communities have been in existence for many millennia, evolving a complex network of ecological interactions. There are hundreds of different kinds of natural communities in Florida if one uses a very fine classification. However, most ecologists prefer a more general scheme consist-

**Table 3. Butterflies found only or mostly in Florida**

| GROUP | SCIENTIFIC NAME | COMMON NAME |
| --- | --- | --- |
| Swallowtails | *Eurytides marcellus floridensis* | Florida Zebra Swallowtail |
| | *Heraclides aristodemus ponceanus* | Schaus' Swallowtail |
| | *Pterourus glaucus australis* | Southern Tiger Swallowtail |
| Whites | *Appias drusilla neumoegenii* | Florida White |
| | *Ascia monuste phileta* | Great Southern White |
| Sulphurs | *Aphrissa statira floridensis* | Florida Statira Sulphur |
| | *Eurema daira daira* | Barred Sulphur |
| | *Phoebis agarithe maxima* | Large Orange Sulphur |
| | *Phoebis sennae eubule* | Cloudless Sulphur |
| Blues | *Brephidium isophthala pseudofea* | Eastern Pigmy Blue |
| | *Hemiargus ceraunus antibubastus* | Ceraunus Blue |
| | *Hemiargus thomasi bethunebakeri* | Miami Blue |
| Hairstreaks | *Eumaeus atala florida* | Florida Atala |
| | *Incisalia henrici margaretae* | Margaret's Elfin |
| | *Mitoura grynea sweadneri* | Sweadner's Hairstreak |
| | *Satyrium liparops liparops* | Florida Striped Hairstreak |
| | *Strymon acis bartrami* | Bartram's Hairstreak |
| | *Strymon columella modesta* | Dotted Hairstreak |
| Hackberry Butterflies | *Asterocampa celtis reinthali* | Reinthal's Hackberry Butterfly |
| | *Asterocampa clyton flora* | Florida Tawny Emperor |
| Leafwing Butterflies | *Anaea troglodyta floridalis* | Florida Leafwing |
| Milkweed Butterflies | *Danaus gilippus berenice* | Florida Queen |
| Longwing Butterflies | *Agraulis vanillae nigrior* | Gulf Fritillary |
| | *Dryas iulia largo* | Julia Butterfly |
| | *Heliconius charitonius tuckeri* | Zebra Longwing |
| Brushfooted Butterflies | *Basilarchia archippus floridensis* | Florida Viceroy |
| | *Eunica tatila tatilista* | Florida Purple Wing |
| Wood Nymphs | *Lethe portlandia floralae* | Florida Pearly Eye |
| | *Megisto cymela viola* | Viola's Wood Satyr |
| Branded Skippers | *Atrytonopsis hianna loammi* | Loamm's Skipper |
| | *Euphyes arpa* | Palmetto Skipper |
| | *Euphyes berryi* | Berry's Skipper |
| | *Euphyes dukesi calhouni* | Calhoun's Skipper |
| | *Euphyes pilatka klotsi* | Klots' Sawgrass Skipper |
| | *Hesperia attalus slossonae* | Slosson's Dotted Skipper |
| | *Hesperia meskei straton* | Gulf Coast Skipper |
| Broadwinged Skippers | *Ephyriades brunneus floridensis* | Florida Dusky Wing |
| | *Erynnis brizo somnus* | Somber Dusky Wing |
| | *Phocides pigmalion okeechobee* | Florida Mangrove Skipper |
| Giant Skippers | *Megathymus cofaqui cofaqui* | Cofaqui Giant Skipper |

ing of a few dozen major types (Myers and Ewel 1990). Plant communities are the habitat for butterflies and other animals. As with plants, butterflies do not occur just anywhere, but each species prefers to live in one or more specific habitats. In order for butterflies to live and breed, the habitat must contain host plants for the caterpillars as well as flowers that produce nectar or other resources for the adults. Butterfly gardening cre-ates habitat for butterflies by providing food for both butterfly caterpillars and adults.

Some butterflies will live only in natural communi-ties. For instance, the Schaus' Swallowtail, a federally endangered species, occurs only in the tropical hard-wood hammocks of the Florida Keys. Even if you plant the host plants in your garden, chances are you will never have Schaus' Swallowtails in your backyard.

However, many other butterflies are weedy. They disperse well and prefer to live in disturbed areas. Weedy butterflies are most likely to do well in your butterfly garden since they are adapted to finding and colonizing ephemeral patches of host plants. If your yard is near a natural area, your butterfly garden will also attract some species that do not normally occur around homes.

Knowing the kinds of natural areas in your neighborhood will help you to decide which host plants to add to your garden. The first step in identifying plant communities is to determine the dominant plant species of the site. Plant communities also vary in structure, such as in the number of layers of vegetation (herb, shrub, and canopy levels). The structure is shaped by climate, soil moisture, fire, and other kinds of disturbance. The following sketches will describe some of the most common plant communities, from very dry uplands to wetlands and human-created environments, all of which are important to butterflies.

## Scrubs

Scrubs are forests or shrub thickets that occur on hills and ridges having excessively drained sandy soils. Fires are uncommon in scrub habitats. Sand Pine scrub has only a few layers of woody vegetation. Sand Pine (*Pinus clausa*) may form the canopy or uppermost layer. Below the canopy there is a characteristic dense shrub layer. Few herbs occur on the forest floor. An interesting variety or phase of this habitat is Rosemary scrub, which is dominated by Florida Rosemary (*Ceratiola ericoides*).

Common plants of scrub communities are Sand Pine, scrub oaks (*Quercus chapmanii, Q. geminata, Q. inopina, Q. myrtifolia*), Silkbay (*Persea humilis*), pawpaws (*Asimina* spp.), Rusty Lyonia (*Lyonia ferruginea*), Florida Rosemary, and Garberia (*Garberia heterophylla*).

Butterflies living in scrub habitats are the Zebra Swallowtail, Palamedes Swallowtail, Spicebush Swallowtail, Barred Sulphur, Little Sulphur, Southern Oak Hairstreak, Eastern Pine Elfin, White-M Hairstreak, Banded Oak Dusky Wing, Horace's Dusky Wing, Juvenal's Dusky Wing, Zarucco Dusky Wing, Northern Cloudy Wing, and Yucca Giant Skipper.

Scrubs are found locally throughout northern and central Florida, and along the coasts as far south as Naples and Fort Lauderdale. Ocala National Forest has the largest tracts of scrub. The U.S. Fish and Wildlife Service is also working toward creating a National Scrub Preserve on the Lake Wales Ridge. Other examples of scrub can be seen at the Archbold Biological Station (Lake Placid), Jonathan Dickinson State Park (Hobe Sound), Cedar Key State Scrub Preserve, Rookery Bay National Estuarine Research Reserve (Naples), and coastal areas of the Panhandle.

## Sandhills

Sandhill communities are forests on excessively drained sandy soils. They occur on hills and ridges where wildfires are frequent. Typical sandhills have large, widely spaced Longleaf Pine trees forming the canopy. Shrubs in the understory are sparse, but the grass and herb layer is diverse. In areas where the pines were harvested but never replanted, Turkey Oak barrens have formed.

Dominant plants of sandhills are Longleaf Pine (*Pinus palustris*), Turkey Oak (*Quercus laevis*), Bluejack Oak (*Q. incana*), Post Oak (*Q. stellata*), pawpaws, Shiny

14. Sand Pine scrub habitat.

15. Sandhill vegetation.

Station (Tallahassee), Welaka State Forest, St. Marys River State Forest (Hilliard), Withlacoochee State Forest (Brooksville), Wekiwa Springs State Park (Apopka), and Goldhead Branch State Park (Keystone Heights).

## Pine Flatwoods

Pine flatwoods are Florida's most common habitat. These are pine forests on broad flats that have poorly drained soils. The canopy is usually Slash Pine (*Pinus elliottii*) or Longleaf Pine with a shrubby understory of Saw Palmetto (*Serenoa repens*) and/or Gallberry (*Ilex glabra*). Flatwoods are often interspersed with swamps and grassy prairies. Fires occur frequently in flatwoods habitats.

Other common woody plants of pine flatwoods are pawpaws (*Asimina reticulata* and *Asimina pygmaea*), Tarflower (*Befaria racemosa*), Fetterbush (*Lyonia lucida*), and Wax Myrtle (*Myrica cerifera*). Flatwoods also have a great variety of grasses and wildflowers.

Blueberry (*Vaccinium myrsinites*), Wiregrass (*Aristida stricta*), Yellow Buttons (*Balduina angustifolia*), Blazing Star (*Liatris* spp.), and many other grasses and wildflowers.

Butterflies that live in sandhill habitats are the Pipevine Swallowtail, Zebra Swallowtail, Barred Sulphur, Little Sulphur, Eastern Dogface, Ceraunus Blue, Frosted Elfin, Gray Hairstreak, Goatweed, Queen, Monarch, Common Buckeye, Pearl Crescent, Abbott's Wood Nymph, Florida Little Skipper, Field Skipper, Slosson's Dotted Skipper, Meske's Skipper, Fiery Skipper, Gray Skipper, Swarthy Skippers, Baracoa Skipper, Tawny Edged Skipper, Whirlabout Skipper, Hoary Edge, Banded Oak Dusky Wing, Horace's Dusky Wing, Juvenal's Dusky Wing, Zarucco Dusky Wing, Southern Cloudy Wing, Confused Cloudy Wing, Northern Cloudy Wing, Cofaqui Giant Skipper, and Yucca Giant Skipper.

Sandhills are found locally in north and central Florida. Good places to see sandhills are Riverside Island at Ocala National Forest, Tall Timbers Research

16. Pine flatwoods habitat.

Butterflies of pine flatwoods are the Zebra Swallow-tail, Tiger Swallowtail, Palamedes Swallowtail, Spice-bush Swallowtail, Little Sulphur, Gray Hairstreak, Common Buckeye, Pearl Crescent, American Painted Lady, Abbott's Wood Nymph, Florida Little Skipper, Field Skipper, Arogos Skipper, Loamm's Skipper, Palmetto Skipper, Berry's Skipper, Dion Skipper, Palatka Skipper, Fiery Skipper, Gray Skipper, Swarthy Skippers, Twin Spot Skipper, Tawny Edged Skipper, Whirlabout Skipper, Horace's Dusky Wing, Zarucco Dusky Wing, Southern Cloudy Wing, Confused Cloudy Wing, and Northern Cloudy Wing.

Examples of pine flatwoods can be found at most parks. Lake Kissimmee State Park (Lake Wales), Faver-Dykes State Park (St. Augustine), Goethe State Forest (Bronson), Myakka River State Park (Sarasota), Jay B. Starkey Wilderness Park (Pasco County), Apalachicola National Forest (Tallahassee), Morningside Nature Center (Gainesville), and Jonathan Dickinson State Park (Hobe Sound) all have large tracts of well-managed flatwoods.

## Tropical Pineland

Another pine-dominated community is the tropical pineland or pine rockland of southern Florida. This community resembles pine flatwoods but has a sparse canopy of gnarled South Florida Slash Pine (*Pinus elliottii* var. *densa*), and the understory is rich in palms and tropical hardwoods. Characteristic plants are Silver Palm (*Coccothrinax argentata*), thatch palms (*Thrinax* spp.), Locustberry (*Byrsonima lucida*), and Pineland Croton (*Croton linearis*). Grassy openings in the pineland usually have an abundance of wildflowers. Tropical pinelands on the mainland may also have the cycad, Coontie (*Zamia pumila*).

Butterflies found in tropical pinelands are the Florida Atala, Bartram's Hairstreak, Florida Leafwing, Rockland Grass Skipper, Red Broken Dash, and Florida Dusky Wing. Some of best remaining areas of tropical pineland are at Long Pine Key in Everglades National Park and the National Key Deer Refuge on Big Pine Key.

## Hammocks

Hammocks are upland forests of broad-leaved trees. They may be further divided, according to the soil moisture, into xeric (very dry), mesic (moist-soil), or hydric (saturated-soil) types. Hammocks have many

17. A hammock.

layers of trees and shrubs. There are usually few grasses and herbs near the ground, but ferns may be abundant if the soil moisture is high. Fires rarely occur in hammocks.

Live Oak (*Quercus virginiana*), Laurel Oak (*Quercus hemisphaerica*), Sweet Gum (*Liquidambar styraciflua*), Hackberry (*Celtis laevigata*), Cabbage Palm (*Sabal palmetto*), Southern Magnolia (*Magnolia grandiflora*), Loblolly Pine (*Pinus taeda*), Shortleaf Pine (*Pinus echinata*), hickories (*Carya* spp.), Flowering Dogwood (*Cornus florida*), Persimmon (*Diospyros virginiana*), Beautyberry (*Callicarpa americana*), Elm (*Ulmus americana*), bays (*Persea* spp.), hawthorns (*Crataegus* spp.), Bluebeech (*Carpinus caroliniana*), Highbush Blueberry (*Vaccinium corymbosum*), Yellow Jessamine (*Gelsemium sempervirens*), Virginia Creeper (*Parthenocissus quinquefolia*), greenbriers (*Smilax* spp.), and Poison Ivy (*Toxicodendron radicans*) are typical woody plants and vines of hammocks. Spanish Moss (*Tillandsia useoides*), Resurrection Fern (*Polypodium polypodioides*), and other epiphytic plants often grow on the branches of the oaks. The understory may have canebrakes, stands of Switch Cane (*Arundinaria gigantea*), or patches of Spikegrass (*Chasmanthium* spp.) and ferns.

Butterflies found within or at the margins of hammocks are the Giant Swallowtail, Tiger Swallowtail, Palamedes Swallowtail, Spicebush Swallowtail, Harvester Butterfly, Spring Azure, Great Purple Hairstreak, Red Banded Hairstreak, Southern Oak Hairstreak, White-M Hairstreak, Banded Hairstreak, King's Hairstreak, Striped Hairstreak, Hackberry Butterfly, Tawny Emperor, Zebra Longwing, Red-Spotted Purple, Silvery Checkerspot, Mourning Cloak, Comma Anglewing, Question Mark, Red Admiral, Gemmed Satyr, Carolina Satyr, Pearly Eye, Viola's Wood Satyr, Cobweb Little Skipper, Bell's Little Skipper, Cuban Palm Skipper, Three-Spotted Skipper, Clouded Skipper, Southern Swamp Skipper, Zabulon Skipper, Little Glassy Wing, Broken Dash, Golden Banded Skipper, Silver Spotted Skipper, Southern Sooty Wing, Long-Tailed Skipper, and Dorantes Skipper. The Pearly Eye and Cobweb Little Skipper feed on Switch Cane and are closely associated with this wild bamboo.

Hammocks are one of the most common plant communities of Florida. They are distributed throughout the state. Nice examples of hammocks occur at Bulow Plantation State Historical Site (Bunnell), San Felasco Hammock (Gainesville), Devil's Millhopper State Geological Site (Gainesville), Wakulla Springs State Park (south of Tallahassee), Torreya State Park (Bristol), Goldhead Branch State Park (Keystone Heights), Highlands Hammock State Park (Sebring), Florida Cavern's State Park (Marianna), Blackwater River State Forest (Milton), Ocala National Forest (Silver Springs), and Blue Springs State Park (Orange City).

Coastal areas of central and northern Florida have maritime hammocks of oaks, Southern Red Cedar (*Juniperus silicicola*), Hackberry, Redbay, and other trees and shrubs. The constant winds and salt spray often prune the trees into unusual shapes. Sweadner's Hairstreak and many other butterflies occur in maritime hammocks. This forest type can be seen at Fort Matanzas National Monument and Anastasia State Recreation Area near St. Augustine.

### Tropical Hammocks

Tropical hardwood hammocks occur in the Florida Keys and coastal areas of the southern mainland. This community is a dense tangle of tropical trees and shrubs such as Gumbo Limbo (*Bursera simaruba*), Poi-

sonwood (*Metopium toxiferum*), Blackbead (*Pithecellobium keyense*), Jamaica Dogwood (*Piscidia piscipula*), Wild Tamarind (*Lysiloma latisiliquum*), Strangler Fig (*Ficus aurea*), Mahogany (*Swietenia mahagoni*), Pigeon Plum (*Coccoloba diversifolia*), Inkwood (*Exothea paniculata*), Lancewood (*Nectandra coriacea*), Paradise Tree (*Simaruba glauca*), Guiana Plum (*Drypetes lateriflora*), Myrsine (*Myrsine guianensis*), Wild Lime (*Zanthoxylum fagara*), Torchwood (*Amyris elemifera*), stoppers (*Eugenia* spp.), Snowberry (*Chiococca alba*), Wild Coffee (*Psychotria nervosa*), Indigo Berry (*Randia aculeata*), and many others.

Tropical hammocks are home to the Bahama Swallowtail, Schaus' Swallowtail, Giant Swallowtail, Florida White, Bush Sulphur, Jamaican Sulphur, Guayacan Sulphur, Large Orange Sulphur, Miami Blue, Cassius Blue, Verde Azul Hairstreak, St. Christopher's Hairstreak, Florida Atala, Martialis Hairstreak, Julia Butterfly, Zebra Long Wing, Dingy Purple Wing, Florida Purple

18. A Florida swamp.

Wing, Ruddy Dagger Wing, Red Broken Dash, and Hammock Skipper.

Parks that have outstanding examples of tropical hammocks are Hugh Taylor Birch State Recreation Area (Fort Lauderdale), Lignumvitae Key State Botanical Site, John D. MacArthur Beach State Park (North Palm Beach), Royal Palm Hammock in Everglades National Park, Matheson Hammock (Miami), Castellow County Park (Goulds), Key Largo Hammocks State Botanical Site, John Pennekamp State Park (Key Largo), and Long Key State Recreation Area.

### Swamps

Swamps are wetland forests that occur in depressions in the flatwoods and along the edges of streams, rivers, and lakes. Swamps may be dominated by Bald Cypress (*Taxodium distichum*), Pond Cypress (*T. ascendens*), or hardwood trees. Shrubs are usually sparse in swamps. Ferns, sedges, and aquatic herbs and grasses may occur in the understory. Evergreen broad-leaved trees (bays) often form bayhead or baygall swamps on wet sites in flatwoods and on seepage slopes. In central and southern Florida, epiphytic plants such as bromeliads grow on cypress and other trees. The parasitic plant Mistletoe (*Phoradendron serotinum*) commonly infects hardwood trees in swamps.

Other plants of swamps are Pop Ash (*Fraxinus caroliniana*), Water Hickory (*Carya aquatica*), Sweet Bay (*Magnolia virginiana*), Black Gum (*Nyssa sylvatica*), Dahoon Holly (*Ilex* cassine), Buttonbush (*Cephalanthus occidentalis*), Cabbage Palm (*Sabal palmetto*), Virginia Willow (*Itea virginica*), Carolina Willow (*Salix caroliniana*), Pond Apple (*Annona glabra*), Swamp Dogwood (*Cornus foemina*), Waterlocust (*Gleditsia aquatica*), Bastard Indigo (*Amorpha fruiticosa*), Titi (*Cyrilla racemiflora*), Carolina Aster (*Aster carolinianus*), Spoonflower (*Peltandra virginica*), Pickerelweed (*Pontederia cordata*), Lizard's Tail (*Saururus cernuus*), Prairie Iris (*Iris hexagona*), Mild Water Pepper (*Polygonum hydropiperoides*), Cinnamon Fern (*Osmunda cinnamomea*), Royal Fern (*Osmunda regalis*), Netted Chain Fern (*Woodwardia areolata*), Swamp Fern (*Blechnum serrulatum*), Savannah Panicum (*Panicum gymnocarpon*), Redtop Panicum (*Panicum rigidulum*), Southern Wild Rice (*Zizaniopsis miliacea*), sedges (*Carex* spp.), and beakrushes (*Rhynchospora* spp.). Wild Taro (*Colocasia esculentum*), a native of Asia, has also become very abundant in Florida's swamps.

Butterflies that occur in swamps are the Tiger Swallowtail, Palamedes Swallowtail, Spicebush Swallowtail, Great Purple Hairstreak, Henry's Elfin, Seminole Crescent, Viceroy, Mourning Cloak, Red Admiral, Berry's Skipper, Dion Skipper, Calhoun's Skipper, Dun Skip-

19. Freshwater marsh habitat.

per, Clouded Skipper, Wild Rice Skipper, and Silver Spotted Skipper.

Swamps are another very common plant community in Florida. They are easily observed by canoe. It's also fun to slog through some of these forests on foot, but beware of the water moccasins! You will find some interesting swamps at the Osceola National Forest (Olustee), Silver River State Park (Silver Springs), Big Cypress National Preserve (Ochopee), Ocala National Forest (Silver Springs), Green Swamp (north of Lakeland), Collier-Seminole State Park (Naples), Corkscrew Swamp Sanctuary (west of Immokalee), Hontoon Island State Park (DeLand), and the grandmother of all swamps, the Fakahatchee Strand State Preserve (Copeland). Atlantic White Cedar (*Chamaecyparis thyoides*) grows in swamps in the Panhandle such as at Apalachicola National Forest (Bristol) and Blackwater River State Park (Holt). This tree is the only host plant for Hessel's Hairstreak.

### Freshwater Marshes

Freshwater marshes are wetlands that lack trees. Plants that grow in marshes are Carolina Willow, Wax Myrtle, Saltbush (*Baccharis halimifolia*), Elderberry (*Sambucus canadensis*), Swamp Hibiscus (*Hibiscus grandiflorus*), Alligator Flag (*Thalia geniculata*), Sawgrass (*Cladium jamaicense*), Bull Rush (*Scirpus* spp.), Soft Rush (*Juncus effusus*), Sand Cordgrass (*Spartina bakeri*), spikerushes (*Eleocharis* spp.), String Lily (*Crinum americanum*), Pickerelweed, arrowheads (*Sagittaria* spp.), bladderworts (*Utricularia* spp.), White Waterlily (*Nymphaea odorata*), Spatterdock (*Nuphar luteum*), Maidencane (*Panicum hemitomon*), American Cupscale (*Sacciolepis striata*), Leather Fern (*Acrostichum danaeifolium*), pennyworts (*Hydrocotyle* spp.), and cattails (*Typha* spp.). Some exotic plants such as Torpedograss (*Panicum repens),* Water Hyacinth (*Eichhornia crassipes*), Water Lettuce (*Pistia stratiotes*), and Alligatorweed (*Alternanathera philoxeroides*) are naturalized pest species of Florida's marshes.

Freshwater marsh butterflies are the Black Swallowtail, Viceroy, Red Admiral, Least Skipperling, Delaware Skipper, Canna Skipper, Palatka Skipper, Ocola Skipper, Howard's Marsh Skipper, and Wild Rice Skipper.

Parks that have large tracts of freshwater marsh are Loxahatchee National Wildlife Refuge (Boynton Beach), Everglades National Park, Myakka River State Park (Sarasota), The Savannas (Fort Pierce), Tosohatchee State Preserve (Christmas), and Paynes Prairie State Preserve (Micanopy).

20. A salt marsh with Salt Cordgrass in the foreground and Black Needle Rush behind.

### Wet Prairies

Wet Prairies are very shallow marshes that often occur in flatwood depressions or on seepage slopes. This community has a diverse flora of grasses and wildflowers. In northern Florida, many wet prairies support carnivorous plants such as pitcher plants, sundews, and butterworts. Some common plants of wet prairies are star rush (*Dichromena* spp.), yellow-eyed grass (*Xyris* spp.), pipeworts (*Eriocaulon* spp.), bog buttons (*Lachnocaulon* spp.), Redroot (*Lachnanthes caroliniana*), Golden Fringed Orchid (*Plantanthera cristata*), grass-pinks (*Calopogon* spp.), and Golden Canna (*Canna flaccida*).

Butterflies of wet prairies are the Black Swallowtail, Soldier, Queen, Monarch, White Peacock, Common Buckeye, Georgia Satyr, Least Skipperling, Delaware Skipper, Berry's Skipper, Dion Skipper, Dun Skipper, Twin Spot Skipper, Canna Skipper, Ocola Skipper, Howard's Marsh Skipper, Cross Line Skipper, and Byssus Skipper.

Look for wet prairies at the Audubon Kissimmee Prairie Sanctuary (north of Okeechobee), Corkscrew Swamp (west of Immokalee), Everglades National Park, Jennings State Forest (Bryceville), and Apalachicola National Forest (Bristol).

### Salt Marshes

Salt marshes are grass- or herb-dominated communities on salty soils near the coast. Saltbush, Christmasberry (*Lycium carolinianum*), Sea Oxeye (*Borrichia frutescens*), Saltgrass (*Distichlis spicata*), Marsh Elder (*Iva frutescens*), Bay Cedar (*Suriana maritima*), Black Needle Rush (*Juncus roemerianus*), Sea Lavender (*Limonium carolinianum*), Smooth Cordgrass (*Spartina alterniflora*), Marsh Hay (*Spartina patens*), and Seashore Dropseed (*Sporobolus virginicus*) are common plants of salt marshes. Extreme salty soils support mostly succulent plants such as Saltwort (*Batis maritima*), glassworts (*Salicornia* spp.), and Sea Purslane (*Sesuvium portulacastrum*).

Butterflies that live in salt marshes are the Great Southern White, Pigmy Blue, Dotted Hairstreak, Martialis Hairstreak, Black Mangrove Buckeye, Salt Marsh Skipper, Beach Skipper, and Howard's Marsh Skipper.

Coastal areas in the vicinity of Yankeetown, Cedar Key, St. Augustine, Amelia Island, Sanibel Island, Guana River State Park (Ponte Vedra Beach), St. Marks National Wildlife Refuge, and Everglades National Park have salt marshes.

### Mangroves

Mangroves are forests that occur on brackish or salty soils. In Florida there are four kinds of mangroves: Red Mangrove (*Rhizophora mangle*), Black Mangrove (*Avicennia germinans*), White Mangrove (*Laguncularia racemosa*), and Buttonwood (*Conocarpus erectus*). These trees may grow in mixed stands, in single-species patches, or in combination with salt-marsh plants. Mangroves are sensitive to cold temperatures and are mostly found in south and central Florida.

Butterflies found around mangroves are the Statira Sulphur, Black Mangrove Buckeye, Salt Marsh Skipper, Beach Skipper, and Mangrove Skipper.

Mangroves can be found at Marco Island, Long Key State Park, Ding Darling National Wildlife Refuge (Sanibel Island), Matheson Hammock (Miami), Chokoloskee, Merritt Island Wildlife Refuge, and Everglades National Park.

### Beaches and Dunes

Coastal beaches and dunes are harsh environments that do not support many plants or butterflies. Typical plants are Coco Plum (*Chrysobalanus icaco*), Beach

21. Red and Black Mangroves surrounding a salt marsh of succulent plants.

22. A weedy pasture.

Croton (*Croton punctatus*), Saw Palmetto, Spanish Bayonet (*Yucca aloifolia*), Golden Creeper (*Ernodia littoralis*), Railroad Vine (*Ipomoea pes-caprae*), Crimsom Dicliptera (*Dicliptera assurgens*), Prickly Pear Cactus (*Opuntia stricta*), passion-flower (*Passiflora* spp.), Partridge Pea (*Cassia* fasciculata), cassia (*Cassia* spp.), Blanket Flower (*Gaillardia pulchella*), Seaside Goldenrod (*Solidago sempervirens*), and Sea Oats (*Uniola paniculata*).

The Great Southern White, Cuban Crescent, Common Buckeye, Monarch, Gulf Fritillary, Beach Skipper, Long-Tailed Skipper, and Yucca Giant Skipper are some of the butterflies that frequent beaches.

Beach and dune communities are common along the Atlantic coast and in the Panhandle of Florida. Canaveral National Seashore (Titusville), Blowing Rocks Preserve, Gulf Islands National Seashore (Gulf Breeze), St. George Island, Anastasia State Recreation Area (St. Augustine), Fort Matanzas National Monument (St. Augustine), Fort Clinch State Park (Fernandina Beach), and Bahia Honda State Recreation Area have good beaches to explore for butterflies.

23. An aerial view of Fort Lauderdale.

### Disturbed Habitats

Huge areas of Florida have been modified in recent times for agriculture, transportation, and human habitation. Weedy disturbed sites are great places to look for butterflies, because many host and nectar plants are weeds. Also, areas where two or more different types of plant communities meet usually have a diversity of butterflies. Weedy butterflies can be found in old fields, pastures, canal banks, roadsides, power-line corridors, and vacant lots. Heavily urban sites may have fewer butterfly species than those in rural settings. However, some butterflies are closely associated with urban areas, especially in southern Florida.

Butterflies that frequent disturbed or urban sites are the Tailless Swallowtail, Black Swallowtail, Giant Swallowtail, Great Southern White, European Cabbage White, Checkered White, Alfalfa Butterfly, Barred Sulphur, Sleepy Orange, Dainty Sulphur, Cloudless Sulphur, Orange-Barred Sulphur, Eastern Tailed Blue, Ceraunus Blue, Cassius Blue, Red-Banded Hairstreak, Fulvous Hairstreak, Dotted Hairstreak, Gray Hairstreak, Tiny Hairstreak, Soldier, Queen, Monarch, Gulf Fritillary, Julia Butterfly, Zebra Long Wing, White Peacock, Viceroy, Variegated Fritillary, Common Buckeye, Caribbean Buckeye, Phaon Crescent, Pearl Crescent, Malachite Butterfly, Red Admiral, American Painted Lady, Cuban Palm Skipper, Field Skipper, Tiny Skipper, Three-Spotted Skipper, Fiery Skipper, Clouded Skipper, Gray Skipper, Ocola Skipper, Baracoa Skipper, Tawny Edged Skipper, Whirlabout Skipper, Red Broken Dash, Silver Spotted Skipper, Horace's Dusky Wing, Zarucco Dusky Wing, Common Sooty Wing, Western Checkered Skipper, Common Checkered Skipper, Tropical Checkered Skipper, Dorantes Skipper, and Long-Tailed Skipper.

## Butterfly Conservation

Butterfly gardening creates or enhances habitat for butterflies in urban landscapes. Planting host and nectar plants is a great benefit to butterflies. Individuals bred in your yard are likely to disperse to other areas and perhaps start new populations. Most of the species that you are likely to find in your garden are common and widely distributed, but you may find some rare butterflies as well. During the early 1970s, the Florida Atala was thought to have gone extinct. After a single colony was rediscovered in Miami, conservationists moved caterpillars to other sites and started new populations. This volunteer effort on the part of amateur lepidopterists was a tremendous success. Today this spectacular tropical butterfly is locally abundant in gardens and natural areas of southeastern Florida (Hammer 1995). However, the habitat requirements of many of Florida's rare, threatened, or endangered butterflies cannot be met in gardens. Preservation of existing natural areas is the only way that they can be saved from extinction. Support of government conservation programs and donations to organizations that are actively purchasing and managing wild areas will help to ensure that Florida's butterfly treasures can be enjoyed by us and future generations.

# Identifying Butterflies

## Scientific and Common Names

Butterflies may have many different names. There is the scientific name that a scientist gave to the species when it was first described. More than 200 years ago, Swedish naturalist Carl Linnaeus invented the current system of naming living organisms. The first valid scientific names began with a book published by Linnaeus in 1753. The scientific name consists of two words: the genus, which is always capitalized, and the specific epithet, which is never capitalized. Usually the name is derived from Latin or Greek. The two words form a unique combination belonging only to that species and no other animal.

Sometimes the same butterfly has unwittingly been described on several occasions and given different names. The oldest name is usually accepted as valid. The newer names or synonyms are not used. A third name may be added to the scientific name to recognize a geographic variant or subspecies. Many of the butterflies in Florida have subspecies names.

The scientific name shows relationships among butterflies, since closely related species have the same genus name. Scientific names may change, because scientists disagree on butterfly relationships, or new relationships are determined. Related butterflies are further grouped into subfamilies, families, and other categories. The names for these groups are derived from Latin, and have standard endings: *-inae* for subfamilies and *-idae* for families. A different system is used for plants, but plant family names always end with *-aceae.*

Common names have been given to our butterflies as well. These are names that may vary from one region to another. Since common names are usually based on English words, they are easier to pronounce and use than the scientific names. However, confusion may sometimes occur because common names do not reflect relationships. Several common names may be used for the same butterfly, and different butterflies may share the same common name. Miller (1992) helped develop a list of common names of North American butterflies. More recently, the North American Butterfly Association has drafted a somewhat different list of common names. Throughout this book, we have tried to give both common and scientific names of the plants and butterflies discussed.

## Butterfly Families

Even if you're a novice at identification, it's relatively easy to determine which family or subfamily a particular butterfly belongs. Size, color pattern, wing shape, and flight behavior are important adult characteristics. Species identification is more difficult, but by knowing fieldmarks and making comparisons with the pictures in this book, you should be able to put names on most of the butterflies in your garden. The color patterns on the upper side of the forewings and underside of the hindwings are very important for species identification.

## A Quick Guide to the Major Butterfly Groups Found in Florida Gardens

### Family Papilionidae (Swallowtails)

**Adults:** Large in size; eyes black and opaque; usually with tails on the hindwings; six legs; flutter the wings when feeding.

**Larvae:** Thickest at the thorax; shoot the smelly, forked, defensive gland (osmeterium) from behind head when provoked; the small caterpillars look like bird droppings; older larvae may have fleshy tubercles along the body or eyespots on the thorax; eat aromatic plants.

**Pupae:** Two points on the head; the back of thorax and head have the form of a sleeping dog; color green or brown; supported by a silk girdle around the middle and a silk button at the rear end.

### Family Pieridae (Whites and Sulphurs)
### Whites (Subfamily Pierinae)

**Adults:** Small to medium-sized; eyes clear with several small black spots; six legs; wings white with black markings.

**Larvae:** Slender; gray with yellow stripes or green; short hairs on the body; eat plants in the Cabbage Family.

**Pupae:** One point on the head; points on the edges of the wing cases; white, green, or brown in color; supported by a silk girdle around middle and a silk button at the rear end.

### Sulphurs (Subfamily Coliadinae)

**Adults:** Small to medium-sized; eyes clear with several

24B. European Cabbage White.

24C. Cloudless Sulphur.

small black spots; six legs; wings yellow or orange (sometimes white).

**Larvae:** Slender; green with yellow side stripes (some with blue markings); short hairs or shiny black cones on the body; eat plants in the Bean Family.

**Pupae:** One point on the head; flattened sideways; green (sometimes pink or purple); supported by a silk girdle around middle and a silk button at the rear end.

### Family Lycaenidae (Blues and Hairstreaks)
### Blues (Subfamily Polyommatinae)

**Adults:** Small in size; eyes black and opaque; six legs; wings blue above (sometimes mostly black or brown); one species with small tails; tiny eyespots on the hindwings.

**Larvae:** Sluglike; head retracted into the body; green, pink, or red (often with white or yellow markings); short hairs on the body; eat flowers and young seeds,

24A. Tiger Swallowtail.

24D. Cassius Blue.

24F. Common Buckeye.

especially of plants in the Bean Family; very slow moving.

**Pupae:** Compact, rounded; green or brown; supported by a silk girdle around middle and a silk button at the rear end.

### Hairstreaks (Subfamily Theclinae)

**Adults:** Small in size; eyes black and opaque; six legs; wings dull or iridescent blue or purple above; one or more small eyespots and usually one or two pairs of slender tails on the hindwings.

**Larvae:** Similar to blues; green, red, or mixed patterns.

**Pupae:** Similar to blues.

### Family Nymphalidae (Brushfooted Butterflies)
### True Brushfooted Butterflies (Subfamily Nymphalinae)

**Adults:** Small to medium-sized; eyes clear with several small black spots; four legs; some with tails or angular wing margins.

**Larvae:** Slender; rows of branching spines on the body; a pair of short or long horns on top of the head; caterpillar sometimes makes a nest of leaves and silk.

**Pupae:** Two points on the head; sometimes with gold or silver markings; small points or a flange on the back; supported only by a silk button at the rear end.

### Hackberry Butterflies (Subfamily Apaturinae)

**Adults:** Medium-sized; eyes clear with several small black spots; four legs; brown with five or six black spots on the hindwing.

**Larvae:** Body thickest at the middle; green with yellow markings; no spines on body; head with short branched horns at the top and short spines on the sides; forked rear end; caterpillar hides in a leaf and silk nest; eat only hackberry.

**Pupae:** Two points on the head; green with yellow markings; flattened sideways; angular; supported only by a silk button at the rear end.

24E. Gray Hairstreak.

24G. Tawny Emperor.

24H. Zebra Longwing.

24J. Carolina Satyr.

### Longwing Butterflies (Subfamily Heliconiinae)

**Adults:** Medium to large in size; eyes clear with several small black spots; four legs; forewings much longer than wide.

**Larvae:** Slender; rows of long, branched spines on the body; a pair of long branched spines at the top of the head; eat only passion-flower vines.

**Pupae:** Two points on the head; resembles a dead leaf; body indented along the back between the thorax and abdomen; metallic silver markings; points or spines on the back of the abdomen; supported only by a silk button at rear the end.

### Milkweed Butterflies (Subfamily Danainae)

**Adults:** Large in size; eyes black; four legs; wings orange or brown with black markings.

**Larvae:** Slender or somewhat thick; colorful (black, white, and yellow); no spines; two or three pairs of long fleshy filaments on the body; eat only plants in the Milkweed Family.

**Pupae:** Compact and rounded; green or pink, with a

black and gold line across the back of the abdomen; gold spots; supported only by a silk button at the rear end.

### Satyrs and Wood Nymphs (Subfamily Satyrinae)

**Adults:** Small to medium-sized; eyes clear with dark spots or stripes; four legs; wings brown with eyespots.

**Larvae:** Slender or somewhat thick; green or brown; no spines; head with two short spines at the top; forked rear end; eat grasses.

**Pupae:** Compact and angular; green or brown; supported only by a silk button at the rear end.

### Family Libytheidae (Snout Butterflies)

**Adults:** Smallish in size; eyes clear with several small black spots; four legs; angular forewings; palpi long and beaklike.

24I. Monarch.

24K. Bachman's Snout Butterfly.

24L. Fiery Skipper.

24N. Yucca Giant Skipper.

**Larvae:** Slender; green with yellow markings; no spines on head or body; resembles a moth caterpillar; eats only hackberry.

**Pupae:** Angular; green with yellow markings; supported only by a silk button at the rear end.

### Family Hesperiidae (Skipper Butterflies)

### Branded Skippers (Subfamily Hesperiinae)

**Adults:** Small to medium-sized; eyes black and opaque; six legs; antenna with a short hook at tip; males often with a dark line or patch near the middle of the forewing; the underside of the hindwing often has a row of pale spots.

**Larvae:** Slender or somewhat thick; green or brown; no spines on the body or head; some develop wax glands on the underside of the body prior to pupation; caterpillar in a folded leaf shelter; eat only grasses.

**Pupae:** Green or brown, sometimes with a single point on the head; tip of proboscis extends beyond the wings; some with short hairs on the abdomen; supported by a silk girdle around the middle and a silk button at the rear end, in a leaf shelter.

### Broadwinged Skippers (Subfamily Pyrginae)

**Adults:** Small to medium-sized; eyes black and opaque; six legs; antenna bent or hooked at tip; males with a flap along the forewing; translucent spots on the forewings; a few species with tails.

**Larvae:** Thick body; green or colorful; some with yellow or orange eyespots on the head; no spines on the body or head; caterpillar in a folded leaf shelter; many eat plants in the Bean Family.

**Pupae:** Green or brown; thick; some are covered by white wax; some with short hairs on the abdomen; supported by a silk girdle around the middle and a silk button at the rear end, in a leaf shelter.

### Giant Skippers (Subfamily Megathyminae)

**Adults:** Medium-sized; robust body; eyes black and opaque or clear red with one black spot; six legs; antenna with a small hook at the tip; wings dark brown with yellow patches.

**Larvae:** Body thickest at thorax; whitish with a reddish-brown head; bores into yucca stems and roots.

**Pupae:** Brown; covered by white wax; located in the larval tunnel underground or in a yucca stem, without silk supports.

24M. Silver Spotted Skipper.

# Butterflies of Florida Gardens

Orange-Barred Sulphurs feeding at Garberia flowers.

## Swallowtails (Family Papilionidae)

### Pipevine Swallowtail

*Battus philenor*

**Adult:** The Pipevine Swallowtail is a fairly large black butterfly with a short tail on each hindwing. There is a row of small whitish spots on the upper hindwing. The underside of the hindwing has a row of large orange spots embedded in a metallic blue patch. Males have extensive blue iridescence on the upper hindwing. Unlike the males, females have very little blue on the upper side, and the white spots extend onto the forewing. Wingspans range from 6.2 to 9.4 cm.

**Field Marks:** Medium to large in size; tails present; the wings are black with shiny blue (male) or with faint whitish spots (female); this is Florida's only primarily black butterfly with a metallic blue patch on the underside of the hindwing.

**Larva:** The caterpillar is velvety black with fleshy protuberances (tubercles). Those on or near the back are short and reddish-orange. The tubercles near the legs are longer and blackish. The two very long front tubercles are used as feelers as the caterpillar moves about. The osmeterium is bright yellow. The Gold Rim caterpillar is similar.

**Pupa:** The chrysalis may be either green with yellow markings or brown.

**Host Plants:** Herbs and vines in the Dutchman's Pipe or Birthwort Family (Aristolochiaceae). Snake Root (*Aristolochia serpenteria*) is the common native host. This herb is so small that all of the leaves on an individual plant are unlikely to support a caterpillar for very long, and the larva must crawl over the ground to find more plants to satisfy its needs. The caterpillars also eat Large-Leaved Pipevine (*Aristolochia durior*) and Wooly Pipevine (*Aristolochia tomentosa*) of the southeastern United States. These plants are more robust than Snake Root and are capable of supporting many caterpillars. They rarely feed on exotic pipevines such as Calico Flower (*Aristolochia elegans*).

Pipevines are protected from most herbivores by foul-tasting aristolochic acids and other chemicals. The swallowtail caterpillars, however, are not affected by these toxins. Both the caterpillars and adults may use chemicals from the host plants for their own protection. The black and orange markings are warning colors. When a predator such as a bird or lizard eats a bad tasting insect with these colors, it gets sick, and quickly learns to avoid such prey in the future.

**Natural History:** The eggs are large, round, and orange.

25. Pipevine Swallowtails (males left, females right; top row upper sides, bottom row undersides).

27. The last-stage caterpillar.

26. A male visiting Paint Brush (*Carphephorus corymbosus*).

28. The pupa.

Females lay the eggs singly or in small clusters on the young growth of the host. The caterpillars live on the host plant and do not make nests. They evert (shoot out) their smelly osmeterium from behind the head when disturbed. Several generations are produced each year. Adults occur from February through November. The pupa is the over-wintering stage. Males have a fast, erratic flight, from 1 to 2 meters above the ground. Females seeking host plants have a slower flight pattern lower to the ground. Males may defend small territories, periodically resting on vegetation and making short flights around the perch.

29. Snake Root (*Aristolochia serpentaria*) with two Pipevine Swallowtail eggs.

**Distribution:** The Pipevine Swallowtail is usually found in sandhills and scrubby flatwoods in northern and central Florida. This butterfly is unlikely to occur in highly urban areas, but may visit gardens in the suburbs and rural settings, especially if sandhill vegetation is nearby. It is seldom very abundant in gardens.

**Note:** *Aristolochia* was the source of the active ingredients in the cure-all "snakeroot oil" sold by traveling peddlers in western America (Crosswhite and Crosswhite 1985). For centuries these plants were also used to aid in birth and the removal of the placenta from the uterus, thus the name "birthwort." The word *Aristolochia* is derived from Greek, meaning "best parturition." The powerful chemicals in *Aristolochia* also cause nausea, gas, and vomiting. Do not eat *Aristolochia* or any other plants unless they are known to be safe for human consumption.

## Gold Rim, Paolydamas, or Tailless Swallowtail

### *Battus polydamas lucayus*

**Adult:** The Gold Rim is a large blackish butterfly with a greenish-yellow band on each wing. The underside of the hindwing is brown with brick-red spots and a small yellow patch. The hindwing is scalloped but, unlike our other swallowtails, does not have tails. Females have slightly wider yellow bands than males. Do not confuse the Gold Rim with Black or Palamedes Swallowtails that have the tails broken off. Wingspans range from 6.7 to 8.9 cm.

**Field Marks:** Medium to medium-large in size; the wings are blackish with yellow bands; without tails.

**Larva:** The brownish caterpillars are thick-bodied with fleshy protuberances (tubercles). The tubercles are short and orange-red in color. The osmeterium is bright yellow.

**Pupa:** The chrysalis may be either brown with orange markings or green with yellow markings.

**Host Plants:** Herbs and vines in the Dutchman's Pipe or Birthwort Family (Aristolochiaceae). The caterpillars feed on the leaves of many species of pipevine (*Aristolochia* spp.), especially exotics such as Calico Flower (*A. elegans*), Giant Pipevine (*A. gigantea*), Pelican Flower (*A. ringens*), and Three-Lobed Pipevine (*A. trilobata*). Burch et al. (1988) also list Rooster Flower (*A. galatea*), *A. grandiflora*, *A. labiata*, and *A. maxima* as being cultivated in Florida, and the Gold Rim probably feeds on these plants as well.

**Natural History:** The eggs are large, round, and orange-brown in color. Females deposit the eggs in small clusters on the leaves of the host plant. The caterpillars feed in groups, especially while small, and do not make nests. If disturbed, the caterpillars display the stinky osmeterium. Many generations are produced each year. Adults can be found all year in central and southern Florida. In northern Florida, the Gold Rim is limited by freezing temperatures during December, January, and February. Hard freezes may temporarily eliminate some populations. The flight is slow and from 1 to 3 meters above the ground.

**Distribution:** The Gold Rim occurs throughout Florida, especially in urban areas. Garden abundance may be moderate to high.

**Note:** If pipevines are planted in the garden, this swallowtail will eventually find the patch and start a colony. Although some individuals may disperse long distances to find new patches of pipevine, most are homebodies that stay close to the garden. It may take several years before a new planting of pipevine is discovered by a dispersing female, depending upon whether other colonies are in the neighborhood or far away. Over several generations, the caterpillars will eat all of the leaves from the pipevine host, then chew the smaller stems, and eventually gnaw the bark from older branches. The caterpillars usually will not kill the plant, but hardly give it a chance to recover. Using fertilizer or compost to boost the soil nutrients will encourage new growth. The reward is dozens of Gold Rim adults flitting in the garden.

## Zebra Swallowtail

### *Eurytides marcellus floridanus*

**Adult:** The Zebra Swallowtail is a fairly large whitish butterfly with black stripes and a pair of long tails. The hindwing also has a red spot near the base of the tail, and on the underside a red stripe through the middle of the wing. The sexes are very similar. This species is one of the first to emerge in spring and these early adults are small, crisply marked, and have short tails. The summer generation is larger and has longer tails. Some individuals appearing in the fall are very large, dark, and have very long tails. Wingspans range from 5.5 to 7.9 cm.

**Field Marks:** Medium to medium-large in size; long tails present; wings white with black stripes, there is a red stripe through the middle of the hindwing below.

**Larva:** Young larvae are black. The mature caterpillars have several color forms, but all have black and yellow behind the head and a transverse (across the body axis) blue, black, and yellow stripe on the thorax that is usually mostly hidden. The main color forms are light green with black sprinkles, green with pale blue and yellow stripes, or brown with white and yellow stripes. The body is thickest at the thorax and strongly tapers toward the rear. The osmeterium is bright yellow.

**Pupa:** The chrysalis is usually uniformly green, but a brown form also occurs.

**Host Plants:** Trees and shrubs in the Custard Apple Family (Annonaceae). The caterpillars eat the young leaves and flowers of pawpaws (*Asimina incarna, A. angustifolia,*

30. Gold Rim Swallowtails (males left, females right; top row upper sides, bottom row undersides).

31. The last-stage caterpillar.

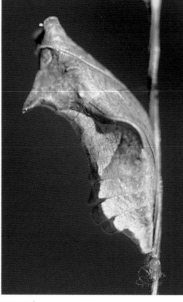

32. A brown pupa.

33. Calico Flower (*Aristolochia elegans*).

34. Zebra Swallowtails (top row spring forms, bottom row summer forms; left column upper side males; middle column upper side females; right column undersides, female on top, male on bottom).

35. A Zebra Swallowtail feeding at Southern Butterfly Weed (*Asclepias tuberosa* subsp. *rolfsii*).

36. Mating Zebra Swallowtails.

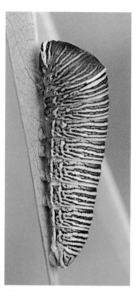

37. A last-stage caterpillar with yellow stripes.

38. A green last-stage caterpillar.

39. A brown last-stage caterpillar.

40. A last-stage caterpillar in defensive pose.

41. A green pupa.

42. A brown pupa.

44. Flatwoods Pawpaw (*Asimina reticulata*).

43. Flag Pawpaw (*Asimina incarna*).

*A. obovata, A. tetramera, A. pygmaea, A. triloba,* and *A. parviflora*) and squirrel-bananas (*Deeringothamnus pulchella* and *D. rugelii*).

**Natural History:** The eggs are large, round, and pale green. Females lay the eggs on tender young leaves, one or two per plant. Use caution if you're raising the caterpillars in captivity. The largest caterpillar will eat the smaller ones if too crowded. If disturbed, the caterpillar puffs up the thorax, prominently displaying the blue, black, and yellow stripe, and shoots out the foul-smelling yellow osmeterium from behind the head. At least three generations occur in Florida. Adults can be found from February through November. The pupa is the overwintering stage. The flight is fast, erratic, and low to the ground. Males sometimes drink from wet soil.

**Distribution:** The Zebra Swallowtail occurs throughout the state in dry pastures, scrubs, sandhills, and scrubby flatwoods habitats. This butterfly is unlikely to be found in highly urban areas, but will visit suburban and rural gardens, especially if areas with pawpaws are in the neighborhood. Abundance in gardens is low.

## Giant Swallowtail

### *Heraclides cresphontes*

**Adult:** The Giant Swallowtail is one of Florida's largest butterflies. The wings above are dark brown with bands of yellow spots. The large yellow spot near the tip of the forewing may be entirely yellow or have a dark center. The undersides of the wings are mostly pale yellow. The hindwing has a red and black eyespot and a tail that is yellow near the tip. On the underside of the hindwing is a blue band and a small orange patch near the center. The sexes are similar, but females are paler yellow and have a narrower yellow band at the base of the hindwing above. Wingspans range from 8.5 to 11.3 cm.

**Field Marks:** Medium-large to large in size; tails present; dark brown wings with yellow bands; yellow undersides; there is a yellow band at base of hindwing above.

**Larva:** Young caterpillars are light brown with white and yellow patches. The shiny skin and blotchy coloration give the caterpillars a bird-dropping appearance. Mature larvae have dull skin and are brown with disruptive white patches on the thorax, middle, and rear end. The thorax is enlarged and bears some black markings. When viewed from the front, the thorax looks like the head of a small animal. The pale rear end has dark markings that form a face pattern as well. The osmeterium is bright red. Giant Swallowtail caterpillars are called Orange Dogs.

**Pupa:** The chrysalis is brown with dark markings and patches of green. It closely resembles a broken twig with lichens.

**Host Plants:** Trees in the Citrus Family (Rutaceae). Native hosts are Wild Lime (*Zanthoxylum fagara*), Hercules Club (*Zanthoxylum clava-herculis*), Torchwood (*Amyris elemifera*), and Wafer Ash (*Ptelea trifoliata*). The larvae also eat the young leaves of Sweet Orange (*Citrus sinensis*), Sour Orange (*Citrus aurantium*), Lemon (*Citrus limon*), Tangerine (*Citrus reticulata*), Key Lime (*Citrus aurantifolia*), Grapefruit (*Citrus paradisi*), Trifoliate Orange (*Poncirus trifoliata,* used as a root stock on which citrus is grafted), Box Thorn (*Severinia buxifolia*), and occasionally Rue (*Ruta graveolens*). Giant Swallowtail females will lay eggs on Nagami Kumquat (*Fortunella margarita*), but the larvae do not seem able to survive on this plant. *Zanthoxylum* spp. and Wafer Ash seem much preferred over other hosts by the ovipositing females.

**Natural History:** The eggs are large, round, and orange in color. Females lay the eggs one or two at a time on the new growth. The young caterpillars eat only young, tender leaves and rest exposed on the upper leaf surfaces. Older larvae more often rest on twigs and branches. The osmeterium is displayed when the caterpillar is provoked. Adults fly all year in south Florida and from February through November in the northern part of the state. The pupa is the overwintering stage. The flight pattern is normally slow and gliding, from 1 to 2 meters above the ground. Males sometimes drink from wet soil.

**Distribution:** This spectacular butterfly is found throughout Florida in or at the edges of hammocks, citrus groves, and urban areas. The Giant Swallowtail frequently can be found in gardens, but is seldom very abundant.

## Black Swallowtail

### *Papilio polyxenes asterius*

**Adult:** The Black Swallowtail is a fairly large black butterfly with yellow bands and tails. The wings are edged by yellow spots on the upper side. The hindwing has a small red and black eyespot near the base of the tail. On the underside of the hindwing there are two rows of orange spots bordering a zone of blue and black. Males have a wide yellow band across the middle of the wings above. The band is reduced to small spots in the female. The upper side of the hindwing of females usually has extensive blue. This is one of the smallest swallowtails in Florida. Wingspans range from 6.9 to 8.4 cm.

**Field Marks:** Medium to medium-large in size; tails present; wings black with yellow bands, edged with yellow spots.

**Larva:** Young caterpillars are black with a white saddle and look like bird droppings. The mature larva is green with black bands and yellow spots. The width of the black

45. Giant Swallowtails (males left, females right; top row upper sides, bottom row undersides).

46. Males puddling at wet soil.

47. The last-stage caterpillar on Wild Lime.

48. Hercules Club (*Zanthoxylum clava-herculis*).

49. Wild Lime (*Zanthoxylum fagara*).

bands varies, and occasionally nearly all black caterpillars can be found. The osmeterium is bright yellow.

**Pupa:** The chrysalis may be green with yellow markings or brown.

**Host Plants:** Herbs in the Carrot or Umbellifer Family (Apiaceae). The caterpillars are especially fond of the leaves, flowers, and young seeds of cultivated umbellifers such as Parsley (*Petroselinum crispum*), Fennel (*Foeniculum vulgare*), Florence Fennel (*Foeniculum dulce*), Lovage (*Levisticum officinale*), Anise (*Pimpinella anisum*), Dill (*Anethum graveolens*), and Carrot (*Daucus carota* var. *sativa*). Other native or naturalized plants used by the Black Swallowtail include Water Hemlock (*Cicuta mexicana*), Water Dropwort (*Oxypolis filiformis*), Mock Bishop's Weed (*Ptilimnium capillaceum*), Roughfruit Scaleseed (*Spermolepis divaricata*), and occasionally Wedge-Leaved Eryngium (*Eryngium cuneifolium*). Curly Parsley seems to be preferred over the flat-leaved Italian variety. Caution: Water Hemlock is extremely poisonous to humans and pets if eaten, and is not recommended for the garden.

**Natural History:** The eggs are large, round, and pale yellow. Females lay the eggs on the leaves of the host. Although not laid in clusters, the female may deposit several eggs on the same plant. The larvae sit exposed on the leaves and stems. Many generations are produced each year. Adults can be found from February through November. The pupa is the overwintering stage. The flight is slow and near the ground when seeking nectar or laying eggs, or fast and higher when dispersing. Males may defend small territories, alternating resting on vegetation with conducting short flights around the area.

**Distribution:** The Black Swallowtail occurs in the vicinity of wet prairies, roadside ditches, disturbed sites, and urban areas throughout the state. It is one of the easiest butterflies to attract to your garden, but the adults are seldom very abundant.

## Tiger Swallowtail

### *Pterourus glaucus glaucus*
### *Pterourous glaucus australis*

**Adult:** The Tiger Swallowtail is a very large yellow butterfly with black borders and stripes. Females come in two color forms. There is a yellow and black form that looks very much like the male, except for a blue flush in the black border on the upper side of the hindwing. The second form is mostly black with the blue flush and an orange spot on the leading edge of the hindwing. The black form may be confused with other dark swallowtails, but the Tiger Swallowtail pattern of stripes is faintly visible. Both forms are about equally abundant. Occasionally, intermediates between the yellow and black forms are seen. Wingspans range from 9.6 to 11.8 cm. The spring generation is the smallest. This is Florida's largest butterfly.

**Field Marks:** Large in size; tails present; wings yellow with black stripes or dark with black stripes faintly visible (dark-form female).

**Larva:** The young caterpillars are dark brown with a white saddle and resemble bird droppings. The last-stage larva is green with rows of small blue spots on the abdomen. The thorax is enlarged and has a pair of small eyespots and a narrow yellow and black transverse line that is usually is mostly hidden. The body is stout. The osmeterium is orange.

**Pupa:** The chrysalis is grayish with dark markings and patches of green. It resembles a broken twig with lichens.

**Host Plants:** Trees in the Olive, Magnolia, and Rose Families (Oleaceae, Magnoliaceae, and Rosaceae). In northern Florida, the Eastern Tiger Swallowtail (*P. glaucus glaucus*) eats the leaves of Pop Ash (*Fraxinus profunda*) and White Ash (*Fraxinus americana*) in the Olive Family, Sweet Bay (*Magnolia virginiana*) and Tulip Tree (*Liriodendron tulipifera*) in the Magnolia Family, and Wild Cherry (*Prunus serotina*) in the Rose Family. The Southern Tiger Swallowtail (*P. glaucus australis*) occurs from Ocala southward and eats only Sweet Bay.

**Natural History:** The eggs are large, round, and green. Females tend to lay the eggs, one per leaf, on the upper side of fully expanded leaves, near the midrib and toward the tip. The caterpillars live in silk-lined curled leaves. When disturbed, the caterpillar puffs up the thorax, prominently displaying the eyespots, yellow and black line, and the yellow osmeterium, giving the appearance of a small snake. When ready to pupate, the color changes from green to

50. Black Swallowtails (males left, females right; top row upper sides, bottom row undersides).

51. Young caterpillars. The middle caterpillar that resembles a bird dropping is one of the first larval stages.

52. The last-stage caterpillar on Water Dropwort (*Oxypolis filiformis*).

53. Melanic (dark) and normal caterpillars.

54. The caterpillar just prior to pupation.

55. A green pupa.

56. A brown pupa.

57. Parsley (*Petroselinum crispum*).

58. Bronze Fennel (*Foeniculum vulgare*).

59. Mock Bishop's Weed (*Ptilimnium capillaceum*).

60. Tiger Swallowtails (males left, females right; top row upper sides, bottom left = underside male, bottom right = upper side dark female).

61. A yellow female visiting Goldenrod.

62. A black female on Flatwoods Plum.

63. A male drinking from wet sand.

64. The last-stage caterpillar on Sweet Bay.

65. The false eyes on the thorax of the last-stage caterpillar.

66. A last-stage caterpillar in its nest on Wild Cherry (*Prunus serotina*).

67. The pupa.

68. Sweet Bay (*Magnolia virginiana*).

69. Pop Ash (*Fraxinus caroliniana*).

brown, and the caterpillar wanders away from the host plant. At least three generations occur each year. Adults can be found from February through November. The pupa is the overwintering stage. The flight is slow and gliding, from 1 meter above the ground to tree-canopy level. Males sometimes drink from wet soil.

**Distribution:** The Tiger Swallowtail inhabits swamps, flatwoods, and hammocks throughout most of the state but is uncommon or absent in extreme southern Florida. It is a frequent garden visitor if the natural habitats are nearby, but is usually much less abundant than the Palamedes or Spicebush Swallowtails.

## Palamedes Swallowtail

### *Pterourus palamedes*

**Adult:** The Palamedes Swallowtail is a very dark brown butterfly with yellow bands on the wings. There is usually a small yellow spot toward the upper middle of the forewing. On the underside of the hindwing, a narrow yellow line parallels the body. The sexes are similar, but females tend to be larger and have some blue on the upper side of the hindwing. Wingspans range from 7.5 to 11.0 cm.

**Field Marks:** Medium-large to large in size; tails present; wings dark brown with yellow bands, edged with yellow spots above; there is a yellow stripe near the base of hindwing on the underside.

**Larva:** The young caterpillars are brown and white with a pair of eyespots on the thorax. They differ from the Spicebush Swallowtail in having an all white rear end. Mature larvae are green above and reddish below with a narrow yellow line between. There is a medium-large pair of eyespots and a small pair of orange spots on the enlarged thorax. The abdomen has rows of small blue spots. The body is stout. The osmeterium is bright yellow.

**Pupa:** The chrysalis is strongly bent away from the substrate and may be either green or brown.

**Host Plants:** Trees in the Laurel Family (Lauraceae). The caterpillars eat the tender young leaves of Redbay (*Persea borbonia*), Swampbay (*Persea palustris*), Pond Spice

70. Palamedes Swallowtails (males left, females right; top row upper sides, bottom row undersides).

71. A young caterpillar raised on Camphor Tree.

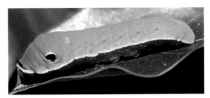

72. The last-stage caterpillar.

73. The false eyes on the last-stage caterpillar.

74. The last-stage caterpillar changes color before wandering to find a pupation site.

75. A green pupa.

76. A brown pupa.

77. Redbay (*Persea borbonia*).

78. Silkbay (*Persea humilis*).

(*Litsea aestivalis*), Silkbay (*Persea humilis*), and Spicebush (*Lindera benzoin*) are probably also eaten. Female Palamedes Swallowtails are not known to lay eggs on the Camphor Tree (*Cinnamomum camphora*), but the caterpillars readily eat the leaves when reared indoors.

**Natural History:** The eggs are large and pale green. Females lay the eggs, one or two at a time, on the new growth. Unlike the Spicebush Swallowtail, the caterpillars do not make nests but live exposed on the leaves and branches. When disturbed, the larva puffs up the thorax and displays the smelly osmeterium. Before pupation, the color changes from green to pale yellow. The larva usually wanders away from the host plant to pupate. Three or more generations occur each year. Adults are present from February through November. The pupa is the overwintering stage. The flight is slow, from 1 to 2 meters above the ground. Males sometimes drink from wet soil.

**Distribution:** The Palamedes Swallowtail occurs in flatwoods and hammocks throughout most of Florida but is usually absent from the Keys. It is one of the most common swallowtails in the state, often occurring in moderate abundance in suburban and rural gardens.

## Spicebush Swallowtail

### *Pterourus troilus*

**Adult:** The Spicebush Swallowtail is a large black butterfly with pale yellowish-green spots along the outer border of the wings. The upper hindwing has a bright orange spot along the leading edge, and a greenish (males) or bluish (females) flush. The underside of the hindwing has two bands of orange spots bordering a black and blue patch. Wingspans range from 7.2 to 9.0 cm.

**Field Marks:** Medium-large to large in size; tails present; wings black with green (male) or blue (female) on the upper hindwings, edged by pale yellowish-green spots above.

**Larva:** Young caterpillars are brown and white with eyespots on the thorax. Unlike the Palamedes Swallowtail, the larvae have a dark patch on the white rear. Mature larvae are yellowish-green above and reddish-brown below. A wide yellow line is present on the sides. The abdomen has rows of small blue spots. The thorax is enlarged and has a pair of large eyespots and large orange spots. The body is stout. The osmeterium is bright yellow. This larva is very similar to that of the Palamedes Swallowtail.

**Pupa:** The chrysalis may be green or brown and is strongly bent away from the substrate.

**Host Plants:** Trees in the Laurel Family (Lauraceae). The larvae eat the young leaves of Sassafras (*Sassafras albidum*), Redbay (*Persea borbonia*), Swampbay (*Persea palustris*), Spicebush (*Lindera benzoin*), and Camphor Tree (*Cinnamomum camphora*). Silkbay (*Persea humilis*)

and Pond Spice (*Litsea aestivalis*) are probably also eaten in Florida.

**Natural History:** The eggs are large and pale green. Females lay the eggs, one or two at a time, on the new growth. Young caterpillars make nests by eating part way through a leaf near the tip and folding the flap over. The inside of the nest is lined with silk. Older caterpillars live in curled leaves that are lined with silk. When disturbed the larva puffs up the thorax and displays the yellow osmeterium. Before pupation, the color changes from green to pale yellow. The larva usually wanders away from the host plant to pupate. Three or more generations occur each year. Adults are present from February through November. The pupa is the overwintering stage. The flight is slow, from 1 to 2 meters above the ground. Males sometimes drink from wet soil.

**Distribution:** The Spicebush Swallowtail is found in flatwoods and hammocks throughout Florida, except for the extreme southern part of the state. It is often moderately common in suburban and rural gardens.

## Whites (Family Pieridae: Subfamily Pierinae)

## Great Southern White

### *Ascia monuste phileta*

**Adult:** The Great Southern White is a white butterfly with a border of black triangles on the upper side of the forewings. The underside of the hindwing is pale yellow (males) or grayish (females). Females have a small dark spot near the middle of the forewing. The wings of the females may be white like the males or mostly pale to dark gray in color. The tips of the antennae are bright blue. Wingspans range from 4.5 to 6.0 cm.

**Field Marks:** Somewhat small to medium in size; wings white or gray (dark form female); antennal tips blue.

**Larva:** The caterpillar is yellow with black stripes and small black platelets. The slender body is sparsely covered with longish hairs.

**Pupa:** The chrysalis is black and white and resembles a bird dropping. The head, thorax, and edges of the wings have small thornlike points.

**Host Plants:** Herbs in the Mustard, Nasturtium, and Saltwort Families (Brassicaceae, Tropaeolaceae, Bataceae). The caterpillars eat the leaves, flowers, and young seed pods of wild mustards (*Brassica* spp.), Pepper Grass (*Lepidium virginicum*), Arugula (*Eruca vesicaria* spp. *sativa*), and Sea Rocket (*Cakile lanceolata*) in the Mustard Family as well as Nasturtium (*Tropaeolum majus,*

79. Spicebush Swallowtails (males left, females right; top row upper sides, bottom row undersides).

80. The leaf shelter of a young caterpillar.

81. The young larva has a dark patch on the rear end.

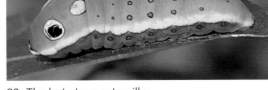

82. The last-stage caterpillar.

83. A green pupa.

84. A brown pupa.

85. Sassafras (*Sassafras albidum*).

86. Swampbay (*Persea palustris*).

Tropaeolaceae) and Saltwort (*Batis maritima,* Bataceae). The latter plant grows in salt marshes and has a salty taste.

**Natural History:** The yellowish eggs are long and narrow. Females deposit the eggs singly or in small groups on the leaves or stems of the host plant. The caterpillars live under the leaves or exposed on the host. Several generations are produced each year. This butterfly experiences population outbreaks from time to time in south Florida. During some years, thousands can be seen flying northward along the coast. Adults of the Great Southern White can be found all year in south Florida, but are limited to the summer months in the northern part of the state. The flight is lazy and low to the ground, especially when seeking nectar or laying eggs. During dispersal or migration, the flight is strong and directed, from 1 to 2 meters above the ground.

**Distribution:** The Great Southern White is mostly a coastal butterfly that breeds in salt marshes. It occurs from the Keys to northern Florida. In central and south-

ern Florida, this butterfly also colonizes inland areas, especially citrus groves with an abundance of Pepper Grass. If you live near the beach, you are likely to have lots of Great Southern Whites visiting your garden.

## European Cabbage White

### *Pieris rapae*

**Adult:** The European Cabbage White is a white butterfly with black spots. The upper side of the forewing is ornamented with one black spot in the male and two in the female. The tip of the forewing is black. There is also a small black spot along the leading edge of the hindwing. The underside of the hindwing is pale yellow. Wingspans range from 4.3 to 4.9 cm.

**Field Marks:** Somewhat small in size; wings white with one or two black spots on upper forewing; the forewing tip is black.

**Larva:** The caterpillar is green with minute black dots. A broken yellow line occurs on each side. The body is slender with numerous, very short hairs, giving the caterpillars a velvety appearance.

**Pupa:** The pupa may be green or brown, and has a short point on the head, thorax, and edges of the wings.

**Host Plants:** Herbs in the Mustard Family (Brassicaceae). The caterpillars eat the leaves of Collards, Cabbage, Cauliflower, Brussels Sprouts, and Broccoli (these are all varieties of *Brassica oleracea*), Turnip (*Brassica rapa*), Wild Mustard (*Brassica campestris*), Wild Radish (*Raphanus raphanistrum*), Pepper Grass (*Lepidium virginicum*), and probably other crucifers (cross-bearers, referring to the four-petaled flowers).

**Natural History:** The eggs are narrow and pointed at the tip. They are white when first laid but change to yellow within a day. Females deposit the eggs singly or in small groups on the leaves, stems, or flower buds of the host plant. The caterpillars live under the leaves or exposed on the host. The last-stage larva may pupate on the host, usually forming a green chrysalis. Or it may wander away to form a brown pupa on fences, the sides of buildings, flower pots, and other substrates. Several generations are produced each year. Adults are seen mostly in the spring and early summer from February through June. The pupa is the overwintering stage. The flight pattern is lazy and near the ground when seeking nectar or laying eggs. Dispersing adults have a strong, directed flight, from 1 to 2 meters above the ground.

**Distribution:** This butterfly occurs in Europe, northern Africa, and Asia and was accidentally introduced into Quebec, Canada, and California probably during the 1860s. It quickly spread throughout the United States as well as through much of Canada and Mexico. This species

87. Great Southern Whites (males left, females right; top row upper sides, bottom left = underside male, bottom right = upper side dark female).

88. The last-stage caterpillar on Wild Mustard.

89. The bird dropping–like pupa.

90. Wild Mustard (*Brassica* sp.).

is found throughout Florida but is uncommon in the southern part of the state. The European Cabbage White is a tremendous pest of cultivated crucifers, and is especially abundant in cabbage-growing areas such as around Hastings in St. Johns County. It frequently occurs in places where the earth has recently been tilled, such as roadsides, cultivated fields, and construction sites. The European Cabbage White also is found in gardens and yards where the host plants are grown. Garden abundance is low to moderate.

91. Cabbage Whites (males left, females right; top row upper sides, bottom row undersides).

92. A Cabbage White sipping nectar from a Radish flower.

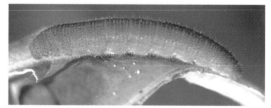

93. The last-stage caterpillar.

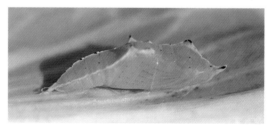

94. A green pupa.

95. Cabbage (*Brassica oleracea*).

## Checkered White

### *Pontia protodice*

**Adult:** The Checkered White is mostly a white butterfly with black spots on the forewings. There is a large, squarish black spot with a white center near the upper middle of the forewing. Females are similar to the males but are darker and have a chainlike grayish band along the outer margin of the hindwing. The underside of the hindwing has greenish markings in the spring generation and grayish markings in the summer and fall broods. Wingspans range from 3.2 to 4.6 cm.

**Field Marks:** Somewhat small in size; wings white; forewing with more than two black spots.

96. Checkered Whites (left column males, middle column females, right column spring forms; bottom row undersides; top right = underside male, bottom right = underside female).

97. The last-stage caterpillar on Pepper Grass.

98. The pupa.

99. Pepper Grass (*Lepidium virginicum*).

**Larva:** The last stage larva is gray with yellow stripes and small black platelets. It resembles the Great Southern White caterpillar. The body is slender with short hairs.

**Pupa:** The pupa is gray with thornlike points on the head, thorax, and edges of the wings.

**Host Plants:** Herbs in the Mustard Family. The caterpillars eat the leaves and young seeds of Pepper Grass (*Lepidium virginicum*).

**Natural History:** The eggs are narrow and pointed. The color is white when first laid, but they quickly change to yellow. Females lay the eggs singly on the leaves or developing seeds of the host plant. The caterpillars live exposed on the leaves and do not build nests. Several generations occur each year. Adults of the Checkered White can be found from late February until early December. The pupa is the overwintering stage. The flight pattern is fast and erratic near the ground.

**Distribution:** The Checkered White is found in disturbed sites such as weedlots, roadsides, and cultivated fields throughout Florida. Garden abundance is low.

# Sulphurs (Family Pieridae: Subfamily Coliadinae)

## Barred Sulphur

### *Eurema daira*

**Adult:** The Barred Sulphur is a small yellow butterfly with black wingtips and a black bar along the lower margin of the forewings. The upper hindwing usually has a black band along the outer margin. Females are paler yellow than males and are sometimes nearly white. The black bar along the lower margin of the forewing is faint or nearly absent in females. The Barred Sulphur also shows considerable seasonal variation. The underside of the hindwing is gray in the summer generation and brown or red from fall and winter. The winter form is also a brighter yellow and has less black, especially on the upper hindwing. Wingspans range from 2.5 to 3.7 cm.

100. Barred Sulphurs (left columns males, right columns females; top row upper sides, bottom row undersides; second and far right columns winter forms)

101. A resting winter-form adult.

102. The last-stage caterpillar on Joint Vetch (*Aeschynomene americana*).

103. The caterpillar just before pupation.

The Little Sulphur (*Eurema lisa*) is similar but lacks the black bar on the upper forewing, and the underside of the hindwing is yellow with an orange spot near the tip.

**Field Marks:** Small to somewhat small in size; wings yellow with black markings; the hindwings are uniform gray, brown, or reddish beneath.

**Larva:** The caterpillar is bright green with a narrow whitish line along each side. The body is slender and has short hairs.

**Pupa:** The pupa is flattened sideways and has a short point on the head. The color is green with small dark spots, and there is a white and black line along the sides of the head and thorax. Occasionally, a form with extensive black markings is seen.

**Host Plants:** Herbs in the Bean Family (Fabaceae). Joint Vetch (*Aeschynomene americana*), Sandhill Joint Vetch (*Aeschynomene viscidula*), Pencilflower (*Stylosanthes biflora*), Tropical Pencilflower (*Stylosanthes hamata*), and,

perhaps occasionally, Hairy Indigo (*Indigofera hirsuta*), Perennial Peanut (*Arachis glabrata*), and vetches (*Vicia* spp.).

**Natural History:** The yellowish eggs are narrow and pointed. Females deposit the eggs singly on the leaves or seeds of the host plant. The caterpillars live exposed on the leaves but blend in well with the green background. The pupa is formed on the host or nearby. Many generations are produced each year. Adults of the Barred Sulphur occur all months of the year but are especially abundant from August through October. This butterfly overwinters in the adult stage. The flight is slow and fluttering, near the ground. Males sometimes drink from wet soil.

**Distribution:** The Barred Sulphur is found in sandhills, weedy fields, and along roadsides. Garden abundance may be moderate to high.

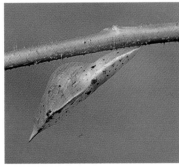

104. A green pupa.

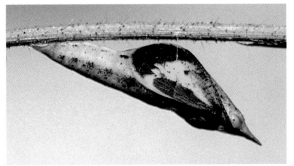

106. The pupa shortly before adult emergence.

105. A darkly patterned pupa.

107. Tropical Pencil Flower (*Stylosanthes hamata*).

## Sleepy Orange

### *Eurema nicippe*

**Adult:** The Sleepy Orange is an orange butterfly with black borders. There is a small black spot near the upper middle of the forewing. Males are a deep, uniform orange color above. The color is paler and streakier in females. The underside of the hindwing is yellow in summer-form adults and reddish in the winter form. Wingspans range from 3.3 to 5.1 cm.

**Field Marks:** Somewhat small to medium in size; wings orange with black borders.

**Larva:** The caterpillar is green with a narrow whitish line along the sides. The body is slender and covered with short hairs, giving the larva a velvety appearance. When viewed in oblique sunlight, the tips of some of the taller hairs shine and look like droplets of liquid.

**Pupa:** The pupa is flattened sideways and is green and leaflike. The head bears a long point. Some individuals have considerable black markings.

**Host Plants:** Herbs and shrubs in the Bean Family (Fabaceae). The larvae eat the leaves of Bahama Senna (*Cassia chapmanii*), Sicklepod (*Cassia obtusifolia*), Coffee Senna (*Cassia occidentalis*), and Christmas Senna (*Cassia bicapsularis*).

**Natural History:** The eggs are slender and pointed, white when first laid, but quickly turning yellow. Females lay the eggs singly on the leaves. The caterpillars live exposed on the leaves of the host. Adults of the Sleepy Orange occur all months of the year but are especially abundant from August to November. The adult is the main overwintering stage. The flight is fast and erratic, near the ground. Males sometimes drink from wet soil.

**Distribution:** The Sleepy Orange is found in disturbed sites such as roadsides, weedlots, and cultivated fields throughout Florida. It is a good disperser and readily colonizes patches of the host plant. Garden abundance may be moderate.

108. Sleepy Oranges (left columns males, right columns females; top row upper sides, bottom row undersides; second and far right columns winter forms).

109. An adult drinking from wet sand.

110. The last-stage caterpillar.

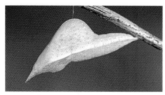

111. The pupa.

112. Sicklepod (*Cassia obtusifolia*).

113. Dainty Sulphurs (males left, females right; top row upper sides, bottom row undersides).

## Dainty Sulphur

### *Nathalis iole*

**Adult:** The Dainty Sulphur is our smallest yellow butterfly. There is a small black dot near the upper middle of the forewing. Males are bright yellow with black markings. Females are more orange above and have more extensive black on the upper hindwing. The leading margin of the hindwing is edged with black. Males also have an orange spot near the base of the hindwing that quickly fades to yellow in museum specimens. The underside of the hindwing is yellow with green markings. Wingspans range from 2.2 to 3.0 cm.

**Field Marks:** Small in size; wings yellow with black markings; black along the leading edge of the upper hindwing; relatively long forewings; greenish undersides.

**Larva:** The caterpillar is green and often has a purple stripe on each side and one on the back. The purple stripes may be absent, relatively narrow, or wide. This coloration perfectly matches the stems of the host plant, which are often green with purple stripes. The front of the thorax bears two small purplish projections.

**Pupa:** The tiny pupa is green, and unlike other members of the Sulphur Family does not have a point on the head.

**Host Plants:** The caterpillars eat the leaves of Spanish Needles (*Bidens alba* var. *radiata*), an herb in the Aster Family (Asteraceae).

**Natural History:** Females lay the yellowish eggs singly on the leaves of seedlings or very small host plants. The caterpillars live exposed on the host, but are very difficult to find due to their small size and coloration. Adults of the Dainty Sulphur occur all months of the year in south Florida. This butterfly is most abundant from August through November in northern Florida. The flight is fast, erratic, and very low to the ground.

**Distribution:** The Dainty Sulphur is found in disturbed sites such as roadsides, weedlots, canal banks, and utility corridors, especially around patches of low vegetation or mown areas. Although it is very abundant in parts of south Florida, this butterfly is rather local and uncommon in the northern part of the state. Garden abundance may be moderate.

114. A resting adult.

116. The pupa.

115. The last-stage caterpillar on Spanish Needles.

117. Spanish Needles (*Bidens alba*).

## Large Orange Sulphur

### *Phoebis agarithe maxima*

**Adult:** This butterfly is mostly orange with reddish-brown markings on the undersides. On the underside of the forewing there is a reddish-brown diagonal line extending to the tip. Females are paler orange or white, with a narrow black outer border, a diagonal line, and a central black spot on the upper side of the forewing. The females also have some small silvery spots near the middle of the wings on the underside, especially on the hindwings. Summer individuals tend to be lightly marked below. The fall and winter generations are usually more heavily marked with reddish-brown. Wingspans range from 4.3 to 7.0 cm.

**Field Marks:** Somewhat small to medium in size; wings orange (some females whitish) with a reddish-brown diagonal line on the underside of the forewing.

**Larva:** The caterpillar is green with a pale yellow line along the sides. Some individuals have numerous small, blue spots.

**Pupa:** The pupa is flattened sideways. The color is green with a white and pink line along the sides. The head has a point.

**Host Plants:** Trees in the Bean Family (Fabaceae). The caterpillars eat the young leaves of Blackbead (*Pithecellobium keyense*), Cat's Claw (*Pithecellobium unguis-cati*), and Wild Tamarind (*Lysiloma latisiliquum*).

**Natural History:** Females lay the slender, yellowish eggs singly on the new growth of the host plant. The caterpillars live exposed on the leaves. This species is difficult to rear in captivity. Several generations are produced each year. Adults of the Large Orange Sulphur occur all year but are most abundant during the summer and fall. The flight is strong and directed from 1 to 4 meters above the ground. Males sometimes drink from wet soil.

**Distribution:** The Large Orange Sulphur is found in tropical and coastal hammocks of southern Florida. Stray specimens may sometimes be found inland or in northern Florida. Garden abundance may be moderate to high.

## Orange-Barred Sulphur

### *Phoebis philea*

**Adult:** The male Orange-Barred Sulphur is yellow with an orange band part way across the middle of the forewing and also along the outer border of the hindwing above. The undersides are yellow with reddish-brown spots that are especially well developed on individuals from the fall and winter generations. Females are usually whitish above but may be pale yellow with a reddish band along the outer border of the hindwing above in the winter form.

118. Large Orange Sulphurs (left column males, middle column females; right column winter forms; top row upper sides, bottom row undersides; top right = female, bottom right = male).

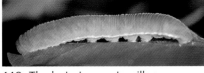

119. The last-stage caterpillar.

120. The pupa.

121. Wild Tamarind (*Lysiloma latisili-quum*).

122. Blackbead (*Pithecellobium keyense*).

The forewings and outer margin of the hindwing have black borders and spots in the female, including a black spot near the middle of the forewing. Females usually have some small silver spots toward the center of the wings below. This species is larger than the Cloudless Sulphur or the Large Orange Sulphur. Wingspans range from 6.3 to 7.9 cm.

**Field Marks:** Medium to medium-large in size; wings yellow with orange bands (typical female whitish), undersides frequently with reddish-brown markings.

**Larva:** The caterpillar is green or yellow with black stripes along the sides. The body is covered with sharp black points. The body color of the caterpillars varies depending upon which part of the host plant has been eaten. Green

123. Orange-Barred Sulphurs (left column males, middle column females, right column winter forms; top row upper sides, bottom row undersides; top right = female, bottom right = male).

124. A male feeding on Madagascar Periwinkle (*Catharanthus roseus*).

125. The last-stage caterpillar.

126. The caterpillar just before pupation.

127. The pupa.

caterpillars have eaten the leaves, while yellow caterpillars fed upon the flowers.

**Pupa:** The leaflike pupa is flattened sideways, with a long point on the head. The color is typically green with whitish markings or occasionally purple with green markings.

**Host Plants:** Trees and shrubs in the Bean Family (Fabaceae). The larvae eat the young leaves and flowers of Candle Plant (*Cassia alata*), Christmas Senna (*Cassia bicapsularis*), Bahama Senna (*Cassia chapmanii*), Golden Shower (*Cassia fistula*), *Cassia didymobotrya*, Glaucous Cassia (*Cassia surattensis*), and probably other woody *Cassia* species.

**Natural History:** The eggs are slender and pointed at the tip. When first laid the color is white, but they quickly change to bright orange. Females lay the eggs one at a time. The caterpillars live exposed on the leaves or flowers

128. Candle Plant (*Cassia alata*).

129. Christmas Senna (*Cassia bicapsularis*).

of the host. Several generations are produced each year. Adults of the Orange-Barred Sulphur are found all year in south and central Florida but are most abundant during the summer rainy season. It regularly colonizes north Florida gardens from August until November but is usually eliminated by hard freezes during the winter. The flight is fast, high, and directed.

**Distribution:** The Orange-Barred Sulphur is found throughout much of South and Central America. It was accidentally introduced into Florida probably during the 1920s. This butterfly occurs mostly in urban areas in close association with the larval host plants. Garden abundance may be moderate to high.

## Cloudless Sulphur

### *Phoebis sennae eubule*

**Adult:** The Cloudless Sulphur is easily recognized by its lemon-yellow color. The undersides are often plain yellow but may be marked with reddish-brown spots in the fall and winter generations. Females have narrow black borders and a black spot near the center of the forewings above. Rarely, the female may be very pale yellow or orange. The undersides of the wings have some small silvery spots near the middle. Wingspans range from 4.8 to 6.5 cm.

**Field Marks:** Medium in size; wings lemon-yellow in color.

**Larva:** The caterpillar may be green or yellow with a yellow stripe along the sides. There may also be varying amounts of blue, from none or small spots along the sides to wide bands across each segment. The body is covered with rows of very short black points.

**Pupa:** The pupa is flattened sideways and is usually green but may be pink or purple with yellow and green markings. The head has a long point.

**Host Plants:** Herbs, shrubs, and trees in the Bean Family (Fabaceae). The caterpillars eat the young leaves and flowers of partridge peas (*Cassia fasciculata* and *Cassia nictitans*), Candle Plant (*Cassia alata*), Christmas Senna (*Cassia bicapsularis*), Bahama Senna (*Cassia chapmanii*), Privet Senna (*Cassia ligustrina*), Glaucous Cassia (*Cassia surattensis*), Coffee Senna (*Cassia occidentalis*), Sicklepod (*Cassia obtusifolia*), and probably other exotic *Cassia* species.

**Natural History:** The eggs are slender and pointed at the tip. Egg color changes from white when first laid to orange. Females lay the eggs singly on the host. The caterpillars live exposed on the host plant. Several generations occur each year. Adults of the Cloudless Sulphur occur all months of the year but are especially abundant from August until November. The flight is strong, high, and directed. Males occasionally drink from wet soil.

**Distribution:** The Cloudless Sulphur may be found in all habitats during the fall migration, but breeds in disturbed areas such as roadsides, weedlots, canal banks, utility corridors, construction sites, and cultivated fields. Garden abundance may be moderate to high.

**Note:** The fall migration of the Cloudless Sulphur is one

130. Cloudless Sulphurs (top row upper sides, bottom row undersides; left column males, middle column females, right column winter forms, top female, bottom male).

131. An adult feeding at Garberia flowers.

134. A green pupa.

135. A pink pupa.

133. A green caterpillar.

132. A yellow and blue caterpillar.

136. Partridge Pea (*Cassia fasciculata*).

of Florida's most spectacular natural events. Each year from mid-August until November countless numbers of Cloudless Sulphurs fly southward into the Florida peninsula from areas further north. The butterflies do not overwinter in groups, as do the Monarchs, but spread throughout central and southern Florida. During the spring, there is a more casual northward dispersal.

## Blues (Family Lycaenidae: Subfamily Polyommatinae)

### Ceraunus or Antillean Blue

#### *Hemiargus ceraunus antibubastus*

**Adult:** The Ceraunus Blue is a small blue butterfly that lacks tails. Males are bright blue above with narrow black borders and whitish wing fringes. The upper hindwing has a black spot along the outer margin. The undersides of the wings are gray with black spots and bars. The hindwing has a black, orange, and metallic blue eyespot along the outer margin. Females are similar, but are mostly black above with blue toward the base of the wings. Wingspans range from 1.5 to 2.4 cm.

**Field Marks:** Small in size; no tails; wings blue above and gray below with a small eyespot on the hindwing.

**Larva:** The color of the caterpillar varies from green with a red stripe along the side to mostly red.

**Pupa:** The pupa is pale green.

**Host Plants:** Herbs and vines in the Bean Family (Fabaceae). The caterpillars eat the flowers and young seeds of Alicia (*Chapmannia floridana*), Partridge Pea (*Cassia fasciculata*), Prostrate Milk Pea (*Galactia regularis*), Twining Milk Pea (*Galactia volubilis*), Carolina Indigo (*Indigofera caroliniana*), Hairy Indigo (*Indigofera hirsuta*), Creeping Indigo (*Indigofera spicata*), Small-Head Yellow Puff (*Neptunia pubescens*), and occasionally Rabbit Bells (*Crotalaria rotundifolia*) and Hemp Sesbania (*Sesbania macrocarpa*).

**Natural History:** The eggs are pale bluish-green and flat. Females lay the eggs singly on the flower buds of the host plant. The larvae live exposed on the host but blend in with the background, and are very difficult to see. Many generations occur each year. Adults of the Ceraunus Blue are found during all months in south Florida, especially during the summer rainy season. In north Florida this butterfly may be found from May through December. The pupa is the overwintering stage. The flight is slow and fluttering near the ground. Adults often perch in a head-down position on vegetation and flowers.

**Distribution:** The Ceraunus Blue occurs in sandhills and open, disturbed sites such as roadsides, weedlots, and fields. Garden abundance is usually low.

137. Ceraunus Blues (males left, females right; top row upper sides, bottom row undersides).

138. A perching adult.

139. A green caterpillar.

140. A reddish caterpillar.

141. The pupa.

142. Creeping Indigo (*Indigofera spicata*).

143. Hairy Indigo (*Indigofera hirsuta*).

## Cassius Blue

### *Leptotes cassius theonus*

**Adult:** The Cassius Blue is a small blue butterfly with two eyespots on the hindwing. The underside is white with dark bands and spots. Males are bright blue above. The females are pale blue with dark borders on the upper wings. Wingspans range from 1.4 to 2.5 cm.

**Field Marks:** Small in size; no tails; wings blue above, white with dark bands below; two small eyespots on the hindwing.

**Larva:** The color of the caterpillar varies from uniform green to patterned forms with red, pink, and green markings.

**Pupa:** The pupa is brown with darker markings.

**Host Plants:** Herbs, vines, shrubs, and trees in the Bean (Fabaceae) and Leadwort (Plumbaginaceae) Families. The caterpillars eat the flowers and young seeds of Rosary Pea (*Abrus precatorius*), milk-peas (*Galactia regularis, Galactia striata*), and Wild Tamarind (*Lysiloma latisiliquum*) in the Bean Family. Leadwort (*Plumbago auriculata* [= *P. capensis*]) and Wild Plumbago (*Plumbago scandens*) are also favored hosts.

**Natural History:** The tiny eggs are bluish green. Females lay the eggs singly on the flowers and young seed pods of the host. The caterpillars live exposed on the host or bore into the immature fruit to eat the developing seeds. Many generations are produced each year. Adults of the Cassius Blue are found all months of the year in south Florida. In central Florida it is more likely to be seen from May through November. This butterfly is intolerant of hard freezes in northern Florida but can occasionally be found in late summer and fall, at least as far north as Gainesville and Jacksonville. Males have a fast, erratic flight and usually fly from 1 to 4 meters above the ground. Females seeking host plants fly more slowly, near the ground or high in the treetops.

**Distribution:** The Cassius Blue is found in dune areas near the beach, at the margins of hammocks, and in shrubby, disturbed sites. Garden abundance may be moderate to high.

144. Cassius Blues (males left, females right; top row upper sides, bottom row undersides).

145. A strongly patterned caterpillar.

146. The pupa.

147. Leadwort (*Plumbago auriculata*).

## Hairstreaks (Family Lycaenidae: Subfamily Theclinae)

### Great Purple Hairstreak

*Atlides halesus*

**Adult:** The Great Purple Hairstreak is a spectacular blue and black butterfly with tails. The male is bright blue above with black borders. There is a black scent patch near the middle of the leading edge of the forewing that produces pheromones used during courtship. The male also has a blue streak on the underside of the forewing. The female has less blue above. The undersides are black with metallic green markings near the tails. The bases of the wings have red spots and the underside of the abdomen is bright red. This species is one of our largest hairstreaks. Wingspans range from 2.6 to 4.2 cm.

**Field Marks:** Small to somewhat small in size; tails present; wings bright blue above; abdomen red below.

**Larva:** The caterpillar is green with a small whitish shield on the thorax. The body is covered with short hairs.

**Pupa:** The pupa is dark brown with two rows of short points along the back. The pupa is able to make squeaking sounds when handled. The sounds are probably intended to scare away potential predators.

**Host Plants:** An herb in the Mistletoe Family (Loranthaceae). The caterpillar eats the leaves of Mistletoe (*Phoradendron serotinum*), a parasite of hardwood trees.

**Natural History:** The eggs are green and flat. Females lay the eggs on the new growth of Mistletoe. The caterpillars live exposed on the host but blend in extremely well with the leaves. The pupa is often formed in leaf litter around the base of the tree. Several generations occur each year. Adults of the Great Purple Hairstreak may be found from February until November. They are especially abundant in the spring on the flowers of wild plums and willows and in the fall on Spanish Needles and Garberia. The pupa is the overwintering stage. This hairstreak is clumsy and slow when crawling about flowers for nectar, but fast and erratic in flight. Great Purple Hairstreaks spend most of their time out of sight in the treetops but often can be found at flowers.

**Distribution:** The Great Purple Hairstreak is found in sandhills, hammocks, and swamps in northern and central Florida. Garden abundance is low.

148. Great Purple Hairstreaks (males left, females right; top row upper sides, bottom row undersides).

149. The last-stage caterpillar.

150. The pupa.

151. Mistletoe (*Phoradendron serotinum*).

## Red-Banded Hairstreak

### *Calycopis cecrops*

**Adult:** The Red-Banded Hairstreak is a small blackish butterfly with tails. The upper sides of the wings are black in males and bluish in females. The underside is grayish with a jagged red and white line and a black eyespot. Each hindwing has two tails. Wingspans range from 2.0 to 2.7 cm.

**Field Marks:** Small in size; tails present; wings with red lines below.

**Larva:** The caterpillar is pinkish-brown with a small dark shield on the thorax. The body is covered with short hairs.

**Pupa:** The pupa is brown with darker markings.

**Host Plants:** The caterpillars mostly eat dead leaves of various shrubs and trees lying on the ground. The Red-Banded Hairstreak is often associated with oaks (*Quercus* spp.), Wax Myrtle (*Myrica cerifera*), Brazilian Pepper (*Schinus terebinthifolius*), Mango (*Mangifera indica*), and Manioc (*Manihot esculenta*). They will also eat living leaves of various trees in captivity.

**Natural History:** The eggs are flat and brownish. Females lay the eggs singly on dead leaves lying on the ground. The caterpillars forage on, and pupate in the leaf litter. Many generations are produced each year. Adults of the Red-Banded Hairstreak occur all months of the year, but are most abundant in the spring (March–May) and fall (August–October). The pupa is the overwintering stage. They often perch on the ground or on shrubs. The flight is fast and erratic. The males frequent the tops of large trees late in the afternoon or on cloudy days and may be seen perching and chasing one another about.

**Distribution:** The Red-Banded Hairstreak is found in hammocks and shrubby disturbed sites throughout Florida. Garden abundance may be moderate to high.

152. Red-Banded Hairstreaks (males left, females right; top row upper sides, bottom row undersides).

153. An adult resting on a leaf.

154. A group of caterpillars.

155. The pupa.

156. Mango (*Mangifera indica*).

## Florida Atala

### *Eumaeus atala florida*

**Adult:** The Atala is one of the most beautiful butterflies in the world. Males are black with metallic green above. Females are black and blue on the upper wings. The undersides of the wings are black with metallic blue spots and a red patch near the abdomen. The abdomen is bright red. The Atala is the largest hairstreak in Florida. Wingspans range from 4.2 to 4.7 cm.

**Field Marks:** Somewhat small in size; without tails; wings black with green or blue above; there is a bright red patch near the abdomen on the underside of the hindwings.

**Larva:** The caterpillar is bright red with two rows of lemon-yellow spots on the back.

**Pupa:** The pupa is brown with small dark spots.

**Host Plants:** Cycads in the Zamia Family (Zamiaceae). The caterpillars eat the young leaves of Coontie (*Zamia pumila*). At Fairchild Tropical Garden, Atala larvae also feed on *Zamia fischeri, Z. furfuracea, Z. loddigesi, Z. fairchildiana, Z. pygmaea, Z. skinneri, Z. vazquessii, Encephalartos villosus, E. hildebrandtii, Macrozamia lucida,* and *Cycas cairnsiana* (Hammer 1996).

**Natural History:** The flat white eggs are laid in clusters on the young shoots of the host. The caterpillars often feed in groups, but do not make nests. Mature larvae frequently gather in groups to pupate. Unlike other hairstreaks, the pupa is suspended only by a silk thread around the middle. Droplets of a bitter-tasting liquid cover the young pupa. Adults readily visit flowers for nectar. Many generations are produced each year. The Florida Atala flies all months of the year. The flight is slow and fluttering, 1 to 2 meters above the ground. Males perch on the leaves of shrubs and make periodic exploratory flights for females around the perch.

**Distribution:** The Florida Atala is found in hammocks, tropical pinelands, and urban areas near patches of the host plants, mostly in Miami-Dade, Broward, and Palm Beach counties. A colony was recently established by accident in Vero Beach, but it has now died out. The Atala is sensitive to freezing temperatures and is unlikely to be established for very long outside of tropical southern Florida. Garden abundance may be moderate to high.

## Fulvous Hairstreak

### *Electrostrymon angelia*

**Adult:** The Fulvous Hairstreak is a small orange and black butterfly with two tails on each hindwing. The upper sides are orange with black borders. Females have less orange above than males. The male also has a black scent patch near the middle of the leading edge of the forewing.

157. Florida Atalas (males left, females right; top row upper sides, bottom row undersides).

158. A perching male.

159. Last-stage caterpillars.

160. A group of pupae.

161. Coontie (*Zamia pumila*).

The undersides are brown. The hindwing has a blotchy white line across the middle and a rather large orange and black eyespot near the base of the tails below. Wingspans range from 1.6 to 2.4 cm.

**Field Marks:** Small in size; tails present; wings orange and black above; one orange and black eyespot on the hindwing below.

**Larva:** The caterpillar closely resembles that of the Red-Banded Hairstreak. The body is reddish-green with two rows of small pale spots on the back. The body is covered with short hairs.

**Pupa:** The pupa is reddish-brown with darker markings.

**Host Plants:** The caterpillars eat the young leaves of Brazilian Pepper (*Schinus terebinthifolius*), a shrub in the Cashew Family (Anacardiaceae).

**Natural History:** The tiny eggs are laid singly on the new growth of the host plant. The caterpillars do not make nests. This butterfly readily visits flowers for nectar. Many generations are produced each year. Adults of the Fulvous Hairstreak occur all months of the year in south Florida, but are most abundant from May through November. The flight is fast and erratic. Males often perch on the leaves of shrubs or trees and make periodic exploratory flights for females around the perch.

**Distribution:** This species has only recently become established in Florida. The Fulvous Hairstreak is found at the margins of hammocks or shrubby areas with an abundance of Brazilian Pepper in south Florida. Garden abundance may be moderate to high.

162. Fulvous Hairstreaks (males left, females right; top row upper sides, bottom row undersides).

163. The last-stage caterpillar.

164. The pupa.

165. Brazilian Pepper (*Schinus terebinthifolius*).

## Tiny Hairstreak

### *Tmolus azia*

**Adult:** The Tiny Hairstreak is a minute black and white butterfly with only one tail on the hindwing. On the upper sides, the forewings are mostly black and the hindwings are white and black. The underside is very pale gray with a narrow red and white line near the middle of the wings. The hindwing has a small round eyespot near the base of the tail. The sexes are similar. This is one of our smallest butterflies. Wingspans range from 1.5 to 1.8 cm.

**Field Marks:** Small in size; tails present; wings black and white above, pale gray with a narrow red and white line through the middle of the wings below.

**Larva:** The caterpillar is pale green with red and white markings. The body has raised bumps bearing short hairs on the back.

**Pupa:** The pupa is brown with darker markings and a pale thorax.

**Host Plants:** The caterpillars eat the flowers of Lead Tree (*Leucaena leucocephala*), a shrub in the Bean Family (Fabaceae).

166. Tiny Hairstreaks (males left, females right; top row upper sides, bottom row undersides).

**Natural History:** The eggs are laid singly on the flower buds of the host. The caterpillars rest exposed on the plant. Adults perch on the leaves and flowers of the foodplant. Many generations are produced each year. Adults of the Tiny Hairstreak occur all months of the year, but are most abundant from May through November. The flight is fast and erratic, from 1 to 2 meters above the ground.

167. The last-stage caterpillar on a flower head of Lead Plant.

168. The pupa.

169. Lead Tree (*Leucaena leucocephala*).

**Distribution:** This butterfly has only recently become established in Florida. The Tiny Hairstreak is found in weedy, disturbed sites in close association with the larval host plant in south and central Florida. Garden abundance may be moderate.

## White-M Hairstreak

### *Parrhasius m-album*

**Adult:** The White-M Hairstreak is bright blue above and has tails on the hindwings. The upper sides of the wings are blue with black borders. Females have less blue than males. The male has a small scent patch midway along the leading margin of the forewing. The undersides are grayish with a narrow white and black line across the middle of the wings. On the hindwing this line is shaped like an "M" near the small red and black eyespot at the base of the tails. Wingspans range from 2.4 to 3.2 cm.
**Field Marks:** Small to somewhat-small in size; tails present; wings blue and black above; there is a white and black line shaped like an "M" on the hindwing below.
**Larva:** The color of the caterpillars varies from green to dull red.
**Pupa:** The pupa is brown with darker markings.
**Host Plants:** Shrubs and trees in the Oak Family (Fagaceae). The caterpillars eat the young leaves of oaks (*Quercus* spp.).
**Natural History:** The eggs are laid singly on the twigs of oaks. The larvae live exposed on the leaves. Several generations are produced each year. Adults of the White-M Hairstreak are found from March through November. The egg is the overwintering stage. During the spring, the adults are especially fond of wild plum and willow flowers. The flight is fast and erratic from near the ground to tree-canopy level. The males frequent the tops of large trees during late afternoon, where they may be seen perching and chasing one another.
**Distribution:** The White-M Hairstreak is found in sand pine scrubs, sandhills, and oak hammocks throughout Florida. Garden abundance is usually low.

## Gray Hairstreak

### *Strymon melinus*

**Adult:** The Gray Hairstreak is a small grayish butterfly with tails on the hindwings. The upper sides are dark gray with a red or orange eyespot at the base of the tail on the hindwing. Females have a blackish patch near the middle of the forewings above. The undersides are pale gray with a white and black line across the middle of the wings and a red eyespot at the base of the tail. Wingspans range from 2.0 to 3.2 cm.

170. White-M Hairstreaks (males left, females right; top row upper sides, bottom row undersides).

171. A green caterpillar.

172. A red caterpillar.

173. The pupa.

174. Laurel Oak (*Quercus hemisphaerica*).

The Columella Hairstreak (*Strymon columella modesta*), a similar species found in southern Florida, lacks the red and black eyespot on the upper side of the hindwings and has black spots below.

**Field Marks:** Small to somewhat small in size; tails present; wings gray in color; there is a red and black eyespot on both sides of the hindwing.

**Larva:** The color of the caterpillar varies from green to bright red. The body is covered by short hairs.

**Pupa:** The pupa is pale brown with darker markings, including a small black spot near the middle of the back.

**Host Plants:** Herbs and vines in the Bean (Fabaceae), Hibiscus (Malvaceae), and Soapberry (Sapindaceae) Families. The caterpillar feeds on the flowers and young seeds of Partridge Pea (*Cassia fasciculata*), beggarweeds (*Desmodium incanum, D. paniculatum, D. viridiflorum*), milk peas (*Galactia regularis, G. volubilis*), Sky-Blue Lupine (*Lupinus diffusus*), Garden Bean (*Phaseolus vulgaris*), and possibly Phasey Bean (*Macroptilium lathyroides*) and Cowpea (*Vigna luteola*) in the Bean Family, Bladder Mallow (*Herissantia crispa*) and Broomweed (*Sida acuta*) in the Hibiscus Family, and Balloon Vine (*Cardiospermum halicacabum*) in the Soapberry Family.

**Natural History:** The pale green eggs are laid singly on the flower buds of the host. The caterpillar lives exposed on the flower stalks or bores into the developing seed pods. Several generations are produced each year. Adults of the Gray Hairstreak are found from February until November in northern Florida and all year in south Florida. The pupa is the overwintering stage. The flight is fast and erratic, from 1 to 2 meters above the ground. The adults often perch head-downward.

**Distribution:** The Gray Hairstreak is found in scrubs, sandhills, flatwoods, and weedy areas throughout Florida. Garden abundance may be moderate.

175. Gray Hairstreaks (males left, females right; top row upper sides, bottom row undersides).

176. The underside of a male Columella Hairstreak.

179. A green caterpillar.

180. The pupa.

177. An adult feeding at Spanish Needles flowers.

181. Prostrate Milk Pea (*Galactia regularis*).

178. A red caterpillar.

## Brushfooted Butterflies (Family Nymphalidae: Subfamily Nymphalinae)

### White Peacock

**Anartia jatrophae guantanamo**

**Adult:** The White Peacock is a white butterfly with dark lines and orange shading. There is a small black spot near the middle of the forewing. The hindwing has two black spots and a very short tail. The sexes are similar, but females are larger with broader wings. Wingspans range from 3.3 to 6.1 cm.

**Field Marks:** Somewhat small to medium in size; wings white with black lines and orange shading; there are two small black spots on the hindwing.

**Larva:** The caterpillar is black with tiny white dots. A row of branched spines lies across each body segment. The bases of the spines are dull red. The head has a pair of

182. White Peacocks (males left, females right; top row upper sides, bottom row undersides).

183. A perching male.

184. The last-stage caterpillar.

185. The pupa.

186. A pupa just prior to adult emergence.

187. Water Hyssop (*Bacopa monnieri*).

long slender spines at the top. These spines are knobbed at the tip.

**Pupa:** The pupa is bright green with some tiny black spots and a black cremaster (supporting stalk).

**Host Plants:** Herbs in the Snapdragon (Scrophulariaceae) and Vervain (Verbenaceae) Families. The main host is Water Hyssop (*Bacopa monnieri*), but Carpetweed (*Phyla nodiflora* [= *Lippia nodiflora*]) is also used.

**Natural History:** The eggs are small and green. The female lays the eggs one at a time on the leaves of the host. The caterpillars live exposed on the leaves and are sometimes abundant enough to defoliate small patches of the plant. When disturbed, the small caterpillars raise the head over the back. There is a small gland on the underside of the thorax that may be used for protection. Many generations are produced each year. Adults of the White Peacock occur all year in south Florida, and are often present from August through December in the northern part of the state. Males perch on low vegetation or the ground and periodically make exploratory flights around the territory. The flight is fast and low to the ground, consisting of rapid wing beats and gliding.

**Distribution:** The White Peacock is found in wet prairies and open disturbed sites in south and central Florida. During the fall, the adults disperse northward and temporarily colonize patches of the host plants. Garden abundance may be moderate to high.

## Viceroy

### *Basilarchia archippus floridensis*

**Adult:** The Viceroy is an orange butterfly with dark wing veins and borders. The black borders contain two rows of small white spots. Viceroys from south and central Florida are usually dark mahogany brown on the upper sides, but in northern Florida bright orange individuals sometimes can be found. The forewing has a short band of white spots near the tip and a small white spot near the base of

the wing. The hindwing has a black line across the middle. The sexes are similar. Wingspans range from 5.6 to 8.5 cm. The Monarch is similar, but lacks the dark line on the hindwing.

The Red-Spotted Purple (*Limenitis arthemis astyanax*) is a very different-looking butterfly that is closely related to the Viceroy. The immature stages are very similar in appearance. Occasionally, spectacular hybrids of the two species can be found. The Red-Spotted Purple eats the leaves of Wild Cherry (*Prunus serotina*), Deerberry (*Vaccinium staminium*), and Carolina Willow (*Salix caroliniana*).

**Field Marks:** Medium to medium-large in size; wings mahogany brown or orange with black borders; there is a short band of white spots near tip of the forewing and a dark line through middle of hindwing.

**Larva:** The young larvae are brown and white and resemble bird droppings. The thorax has a pair of sticklike tubercles. The last-stage caterpillar may be green or brown with a pinkish-white middle.

**Pupa:** The pupa is brown and white. The abdomen has a flangelike structure on the back.

**Host Plants:** Shrubs and trees in the Willow Family (Salicaceae). The caterpillars eat the young leaves of Carolina Willow (*Salix caroliniana*), Black Willow (*Salix nigra*), and Weeping Willow (*Salix babylonica*).

**Natural History:** The green eggs are laid singly on the young leaves of the food plant. During the fall, the young caterpillar eats most of a leaf, beginning with the tip. The margins of the remainder, near the base of the leaf, are tied together with silk to make a shelter. Silk is also applied to the petiole and stem to make sure the shelter remains attached to the tree. The young larva overwinters in the shelter or hibernaculum, then completes its development the following spring when the young leaves emerge. Older larvae live exposed on the leaves. Several generations occur each year. Adults of the Viceroy are found from April through November. The flight consists of rapid wing beats and gliding, from 1 to 2 meters above the ground. Males perch on the leaves of shrubs and trees and make periodic exploratory flights for females around the territory. Adults sometimes drink from wet soil and readily visit fermenting fruit.

**Distribution:** The Viceroy is found in wetlands with willows throughout Florida. It also readily colonizes Weeping Willows in urban areas. Garden abundance is low.

**Note:** Two different forms of the Viceroy occur in Florida and blend together in the northern part of the state. A bright orange form resembling the Eastern Viceroy (*Basilarchia archippus archippus*) is sometimes encountered in northern Florida. In central and south Florida, only the Florida Viceroy (*Basilarchia archippus floridensis*), which is mahogany brown, occurs.

193. Florida Viceroys (males left, females right; top row upper sides, bottom row undersides).

194. Red-Spotted Purples (males; top = upper side, bottom = underside).

195. A mating pair of Viceroys.

199. A brownish last-stage caterpillar.

200. A caterpillar just before pupation.

201. The pupa.

196. The overwintering shelter or hibernaculum of the young larva.

197. The young caterpillar resembles a bird dropping.

198. A green last-stage caterpillar.

202. Carolina Willow (*Salix caroliniana*).

# Common Buckeye

## *Junonia coenia*

**Adult:** The Common Buckeye is a brownish butterfly with large eyespots on the hindwings. The forewing above has two red bars, an eyespot, and a white band that extends around the inner side of the eyespot. The upper side of the hindwing has two larger eyespots and an orange band along the outer margin. The undersides of the wings are pale brown with eyespots. The sexes are similar, but females are larger and have broader wings. Individuals from the fall and winter generations are reddish brown below. Wingspans range from 3.3 to 5.1 cm.

There are two other buckeye species in Florida. The Black Mangrove Buckeye (*Junonia evarete*) is a frequently encountered species in coastal areas of central and south Florida near the larval host plant, Black Mangrove (*Avicennia germinans*). The pale band enclosing the eyespot on the forewing is orange on the Black Mangrove Buckeye. The Caribbean Buckeye (*Junonia genoveva*) is a rare species found in weedlots of the upper Keys and southern Miami-Dade County. The pale band on the forewing does not include the eyespot and is pinkish. Minno and Emmel's *Butterflies of the Florida Keys* (1993) shows examples for comparison.

**Field Marks:** Somewhat small to medium in size; forewings with two red bars; hindwings with two large eyespots; the white band on the forewing extends around the inner side of the eyespot.

**Larva:** The caterpillar is black and white with orange markings. The body has a row of branched spines across each segment. There is a pair of very short spines on the top of the head.

**Pupa:** The pupa is pink and white with dark markings, including an eyespot on the wing cases.

**Host Plants:** Herbs in the Snapdragon (Scrophulariaceae), Plantain (Plantaginaceae), Vervain (Verbenaceae), and Acanthus (Acanthaceae) Families. The caterpillars eat the leaves and flowers of gerardia or false foxglove (*Agalinis fasciculata, A. purpurea*), Blueheart (*Buchnera americana*), toadflax (*Linaria canadensis, L. floridana*), and seymeria (*Seymeria cassioides, S. pectinata*) in the Snapdragon Family; plantain (*Plantago lanceolata, P. virginica*) in the Plantain Family; Carpetweed (*Phyla nodiflora*) in the Vervain Family; and twinflower (*Dyschoriste humistrata* and *D. oblongifolia*) in the Acanthus Family. Wild Petunia (*Ruellia caroliniensis*) in the Acanthus Family also may be used occasionally.

**Natural History:** The small, pale green eggs are laid singly on the leaves of the food plant. The caterpillars live exposed on the host. Many generations are produced each year. Adults of the Common Buckeye are found all months of the year but are most abundant in the fall (August–October). Males perch on low vegetation or the ground and periodically make exploratory flights around the territory. The flight is fast and low to the ground, consisting of rapid wing beats and gliding. Females also fly low to the ground but are slower and more fluttering, es-

188. Common Buckeyes (left column males, top = upper side, bottom = underside; middle column females, top = upper side, bottom = underside; right column winter forms, top = underside male, bottom = underside female).

189. An adult perching on a finger.

190. The last-stage caterpillar.

191. The pupa.

192. Cluster-Leaf Gerardia (*Agalinis fasciculata*).

pecially when investigating potential host plants on which to lay eggs. This species migrates southward through Florida in large numbers during the fall.

**Distribution:** The Common Buckeye is found in scrubs, sandhills, beaches, wet prairies, and many other natural habitats, as well as in open, disturbed sites such as roadsides, weedlots, canal banks, utility corridors, citrus groves, and recently harvested pine plantations. Garden abundance may be moderate.

## Phaon Crescent

### *Phyciodes phaon*

**Adult:** The Phaon Crescent is a small orange butterfly with black borders and lines on the upper sides of the wings. There is a yellow band across the middle of the forewing. The underside of the hindwing is whitish with dark brown markings. The fall and winter generations are mostly brownish on the hindwing below. The sexes are similar. Wingspans range from 2.3 to 3.1 cm.

**Field Marks:** Small to somewhat small in size; wings orange with black markings; there is a yellow band across the middle of the forewing.

**Larva:** The caterpillars are light brown with darker brown stripes. There is a row of short, branched spines across each segment of the body.

**Pupa:** The pupa is brown with some darker markings.

**Host Plants:** The main host plant is an herb in the Vervain Family (Verbenaceae), Carpetweed (*Phyla nodiflora* [= *Lippia nodiflora*]). A related plant sometimes used as a medicinal tea, *Phyla dulcis,* may also be a food plant.

**Natural History:** The small yellowish eggs are laid in clusters on the undersides of the host leaves. The caterpillars eat the leaves of the host and live together under a silken web when small. Older larvae become more solitary. Many generations are produced each year. Adults of the Phaon Crescent occur all months of the year. The adults overwinter and actively visit flowers on warm days. The flight is low to the ground and moderately fast or fluttering. They frequently perch on low vegetation or flowers.

**Distribution:** The Phaon Crescent is found in disturbed areas such as roadsides, weedlots, canal banks, and utility corridors throughout Florida, usually in close association with the larval host plant. Garden abundance may be moderate to high.

203. Phaon Crescents (left columns males; right columns females; top row upper sides, bottom row undersides; second and far right columns winter forms).

204. A group of last-stage caterpillars.

205. The pupa.

206. Carpetweed (*Phyla nodiflora*).

## Pearl Crescent

### *Phyciodes tharos*

**Adult:** The Pearl Crescent is a rather small orange and black butterfly. It is similar to the Phaon Crescent but lacks a yellow band across the forewing. The underside of the hindwing is pale yellow with brown markings. The fall and winter generations are mostly brown on the underside of the hindwings. The sexes are similar. Wingspans range from 2.5 to 3.5 cm. The Phaon Crescent is similar.

**Field Marks:** Small to somewhat small in size; wings orange with black markings.

**Larva:** The caterpillars are black with white stripes along the sides. Each segment of the body has a transverse row of short, branched spines.

**Pupa:** The pupa is brown with dark markings.

**Host Plants:** Herbs in the Aster Family (Asteraceae). The caterpillars eat the leaves of Bushy Aster (*Aster dumosus*) and other *Aster* species.

207. Pearl Crescents (left columns males, right columns females; top row upper sides, bottom row undersides; second and far right columns winter forms).

*Left:* 208. Last-stage caterpillars.

*Above:* 209. The pupa.

*Below:* 210. Bushy Aster (*Aster dumosus*).

**Natural History:** The yellowish eggs are laid on the undersides of the leaves of the host. The caterpillars live together under a silken web, especially when small. Several generations are produced each year. Adults of the Pearl Crescent occur all months of the year. The adults overwinter and actively visit flowers on warm days. The flight is low to the ground and moderately fast. Males often patrol a territory for females. They frequently perch on low vegetation or flowers.

**Distribution:** The Pearl Crescent is found in sandhills, flatwoods, and open disturbed areas such as roadsides, weedlots, canal banks, and utility corridors throughout Florida, usually in close association with the larval host plant. Garden abundance is usually low.

## Question Mark

### *Polygonia interrogationis*

**Adult:** The Question Mark is a brownish butterfly with a short tail on the hindwing. The margins of the wings have an irregular, tattered appearance. The undersides are brown with a silver question mark on the hindwing. The Question Mark resembles a dead leaf when perched with the wings closed. The upper sides of the wings are orange-brown with black spots. The hindwing is black above on individuals produced during the summer generation. Wingspans range from 5.2 to 6.4 cm.

The Comma Anglewing (*Polygonia comma*) is a similar species that sometimes occurs in northern Florida. It can be distinguished from the Question Mark by a silver comma on the underside of the hindwing.

**Field Marks:** Medium in size; wings orange-brown and black above; irregular wing margins; short tails present; and there is a silver question mark on the hindwing below.

**Larva:** The caterpillar is variegated black or gray with white stripes and small spots. There is a row of branched spines across each body segment. The spines may be pale yellow or orange. The dark reddish-brown head bears a pair of short spines at the top.

**Pupa:** The pupa is pale brown with points and silver markings on the back of the thorax and abdomen. It resembles a dead leaf.

**Host Plants:** Trees in the Elm Family (Ulmaceae). The caterpillar eats the leaves of American Elm (*Ulmus americana*), Winged Elm (*Ulmus alata*), and Hackberry (*Celtis laevigata*).

**Natural History:** The dark green eggs are laid singly or in short stacks, one top of another, on the young leaves of the host plant. The small larvae cling to the undersides of the leaves. They tend to eat holes toward the middle of the leaf. Older larvae rest on the twigs or foliage of the host. At rest the head is turned toward one side. Several generations are produced each year. Adults of the Question Mark occur all months of the year. The adults overwinter in protected sites such as wood piles. The flight is rapid, from near the ground to tree-canopy level. Males perch on leaves at forest edges, sunspots, or clearings and make periodic exploratory flights around the territory for females. The adults readily come to fermenting sap flows or fruit, and occasionally to fresh dung.

**Distribution:** The Question Mark is found in hardwood swamps and hammocks in northern and central Florida. Garden abundance is usually low.

## Malachite Butterfly

### *Siproeta stelenes biplagiata*

**Adult:** The Malachite is the only Florida butterfly with patches of green on the wings. The upper sides are green with dark brown borders. Females are a paler green than males. There is a short tail on the hindwing. The wings are mostly orange and green below. It is a most beautiful butterfly to behold. Wingspans range from 7.0 to 8.2 cm.

**Field Marks:** Medium-large in size; wings dark brown with green patches.

**Larva:** The caterpillar is velvety black. There is a row of long, branched spines across each body segment. The

211. Question Marks (left column males, top = upper side, bottom = underside; right column females, top = upper side summer form; bottom = upper side winter form).

212. A perching Question Mark.

213. The last-stage caterpillar.

214. The pupa.

215. American Elm (*Ulmus americana*).

spines on the back are orange. The head is black with a long pair of spines at the top.

**Pupa:** The pupa is green with minute black spots and a black cremaster. There are a few yellow spines on the back. The last stage larva spins a very long pad of silk from which the pupa hangs.

**Host Plants:** An herb in the Acanthus Family (Acanthaceae). The caterpillars eat the leaves and flower bracts of the Green Shrimp Plant (*Blechum brownei*).

**Natural History:** The green eggs are laid singly on the leaves of the food plant. The larvae hide among the leaves and do not make nests. Many generations are produced each year. Adults of the Malachite occur during all months. The flight is moderately fast, from 1 to 2 meters above the ground. Males perch on the leaves of shrubs and trees and make periodic exploratory flights for females around the territory.

**Distribution:** The Malachite is found at the edges of hammocks where the host plant is abundant, especially adjacent to poorly kept citrus and avocado groves. This butterfly is most abundant in southern Miami-Dade County, but also occurs in Monroe, Broward, and Palm Beach counties. It has occasionally been reported from the Gulf coast as far north as Sarasota. Garden abundance may be moderate.

## Red Admiral

### *Vanessa atalanta rubria*

**Adult:** The Red Admiral is a black butterfly with a red band across the forewing and another along the outer margin of the hindwing. There are some white spots near the tip of the forewing. The sexes are similar. Wingspans range from 4.4 to 5.4 cm.

**Field Marks:** Somewhat small to medium in size; wings black with red bands.

**Larva:** The caterpillar is usually black with numerous tiny white spots and a white line or row of spots along the sides. There is a transverse row of branched spines on each body segment. The bases of the spines are orange. The head is black with a very short pair of spines at the top. Occasionally, the larvae are grayish with a black head.

**Pupa:** The pupa is gray with short spines on the back, some of which are tipped with gold.

**Host Plants:** Herbs in the Nettle Family (Urticaceae). The caterpillars feed on the leaves of False Nettle (*Boehmeria cylindrica*), Burning Nettle (*Urtica urens*), and Pellitory (*Parietaria floridana*).

**Natural History:** The green eggs are laid singly on the leaves of the food plant. The caterpillar ties together the edges of a single leaf of nettle, or many leaves of Pellitory, to make a nest. Several generations are produced each year.

216. Malachites (males left, females right; top row upper sides, bottom row undersides).

218. The pupa.

219. A pupa just before emergence of the adult.

217. The last-stage caterpillar.

220. Green Shrimp Plant (*Blechum brownei*).

221. Red Admirals (males left, females right; top row upper sides, bottom row undersides).

222. An adult sipping water from damp sand.

224. A pale caterpillar.

225. The pupa.

223. The typical caterpillar.

226. False Nettle (*Boehmeria cylindrica*).

227. Pellitory (*Parietaria floridana*).

Adults of the Red Admiral occur all months of the year but hibernate in sheltered areas during the winter. The flight is rapid, from near the ground to tree-canopy level. Males perch in sunspots on the ground, or on leaves along forest edges and clearings and make periodic exploratory

flights for females around the territory. This butterfly sometimes drinks from wet soil and frequently visits fermenting sap flows, fruit, and fresh dung.

**Distribution:** The Red Admiral is found in hammocks, marshes, swamps, and along canals throughout Florida. Garden abundance is low to moderate.

## American Painted Lady

### *Vanessa virginiensis*

**Adult:** The American Painted Lady is an orange-brown butterfly with dark borders and markings on the wings above. The underside of the hindwing has cobweblike lines and two relatively large eyespots. The upper hindwing has a few small blue spots. Females have slightly broader wings than males. Wingspans range from 4.0 to 6.0 cm.

The closely related Painted Lady (*Vanessa cardui*) is similar, but the wings are paler orange. The eyespots on the underside of the hindwing are also much smaller than those of the American Painted Lady. The Painted Lady is a migratory butterfly that occurs in low abundance during the fall in Florida.

**Field Marks:** Somewhat-small to medium in size; wings orange-brown with dark borders; small blue spots are present on the upper hindwing, and there are two large eyespots on hindwing below.

**Larva:** The caterpillar is yellow with black bands. There are two rows of white spots on the back. Each body segment has a transverse row of branched spines with reddish bases. The head is black and has a short pair of spines at the top.

**Pupa:** The pupa is green or gray with dark markings.

**Host Plants:** Herbs in the Aster Family (Asteraceae). The caterpillars eat the leaves and flower parts of Sweet Everlasting (*Gnaphalium obtusifolium*), Narrow-Leaved Cudweed (*Gnaphalium falcatum*), Wandering Cudweed (*Gnaphalium pensylvanicum*), and Purple Cudweed (*Gnaphalium purpureum*).

**Natural History:** The eggs are laid one at a time on the leaves or flowers of the food plant. The caterpillar lives in a nest made of silk, plant hairs, and flower fragments. Several generations occur each year. Adults of the American Painted Lady occur all months of the year but are most common during the spring and fall. The flight is rapid and near the ground. The adults overwinter in sheltered places but may be active on warm winter days.

**Distribution:** The American Painted Lady is found in pine flatwoods, at the edges of hammocks, and in open disturbed areas such as weedy yards, pastures, roadsides, and fields. Garden abundance is low.

228. American Painted Ladies (males left, females right; top row upper sides, bottom row undersides).

229. The last-stage caterpillar.

230. The larval nest is made of silk and flower fragments.

231. A green pupa.

232. A gray pupa.

233. Wandering Cudweed (*Gnaphalium pensylvanicum*).

## Hackberry Butterflies (Family Nymphalidae: Subfamily Apaturinae)

### Hackberry Butterfly

*Asterocampa celtis celtis*
*Asterocampa celtis reinthali*

**Adult:** The Hackberry Butterfly is light brown with white spots on the forewing. There is also a small eyespot toward the outer margin of the wing. The hindwing has five to six small eyespots. The ones on the underside of the wing have green centers. Females are larger, and have broader wings than males. Wingspans range from 4.4 to 6.2 cm. The Tawny Emperor is a similar species.

**Field Marks:** Somewhat small to medium in size; wings brown; white spots present on the forewings; small eyespots present on the hindwing, and one on the forewing.

**Larva:** The caterpillar is green with tiny yellow spots. Two narrow yellow lines on the back frame a row of small yellow spots. The rear end has a pair of short tails. The head is black with light stripes and has a pair of branching spines at the top.

**Pupa:** The green pupa is flattened sideways and is marked with narrow yellow lines.

**Host Plants:** The caterpillars eat the leaves of a tree in the Elm Family (Ulmaceae), Hackberry (*Celtis laevigata*).

**Natural History:** The whitish eggs are laid singly or in small clusters on the undersides of the leaves of the host. The caterpillar makes a nest of leaves tied together with silk. The young caterpillars overwinter in leaf nests on the tree. Two or three generations are produced each year. Adults of the Hackberry Butterfly occur from March to November. The flight is rapid, from about 1 meter above the ground to tree-canopy level. Males perch on leaves along forest edges, in sunspots, or at the edges of clearings and make periodic exploratory flights around the territory for females. They may land on your head or an out-

234. Hackberry Butterflies (males left, females right; top row upper sides, bottom row undersides).

235. The last-stage caterpillar.    236. The pupa.

237. Hackberry (*Celtis laevigata*).

stretched hand if you stand motionless in the center of the territory. This butterfly is easily attracted to fermenting fruit and sap flows.

**Distribution:** The Hackberry Butterfly is found in hammocks, usually in close association with Hackberry trees, in northern and central Florida. Garden abundance may be moderate.

**Note:** There are two forms of the Hackberry Butterfly in Florida. The Panhandle region is inhabited by the Eastern Hackberry Butterfly (*Asterocampa celtis celtis*). A larger and darker form, Reinthal's Hackberry Butterfly (*Asterocampa celtis reinthali*) is found in peninsular Florida.

## Tawny Emperor

### *Asterocampa clyton clyton*
### *Asterocampa clyton flora*

**Adult:** The Tawny Emperor is an orange-brown butterfly with dark lines and spots on the wings. The upper side of the forewing also has bands of yellowish spots. The undersides are pinkish-brown with faint eyespots. The males are only about half the size of females. Wingspans range from 4.2 to 6.8 cm. The Hackberry Butterfly is a similar species.

**Field Marks:** Somewhat small to medium in size; wings orange-brown above; small spots are present on the hindwing.

**Larva:** The caterpillar is green with broad yellow stripes edged with white on the back and a narrow yellow stripe along the sides. The rear end has a pair of short tails. The head is green with black stripes and bears a pair of short, branched spines at the top.

**Pupa:** The green pupa is flattened sideways and is marked with yellow lines.

**Host Plants:** The caterpillars eat the leaves of a tree in the Elm Family (Ulmaceae), Hackberry (*Celtis laevigata*).

**Natural History:** The whitish eggs are laid in clusters on the undersides of the leaves of the host. The young caterpillars live together in a nest made of leaves tied together with silk. During the fall, the young larvae attach the leaf nest to the twig with silk and overwinter in this shelter. Overwintering caterpillars change color from green to brown. When the new leaves appear on the host tree during the spring, the larvae disperse and form individual nests. Two or three generations are produced each year. Adults of the Tawny Emperor occur from March to November. The flight is rapid, from about 1 meter above the ground to tree-canopy level. Males perch on leaves at forest edges, in sunspots, or around clearings and make periodic exploratory flights for females around the territory. This butterfly is easily attracted to fermenting fruit or sap flows.

**Distribution:** The Tawny Emperor is found in hammocks, and in open disturbed areas with an abundance of small to medium sized hackberry trees. Garden abundance may be moderate.

**Note:** Two forms of the Tawny Emperor occur in Florida. The typical Tawny Emperor (*Asterocampa clyton clyton*) is found in the Panhandle area. The Florida Tawny Emperor (*Asterocampa clyton flora*) occurs in peninsular Florida.

238. Tawny Emperors (males left, females right; top row upper sides, bottom row undersides).

240. The last-stage caterpillar.

239. The overwintering shelter is made by the young larvae of hackberry leaves and silk.

242. Hackberry (*Celtis laevigata*).

241. The pupa.

## Longwing Butterflies (Family Nymphalidae: Subfamily Heliconiinae)

### Gulf Fritillary

*Agraulis vanillae nigrior*

**Adult:** The Gulf Fritillary is an orange butterfly with black borders, lines, and spots on the upper sides of the wings. There are a few white spots near the base of the forewing. The hindwing has numerous, elongate silver spots and yellow streaks below. Females are larger and duller orange than the males. Wingspans range from 4.9 to 7.4 cm.

The Variegated Fritillary (*Euptoieta claudia*) is a somewhat similar-looking brushfooted butterfly that also eats Passion-Flower during the larval stages. The larva is bright orange with white and black lines and rows of black spines on the body. There is also a pair of sticklike tubercles on the first thoracic segment. Although the Variegated Fritillary is an abundant species throughout much of the South, it is local and uncommon in peninsular Florida.

**Field Marks:** Medium to medium-large in size; wings orange above, with many large silver spots below.

**Larva:** The caterpillar is orange with dark green stripes.

Each body segment has a transverse row of long black spines. The head has a similar pair of spines at the top.

**Pupa:** The pupa is light brown with pinkish-white patches on the abdomen. It closely resembles a dead leaf.

**Host Plants:** Vines in the Passion-Flower Family (Passifloraceae). The caterpillars eat the leaves of Corky-Stemmed Passion-Flower (*Passiflora suberosa*), Maypop (*Passiflora incarnata*), Yellow Passion-Flower (*Passiflora lutea*), and Incense Passion-Flower (*Passiflora* 'Incense'). The larvae do poorly on Red Passion-Flower (*Passiflora coccinea*) and Purple Granadilla (*Passiflora edulis*).

**Natural History:** The eggs are elongate and yellow. Females lay the eggs one at a time on the tendrils and young leaves of the food plant, usually in sunny locations. The caterpillars live exposed on the plant. Small larvae sometimes rest at the tips of tendrils to avoid ant predators. Many generations are produced each year. Adults of the Gulf Fritillary occur all months of the year in south Florida. Although this butterfly may be found from April through December in the northern part of the state, August through October is the peak abundance period. The flight is swift, usually from 1 to 2 meters above the ground. During late summer and fall countless numbers of Gulf Fritillaries migrate southward into Florida from throughout the eastern United States.

243. Gulf Fritillaries (males left, females right; top row upper sides, bottom row undersides).

244. Variegated Fritillaries (males; top = upper side, bottom = underside).

246. A Gulf Fritillary visiting Mexican Sunflower.

245. The silvery underside of a Gulf Fritillary.

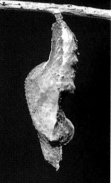

247. The last-stage caterpillar.

248. The pupa.

249. Corky-Stemmed Passion-Flower (*Passiflora suberosa*).

**Distribution:** The Gulf Fritillary is found in many different habitats, especially during the fall, but breeds in weedy fields, pastures, and disturbed sites where the host plant grows. Garden abundance may be moderate to high.

**Note:** Passion-Flower vines have special glands called extrafloral nectaries near the base of the leaves that produce sweet liquids attractive to ants. The ants also eat the eggs and caterpillars of butterflies, and thus help protect the plant from herbivores. *Cassia* species also have extrafloral nectaries.

## Julia Butterfly

### *Dryas iulia largo*

**Adult:** The Julia is a bright orange butterfly with few markings. The males are bright orange with some black spots near the tip of the forewing. The hindwing has a narrow black band along the margin. Females are similar but are duller orange. They also have a complete black band near the tip of the forewing and a black streak along the lower wing margin on the upper side. The undersides of the wings are light brown with a white streak at the base of the hindwing. Wingspans range from 7.1 to 8.1 cm.

**Field Marks:** Medium-large in size; wings orange above; long forewings with a black band or spots near the tip.

**Larva:** The caterpillar is black with a row of white spots on the back and along the sides. There is a row of black branched spines across each body segment. The head is orange with black spots and has a pair of black spines at the top.

**Pupa:** The pupa is brown with small flanges and a few silver spots on the back.

**Host Plants:** Vines in the Passion-Flower Family (Passifloraceae). The caterpillars eat the leaves of Corky-Stemmed Passion-Flower (*Passiflora suberosa*), Many-Flowered Passion-Flower (*Passiflora multiflora*), and probably other passion-flower species.

**Natural History:** The elongate yellow eggs are laid singly on the new growth of the host. Females prefer to lay eggs on plants in the shade. The caterpillars live exposed on the plant. Many generations are produced each year. Adults of the Julia occur all months of the year, but are most abundant from August through October. The flight is swift, from 1 to 2 meters above the ground.

**Distribution:** The Julia is found at the edges of hammocks and in shrubby disturbed areas of southern Florida. Garden abundance may be moderate.

## Zebra Longwing

### *Heliconius charitonius tuckeri*

**Adult:** The Zebra Longwing is a black butterfly with yellow stripes. The forewings are long and narrow. There are some small red spots near the base of the hindwing on the underside. Males and females are similar. Wingspans range from 4.9 to 8.8 cm.

**Field Marks:** Medium to medium-large in size; long forewings; wings black with yellow stripes.

**Larva:** Young caterpillars are orange and resemble the Gulf Fritillary. Older larvae are white with rows of long black spines and shiny black plates on the body. The head is white with black markings and has a pair of long black spines at the top.

**Pupa:** The pupa is brown with spines along the front edge of the wingcases. Thornlike spines and silver spots occur on the back. Overall, the pupa resembles a dead leaf. The head has a pair of long leaflike appendages. When viewed from the back these appendages resemble jaws. A pair of silver spots and the antennal cases on the back of the head give the appearance of the eyes, mouth, and jaws of some small, vicious animal.

250. Julia Butterflies (males left, females right; top row upper sides, bottom row undersides).

251. A perching male.

252. The last-stage caterpillar.

253. The pupa.

**Host Plants:** Vines in the Passion-Flower Family (Passifloraceae). The caterpillars eat the leaves of some, but not all *Passiflora* species, especially Corky-Stemmed Passion-Flower (*Passiflora suberosa*), Maypop (*Passiflora incarnata*), Yellow Passion-Flower (*Passiflora lutea*), and Incense Passion-Flower (*Passiflora 'Incense'*).
**Natural History:** The elongate yellow eggs are laid in small groups on the young leaves of the food plant. Fe-

254. The Incense Passion-Flower (*Passiflora 'Incense'*) is a hybrid between *Passiflora incarnata* and *Passiflora cincinnata*.

males prefer to lay eggs on plants in the shade. The caterpillars live exposed on the leaves and stems. Many generations are produced each year. Adults of the Zebra Longwing occur all months of the year in south and central Florida. The populations in northern Florida are usually killed by freezing temperatures during the winter. Luckily, this butterfly disperses well, and often re-colonizes the northern areas by late summer. The flight is slow and fluttering, from 1 to 2 meters above the ground. The Zebra Longwing is unusual in several aspects of adult behavior, such as pupal mating. One or more males often find and perch on or near the pupa of a female that is ready to emerge. Apparently, a pheromone attracts the males. As the female begins to emerge, the males attempt to thrust their abdomens into the pupal case. One male (usually the largest) will succeed and couple with the female. Then they mate as the female expands and dries her wings. Another unusual behavior is pollen feeding. Females visit flowers not only to sip nectar, but to gather a ball of pollen at the tip of the proboscis. Regurgitated enzymes digest some of the pollen into smaller components, especially proteins, that can be used for producing eggs. A third common behavior is roosting aggregations. In late afternoon, adults of the Zebra Longwing seek out a perch on which to spend the night. Frequently many of the butterflies will cluster on the same perch, night after night for many weeks.

**Distribution:** The Zebra Longwing is found in hammocks and shrubby disturbed sites throughout Florida but is uncommon in the western panhandle region. Garden abundance may be moderate to high.

**Note:** The Zebra Longwing became the official state butterfly of Florida by an April 1996 vote of the legislature.

255. Zebra Longwings (males left, females right; top row upper sides, bottom row undersides).

256. The last-stage caterpillar.

257. The pupa.

258. The false jaws and face pattern on the back of the pupa.

259. Maypop (*Passiflora incarnata*).

## Milkweed Butterflies (Family Nymphalidae: Subfamily Danainae)

### Queen Butterfly

*Danaus gilippus berenice*

**Adult:** The Queen is a brown butterfly with black borders that contain small white spots. There are larger white spots near the tip and outer margin of the forewing. The veins on the underside of the hindwing are outlined in black and gray. Wingspans range from 6.4 to 7.6 cm.

The Soldier (*Danaus eresimus tethys*) is a similar species found in south and central Florida. The Soldier is orange-brown in color and has a row of faint spots on the underside of the hindwing.

**Field Marks:** Medium to medium-large in size; wings mahogany brown with black borders; white spots present on the forewing.

**Larva:** The caterpillar is transversely striped with black and white. Each segment of the body has a wide black band containing a lemon-yellow stripe or spots on the back. Sometimes, the yellow is absent. There are three pairs of long fleshy filaments on the body. The head is white with black stripes.

**Pupa:** The pupa is green or pink with gold spots. There is only one pair of gold spots on the head. The back of the abdomen has a black and gold line. The cremaster is black with a horseshoe-shaped mark extending onto the front of the tip of the abdomen.

**Host Plants:** Herbs and vines in the Milkweed Family (Asclepiadaceae). The caterpillars eat the leaves, flowers, and stems of White Vine (*Sarcostemma clausum*), Strangler Vine (*Morrenia odorata*), Coastal Cynanchum (*Cynanchum angustifolium*), Scarlet Milkweed (*Asclepias curassavica*), Curtiss' Milkweed (*Asclepias curtissii*), Sandhill Milkweed (*Asclepias humistrata*), Pink Swamp Milkweed (*Asclepias incarnata*), Lance-Leaved Milkweed (*Asclepias lanceolata*), White Swamp Milkweed (*Asclepias perennis*), Velvet-Leaf Milkweed (*Asclepias tomentosa*), and Southern Butterfly Weed (*Asclepias tuberosa* subsp. *rolfsii*).

**Natural History:** The whitish eggs are laid singly on the leaves and flowers of the host. The caterpillars live exposed on the host plant but often hide on the lower stem while at rest. Males of the adult butterfly have a black

260. Queen Butterflies (males left, females right; top row upper sides, bottom row undersides).

261. Soldier Butterflies (males; top = upper side, bottom = underside).

262. A Queen visiting Zinnias.

263. The last-stage caterpillar.

264. A green pupa.

265. A pink pupa.

266. Scarlet Milkweed (*Asclepias curassavicum*).

gland near the middle of the hindwing on the upper side. This gland produces pheromones used during courtship. At the tip of the abdomen, the males also have a pair of hair pencils (clusters of stiff hairs) that are usually hidden from view. While perched with the wings closed over the back, the male bends the tip of the abdomen upward and inserts the hair pencils into the gland on the hindwing. During courtship, the male hovers near the female and spreads out the hair pencils to disperse the pheromone. Several generations are produced each year. Adults of the Queen occur all months of the year in south Florida. In north Florida, this butterfly may be seen from March through October. The normal flight is slow and fluttering, from 1 to 2 meters above the ground.

**Distribution:** The Queen is found in sandhills, wet prairies, and disturbed sites such as roadsides, levees, utility corridors, and weedlots throughout Florida. Garden abundance may be moderate to high.

## Monarch Butterfly

### *Danaus plexippus*

**Adult:** Nearly everyone is familiar with the orange and black Monarch Butterfly. The upper sides are bright orange with black borders and veins. The borders also contain tiny white spots. The undersides are similar, but paler. Females are duller orange above, and lack the black gland found on males near the middle of the hindwing. Like our other milkweed butterflies, male Monarchs have a pair of short hair pencils at the tip of the abdomen that they insert into the wing glands for the dissemination of pheromones during courtship. Wingspans range from 8.1 to 10.0 cm.

**Field Marks:** Medium-large to large in size; wings orange with black borders and veins.

**Larva:** The caterpillar is transversely striped with white, black, and yellow. The body has two pairs of long fleshy filaments, one pair on the thorax and the other toward the rear end. The head is white with black stripes.

**Pupa:** The pupa is green with gold spots. Unlike the Queen Butterfly, there are two pairs of gold spots on the head. The back of the abdomen has a black and gold line. The cremaster is black with one black spot on the back of the abdomen and two on the front.

**Host Plants:** Herbs and vines in the Milkweed Family (Asclepiadaceae). The caterpillars eat the leaves, flowers, and stems of White Vine (*Sarcostemma clausum*), Strangler Vine (*Morrenia odorata*), Scarlet Milkweed (*Asclepias curassavica*), Curtiss' Milkweed (*Asclepias curtissii*), Sandhill Milkweed (*Asclepias humistrata*), Pink Swamp Milkweed (*Asclepias incarnata*), Florida Milkweed (*Asclepias longifolia*), White Swamp Milkweed (*Asclepias perennis*), Velvet-Leaf Milkweed (*Asclepias tomentosa*), and Southern Butterfly Weed (*Asclepias tuberosa* subsp. *rolfsii*).

**Natural History:** The whitish eggs are laid singly on the leaves or flowers of the host. The caterpillars live exposed on the leaves; however, older larvae often crawl to the base of the plant to rest between feeding periods. The larger larvae will eat eggs and smaller Monarch caterpillars. Several to many generations are produced each year. Adults of the Monarch are found in Florida mostly during the spring (March through May) and fall (August through December) migration. However, in south and central Florida, small resident or non-migratory populations occur, and this butterfly may be seen all months of the year. The flight is usually slow, from 1 to 2 meters above the ground. The flight is often higher and more gliding while migrating. Males sometimes exhibit territorial behavior and may perch on low vegetation or the ground or make periodic flights around the territory for females. The adults are fond of visiting the flowers of Seaside Goldenrod (*Solidago sempervirens*), Saltbush (*Baccharis halimifolia*), and Carolina Aster (*Aster carolinianus*) during the fall.

**Distribution:** The Monarch is found in many open habitat types, especially sandhills, flatwoods, wet prairies, beaches, and disturbed sites such as pastures and weedlots throughout Florida. Garden abundance may be moderate to high.

**Note:** Every year the Monarch Butterfly undertakes a migration from overwintering sites in central Mexico to southern Canada and back again. This spectacular feat is accomplished in several generations. After enduring a winter of near-freezing temperatures on a few mountains in Mexico, the Monarchs mate and disperse northward. Females lay eggs along the way, eventually reaching southern Texas. The offspring of these Monarchs continue the northward dispersal, and after several generations, eventually reach southern Canada by late summer. Individuals produced in the fall then fly southward to the overwintering sites in Mexico to pass the winter. Large numbers of Monarchs can be seen along the St. Johns River and in the Big Bend area of the Panhandle such as at St. Marks National Wildlife Refuge during October and November. Sometimes many Monarchs will temporarily roost together in trees while on the fall migration.

267. Monarch Butterflies (males left, females right; top row upper sides, bottom row undersides).

268. A Monarch visiting Pentas flowers.

269. The last-stage caterpillar.

270. The pupa.

271. Sandhill Milkweed (*Asclepias humistrata*).

## Satyrs and Wood Nymphs
## (Family Nymphalidae: Subfamily Satyrinae)

### Carolina Satyr

#### *Hermeuptychia sosybius*

**Adult:** The Carolina Satyr is a small brown butterfly with eyespots only on the undersides of the wings. The upper sides are plain brown. The wings have two dark brown lines, and a row of small eyespots along the outer margin below. The sexes are similar. Wingspans range from 2.7 to 3.6 cm.

**Field Marks:** Small to somewhat small in size; wings brown with small eyespots along outer margin below.

**Larva:** The caterpillar is green with a row of small white spots on the sides. The body has a pair of short tails at the tip and is covered with short hairs.

**Pupa:** The pupa is green with dark markings.

**Host Plants:** Grasses (Poaceae). The caterpillars eat the leaves of St. Augustinegrass (*Stenotaphrum secundatum*), Signalgrass (*Brachiaria subquadripara*), Sour Paspalum (*Paspalum conjugatum*), probably spikegrasses (*Chasmanthium* spp.), and other grasses.

**Natural History:** The round, green eggs are laid singly on grass leaves. The caterpillars live exposed on the plant. When disturbed, they curl the head and rear end together and drop to the ground. The larvae are very sedentary and lead quiet lives. Most feeding probably occurs at night. Many generations are produced each year. Adults of the Carolina Satyr occur all months of the year. The flight is fluttering and erratic near the ground. This butterfly often perches near the ground, then zigzags through grasses and other vegetation. The Carolina Satyr only occasionally visits flowers for nectar, especially during the fall, but often comes to fermenting fruit.

**Distribution:** The Carolina Satyr is found in shaded, grassy areas, especially in hammocks and shrubby disturbed sites throughout Florida. Garden abundance may be moderate to high if shade and grasses are available.

272. Carolina Satyrs (males left, females right; top row upper sides, bottom row undersides).

273. The adults often perch on the ground.

274. The last-stage caterpillar.

275. The pupa.

276. St. Augustinegrass (*Stenotaphrum secundatum*).

## Viola's Wood Satyr

*Megisto cymela viola*
*Megisto cymela cymela*

**Adult:** Viola's Wood Satyr is a small brown butterfly with eyespots on both sides of the wings. The eyespots are surrounded by a yellow ring and have metallic silver centers. The undersides of the wings are paler brown with two dark brown lines and eyespots. The sexes are similar, but females are larger, paler brown, and have larger eyespots than males. Wingspans range from 3.4 to 4.5 cm.
**Field Marks:** Somewhat small in size; wings brown with relatively large eyespots on both sides of the wings.

**Larva:** The caterpillar is brown with a dark stripe on the back. The rear end has a pair of short tails. The head bears a pair of short spines on the top.
**Pupa:** The pupa is dark brown with white lines.
**Host Plants:** Grasses (Poaceae). The caterpillars eat the leaves of various grasses. They can be reared on St. Augustinegrass (*Stenotaphrum secundatum*) and other grasses.
**Natural History:** The round, greenish eggs are laid one at a time on the leaves of grasses. The caterpillars are probably mostly active at night. Adults of Viola's Wood Satyr occur only in the spring and early summer from March through May. The flight is bobbing and erratic, usually near the ground. If disturbed this butterfly heads for thickets in which to hide. The adults do not visit flowers, but readily come to fermenting fruit.
**Distribution:** Viola's Wood Satyr is found in hammocks in north and central Florida. Garden abundance is usually low.
**Note:** The Little Wood Satyr (*Megisto cymela cymela*) occurs in the Panhandle area and is replaced by Viola's Wood Satyr (*Megisto cymela viola*) in peninsular Florida.

# Snout Butterflies (Family Libytheidae)

## Bachman's Snout Butterfly

*Libytheana bachmanii*

**Adult:** Bachman's Snout Butterfly is black with orange patches on the upper wings. The forewing has a few white spots near the tip. The color of the underside of the hindwing varies from uniform gray to variegated patterns of dark brown and white. The long, beaklike palpi distinguish this butterfly from all others in Florida. Wingspans range from 3.4 to 4.6 cm.
**Field Marks:** Somewhat small in size; wings black with orange patches; there are some white spots near tip of forewing; long palpi.
**Larva:** The caterpillar is green with yellow spots and a yellow stripe down the back and along the sides. There is a pair of small black spots on the thorax.
**Pupa:** The pupa is green with a diagonal yellow stripe.
**Host Plants:** The caterpillars eat the leaves of a tree in the Elm Family (Ulmaceae), Hackberry (*Celtis laevigata*).
**Natural History:** The small pale yellow eggs are laid in the axils of very young leaves of Hackberry. They closely resemble leaf buds. The caterpillars live exposed on the leaves. Several generations are produced each year. Adults of Bachman's Snout Butterfly occur from April through October. The flight is somewhat fast and erratic, from 1

277. Viola's Wood Satyrs (males left, females right; top row upper sides, bottom row undersides).

278. The last-stage caterpillar.

279. The pupa.

meter above the ground to tree-canopy level. They resemble dead leaves when perching on twigs. Unlike most butterflies, the antennae are held forward along the palpi while at rest. The adults sometimes sip water from wet soil.

**Distribution:** Bachman's Snout Butterfly is found at the edges of hammocks and shrubby disturbed sites with Hackberry trees in north and central Florida. This butterfly is occasionally found in south Florida, especially during late summer and fall. Garden abundance is usually low.

## Branded Skippers (Family Hesperiidae: Subfamily Hesperiinae)

### Monk or Cuban Palm Skipper

*Asbolis capucinus*

**Adult:** The Monk Skipper is a dark brown butterfly with few markings. The forewings have a faint yellowish spot near the center, both on the upper and lower surfaces. Males have a black, curved stigma (line of pheromone producing scales) in the middle of the forewing. Wingspans range from 3.9 to 4.9 cm.

**Field Marks:** Somewhat small in size; wings dark brown; a faint yellow spot present in the middle of the forewing.

**Larva:** The caterpillar is yellowish green with black spiracles, a black collar, and a black line edging the rear end. When viewed from behind the markings on the rear form a false face. The head is orange.

**Pupa:** The pupa is green with dark shading.

**Host Plants:** Palms (Arecaceae). The caterpillar eats the leaves of Coconut Palm (*Cocos nucifera*), Silver Palm (*Coccothrinax argentata*), Thatch Palm (*Thrinax radiata*),

280. Bachman's Snout Butterflies (left column males, top = upper side, bottom = underside; middle column females, top = upper side, bottom = underside; right column patterned forms, top = underside male, bottom = underside female).

281. Snout Butterflies hold the antennae straight ahead while perched.

282. The last-stage caterpillar.

283. The pupa.

284. Hackberry (*Celtis laevigata*).

Saw Palmetto (*Serenoa repens*), Areca Palm (*Chrysalido-carpus lutescens*), Christmas Palm (*Veitchia merrillii*), and probably other palms.

**Natural History:** The pale green eggs are laid singly on the leaves of the host. The caterpillar lives in a shelter made by tying the margins of a leaflet together and lining the interior of the nest with silk. The last stage larva produces an abundance of wax from special glands on the underside of the body. The wax is used to coat the inside of the shelter prior to pupation. Many generations are produced each year. Adults of the Monk Skipper occur all months of the year in south Florida. The flight is fast, from 1 meter above the ground to tree-canopy level. Males perch on the leaves of trees and make exploratory flights around the territory for females.

**Distribution:** The Monk Skipper is found in hammocks and urban areas with palms in south and central Florida. Garden abundance is low to moderate.

## Canna or Brazilian Skipper

### *Calpodes ethlius*

**Adult:** The Canna Skipper is a dark brown butterfly with semi-transparent spots on the wings, including three near the middle of the hindwing. Males and females are similar. Wingspans range from 4.5 to 5.3 cm.

**Field Marks:** Somewhat small to medium in size; wings brown with semi-transparent spots; long, pointed forewings.

285. Monk Skippers (males left, females right; top row upper sides, bottom row undersides).

286. The last-stage caterpillar.

287. The pupa.

288. Coconut Palm (*Cocos nucifera*).

**Larva:** The caterpillar is transparent allowing for easy viewing of the heart along the back, breathing tubes, and other internal organs. The head is tan with a black spot in the middle and on each side of the mouth.

**Pupa:** The pupa is pale green with tiny black spots on the back. The head has a brown, curved point on the front. The proboscis is extremely long, extending beyond the tip of the abdomen.

**Host Plants:** Herbs in the Canna (Cannaceae), Arrowroot (Marantaceae), and Ginger (Zingiberaceae) Families. The caterpillars eat the leaves of Golden Canna (*Canna flaccida*), Indian Shot (*Canna indica*), and canna hybrids. They also readily eat Alligator Flag (*Thalia geniculata*) in the Arrowroot Family and occasionally large-leaved exotic gingers such as *Curcuma* sp.

**Natural History:** The small gray eggs are laid singly on the leaves of the host. The young caterpillars eat two slits along the leaf margin, then fold over the resulting flap to make a shelter. The flap and interior of the shelter are lined with silk. The last stage larva develops wax glands on the underside of the body, between the last two pairs of legs. The wax is used to coat the inside of the shelter before pupation. Many generations are produced each year. Adults of the Canna Skipper occur all months of the year in south Florida. This butterfly cannot tolerate freezing temperatures. In the northern part of the state, it is most often seen in late summer and fall. The flight is fast, from 1 to 2 meters above the ground. Males will perch on low vegetation and make periodic flights around the territory for females. The adults visit deep-throated flowers, such as morning glories, often crawling into the flower to reach the nectar.

**Distribution:** The Canna Skipper is found in marshes, wet prairies, and urban areas throughout the state. Although the adults are usually scarce, the immature stages are often abundant on cannas.

## Three-Spotted Skipper

### *Cymaenes tripunctus*

**Adult:** The Three-Spotted Skipper is a small brown butterfly with whitish spots on the forewing. There is a band of indistinct spots on the underside of the hindwing. Males and females are similar. Unlike many other brown skippers, the antennae are very long, about three-fourths the length of the forewing. Wingspans range from 2.4 to 3.0 cm.

**Field Marks:** Small in size; wings brown with small whitish spots on forewing; indistinct pale spots present on the underside of the hindwing; long antennae.

**Larva:** The caterpillar is green, frosted with white. The head is white with black lines on the sides and front.

**Pupa:** The pupa is green with a long point on the front of the head.

**Host Plants:** Grasses (Poaceae). The caterpillar eats the leaves of Common Bamboo (*Bambusa vulgaris*), Paragrass

289. Canna Skippers (males left, females right; top row upper sides, bottom row undersides).

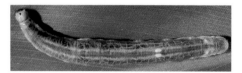

290. The last-stage caterpillar.

291. The pupa.

292. Golden Canna (*Canna flaccida*).

(*Brachiaria mutica*), Crabgrass (*Digitaria sanguinalis*), Guineagrass (*Panicum maximum*), Thin Paspalum (*Paspalum setaceum*), Sugarcane (*Saccharum officinarum*), and Eastern Gamagrass (*Tripsacum dactyloides*).

**Natural History:** The green eggs are laid singly on grass leaves. The young caterpillar eats a slit partly through a leaf, near the tip, and folds the flap over to make a shelter. Larger larvae tie the leaf edges together to make a shelter in which to hide. The last stage larva produces wax from glands on the underside of the body between the last two pairs of legs. The pupa is formed on the underside of a leaf that has been partially tied with silk. Many generations are produced each year. Adults of the Three-Spotted Skipper occur all months of the year. The flight is somewhat fast near the ground. Males perch on vegetation and make periodic flights around the territory.

**Distribution:** The Three-Spotted Skipper is found in or at the edges of hammocks in south Florida. Garden abundance may be moderate to high.

293. Three-Spotted Skippers (males left, females right; top row upper sides, bottom row undersides).

294. The last-stage caterpillar.

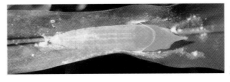

295. The pupa.

296. Eastern Gamagrass (*Tripsacum dactyloides*).

## Fiery Skipper

### *Hylephila phyleus*

**Adult:** The Fiery Skipper is a small golden butterfly with black markings. The male is mostly golden-yellow with black wedge-shaped marks on the outer borders of the wings above. There is a black stigma in the middle of the forewing. Females are mostly dark above with yellowish spots. The underside of the hindwing is yellow in males or yellowish-brown in females, with small black spots. The antennae are short, less than half the length of the forewing. Wingspans range from 2.3 to 3.5 cm.

**Field Marks:** Small to somewhat small in size; short antennae; small black spots on the underside of the hindwing.

**Larva:** The caterpillar is greenish brown with a black head.

**Pupa:** The pupa is tan with dark markings. The large dark thoracic spiracle covers look like eyes, and when viewed from the front the pupa resembles the head of a small animal.

**Host Plants:** Grasses (Poaceae). The caterpillar eats the leaves of grasses such as Bermudagrass (*Cynodon dactylon*) and St. Augustinegrass (*Stenotaphrum secundatum*).

**Natural History:** The whitish eggs are laid singly on the leaves of grasses. The caterpillar makes a tubular nest of silk, droppings, and plant debris near the ground. Many generations are produced each year. Adults of the Fiery Skipper are found all months of the year. The flight is fast and near the ground. Males perch on low vegetation and make periodic flights around the territory to look for females.

**Distribution:** The Fiery Skipper is found in sandhills, flatwoods, and open disturbed areas such as roadsides, weedlots, old fields, levees, and utility corridors throughout Florida. Garden abundance may be moderate.

## Clouded Skipper

### *Lerema accius*

**Adult:** The Clouded Skipper is a dark brown butterfly with small white spots on the forewings. The males have a long stigma near the middle of the forewing. The underside of the hindwing is brown, shaded with blue, and has a dark patch near the middle. The antennae are relatively long, equal to about half the length of the forewing. Wingspans range from 2.6 to 3.6 cm.

**Field Marks:** Small to somewhat in size; dark brown with small white spots on forewings; there is a dark patch on the underside of the hindwing; long antennae.

**Larva:** The caterpillar is green, frosted with white. The head is white with dark brown lines on the sides, and on the face. The central line is light brown at the top of the head.

**Pupa:** The pupa is green with a long point on the front of the head.

**Host Plants:** Grasses (Poaceae). The caterpillar eats the leaves of many different grasses including Switch Cane (*Arundinaria gigantea*), Giant Reed (*Arundo donax*), Paragrass (*Brachiaria mutica*), Longleaf Chasmanthium (*Chasmanthium sessiliflorum*), Barnyardgrass (*Echinochloa crusgalli*), Sugarcane Plumegrass (*Erianthus giganteus*), Guineagrass (*Panicum maximum*), Redtop Panicum (*Panicum rigidulum*), Florida Paspalum (*Paspalum floridanum*), Elephantgrass (*Pennisetum purpureum*), Red Fountaingrass (*Pennisetum setaceum* var. *rubrum*), Golden Bamboo (*Phyllostachys aurea*), Arrow Bamboo (*Pseudosasa japonica*), Sugarcane (*Saccharum officinarum*), Coral Foxtail (*Setaria macrosperma*), Grain Sorghum (*Sorghum bicolor*), Johnsongrass (*Sorghum halepense*), St. Augustinegrass (*Stenotaphrum secundatum*), Purpletop (*Tridens flavus*), Eastern Gamagrass (*Tripsacum dactyloides*), Corn (*Zea mays*), and Southern Wild Rice (*Zizaniopsis miliacea*).

**Natural History:** The pale green eggs are laid singly on the grass leaves. Young caterpillars make shelters near the tips of leaves, but larger larvae tie the edges of a leaf together. The last-stage larva develops wax glands on the underside of the body between the last two pairs of legs. Pupation

297. Fiery Skippers (males left, females right; top row upper sides, bottom row undersides).

298. A female visiting Summer Farewell flowers.

299. The last-stage caterpillar.

300. The pupa.

301. Bermudagrass (*Cynodon dactylon*).

302. Clouded Skippers (males left, females right; top row upper sides, bottom row undersides).

303. The last-stage caterpillar.

304. The pupa is formed on the underside of a folded grass leaf.

305. The pupa.

306. Variegated Giant Reed (*Arundo donax* var. *versicolor*).

takes place on the underside of a partially folded leaf. The wax is smeared over the leaf surface before pupating. Many generations are produced each year. Adults of the Clouded Skipper occur all months of the year in south Florida. The flight is somewhat fast and near the ground. Males perch on vegetation but make periodic flights around the territory to find females.

**Distribution:** The Clouded Skipper is found in swamps, hammocks, and shrubby or wooded disturbed sites throughout Florida. Garden abundance is usually low.

## Ocola Skipper

*Panoquina ocola*

**Adult:** The Ocola Skipper is a small brown butterfly with white spots on long, narrow forewings. The underside of the hindwing is brown with a row of very indistinct spots. Occasional individuals have a purplish sheen on the underside of the hind wings. The antennae are less than half the length of the forewing. Wingspans range from 2.6 to 3.5 cm.

**Field Marks:** Small to somewhat small in size; brown with whitish spots on forewing; long and narrow forewings; short antennae.

**Larva:** The caterpillar is green with yellowish stripes on the body.

**Pupa:** The pupa is green with a few white stripes on the abdomen, and a long point on the front of the head.

**Host Plants:** Grasses (Poaceae). The caterpillars eat the leaves of aquatic grasses such as Southern Cutgrass (*Leersia hexandra*), Rice (*Oryza sativa*), and Torpedograss (*Panicum repens*).

**Natural History:** The green eggs are laid singly on grass leaves. The caterpillars live exposed on the plants and, unlike most skippers, do not make shelters. Many generations are produced each year. Adults of the Ocola Skipper occur all months of the year, but are most abundant during late summer and fall. The flight is somewhat fast, usually near the ground. This species migrates southward into Florida during the fall in large numbers.

**Distribution:** The Ocola Skipper is found in marshes, wet prairies, at the margins of lakes and ponds, and in disturbed sites such as roadsides, weedlots, levees, old fields, and utility corridors throughout Florida. Garden abundance may be moderate to high.

307. Ocola Skippers (males left, females right; top row upper sides, bottom row undersides).

308. The last-stage caterpillar.

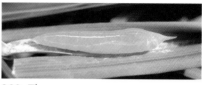

309. The pupa.

310. Southern Cutgrass (*Leersia hexandra*).

## Baracoa Skipper

### *Polites baracoa*

**Adult:** The Baracoa Skipper is a small brown butterfly with golden patches along the front edge of the forewing. Males have a dark stigma near the middle of the forewing above. The underside of the hindwing is light brown with a curved row of pale spots near the middle. Wingspans range from 2.0 to 2.6 cm.

**Field Marks:** Small in size; brown with golden yellow along forewing; with a row of pale spots on the underside of the hindwing.

**Larva:** The caterpillar is brown with dark stripes on the body. The head is black with two pale lines near the top. The rear end is black with white lines.

**Pupa:** The pupa is cream-colored with dark markings.

**Host Plants:** Grasses (Poaceae). The caterpillar eats the leaves of grasses such as Bermudagrass (*Cynodon dactylon*).

**Natural History:** The small whitish eggs are laid singly on the leaves of grasses. The caterpillar lives in a nest of grass leaves tied together with silk. Many generations are produced each year. Adults of the Baracoa Skipper occur all months of the year in south Florida. The flight is fast and near the ground. Males perch on low vegetation or the ground and make periodic flights around the territory for females.

**Distribution:** The Baracoa Skipper is found in urban areas and disturbed sites, especially weedy lawns, in south Florida. It is rare in the upper Keys. In the central and northern areas of the state, this butterfly is found only in dry natural areas such as sandhills and scrubby flatwoods, and is unlikely to occur in gardens. Garden abundance may be moderate in Miami-Dade County.

## Whirlabout Skipper

### *Polites vibex*

**Adult:** The Whirlabout Skipper is a small, golden-yellow butterfly. Males have a dark stigma on the middle of the forewing and black wedge-shaped spots along the outer margin. Females are black above with small yellow spots. The underside of the hindwing is yellow in the male, and greenish in the female, with four large dark spots. Wingspans range from 2.5 to 3.0 cm.

**Field Marks:** Small in size; wings golden yellow (males) or black (females); with four large dark spots on the underside of the hindwing.

**Larva:** The caterpillar is pale green with a black head.

**Pupa:** The pupa is green with some dark shading.

**Host Plants:** Grasses (Poaceae). The caterpillars eat the leaves of Bermudagrass (*Cynodon dactylon*), Crabgrass (*Digitaria villosa*), Thin Paspalum (*Paspalum setaceum*), St. Augustinegrass (*Stenotaphrum secundatum*), and probably other grasses.

**Natural History:** The whitish eggs are laid singly on grass leaves. The larvae tie leaves together with silk to make shelters in which to hide. Many generations are produced each year. Adults of the Whirlabout occur all months of the year. The flight is fast and erratic, near the ground. Males perch on vegetation or the ground and make exploratory flights around the territory for females. While perched, males often hold the wings in a characteristic pattern with the forewings up and the hindwings down.

**Distribution:** The Whirlabout Skipper is found in scrubs, sandhills, flatwoods, and weedy disturbed areas such as roadsides, weedlots, old fields, and utility corridors throughout Florida. Garden abundance may be moderate.

311. Baracoa Skippers (males left, females right; top row upper sides, bottom row undersides).

312. The last-stage caterpillar.

313. The pupa.

## Broadwinged Skippers (Family Hesperiidae: Subfamily Pyrginae)

### Silver Spotted Skipper

*Epargyreus clarus*

**Adult:** The Silver Spotted Skipper is a brown butterfly with a band of golden spots across the forewing. The underside of the hindwing has a large, silvery-white patch. Males and females are similar. Wingspans range from 4.6 to 5.8 cm.

**Field Marks:** Somewhat small to medium in size; wings brown; golden spots present on the forewing; underside of the hindwing with a silvery patch.

**Larva:** The caterpillar is yellow with faint black bands across each body segment. The first body segment, just behind the head, is black above and bright red below. The head is dark reddish-brown with two yellow eye patches near the mouth.

**Pupa:** The pupa is thickest about the middle and is dark brown with a waxy surface. The black thoracic spiracle covers resemble eyes. When viewed from the front, the pupa resembles the face of a manatee.

**Host Plants:** Herbs, vines, shrubs and trees in the Bean Family (Fabaceae). The caterpillars eat the leaves of Bastard Indigo (*Amorpha fruticosa*), Hog Peanut (*Amphicarpa bracteata*), Groundnut (*Apios americana*), Butterfly Pea (*Clitoria mariana*), beggarweeds (*Desmodium paniculatum* and *D. tortuosum*), milk peas (*Galactia regularis* and *G. volubilis*), Honey Locust (*Gleditsia triacanthos*), Kudzu (*Pueraria lobata*), Black Locust (*Robinia pseudo-acacia*), and occasionally Soybean (*Glycine max*), American Wist-

314. Whirlabout Skippers (males left, females right; top row upper sides, bottom row undersides).

315. The Whirlabout frequently perches with the forewings up and the hindwings down.

316. An adult visiting Zinnias.

317. The last-stage caterpillar.

318. The pupa.

319. Southern Crabgrass (*Digitaria ciliaris*).

eria (*Wisteria frutescens*), and Chinese Wisteria (*Wisteria sinensis*).

**Natural History:** The eggs are pale green and dome-shaped. Females lay the eggs singly on the host plant or occasionally on nearby plants. The young caterpillars eat two strips out of the leaf margin and fold the resulting flap over to make a shelter. The flap is crumpled a bit to make the nest roomier, and the interior is lined with silk. The caterpillar sits upside down on the roof of the shelter. Older caterpillars tie one or more leaves together to make a nest. Several generations are produced each year. Adults of the Silver Spotted Skipper occur from March through October. The flight is fast and powerful, from 1 to 2 meters above the ground. Males perch on the leaves of shrubs at forest edges and make exploratory flights around the territory looking for females. The adults sometimes sip moisture from wet soil.

**Distribution:** The Silver Spotted Skipper is found at the edges of hammocks and swamps in north and central Florida. It is also found occasionally in the southern part of the state. Garden abundance is usually low.

320. Silver Spotted Skippers (males left, females right; top row upper sides, bottom row undersides).

321. A male puddling.

322. The last-stage caterpillar.

323. The pupa.

324. Bastard Indigo (*Amorpha fruiticosa*).

## Horace's Dusky Wing

### *Erynnis horatius*

**Adult:** Horace's Dusky Wing is a drab brown butterfly with black markings and white spots on the forewings. Males have a narrow patch of androconial scales covered by a flap along the leading edge of the forewing. The upper forewings also have numerous short, grayish hairs. The underside of the hindwing is brown with small faint spots. Females are patterned very differently from the males. They are paler brown with larger white spots, have distinctly contrasting black bars, and lack the grayish hairs on the forewings. The underside of the wings is also paler with rows of small whitish spots. Wingspans range from 3.4 to 4.1 cm.

Juvenal's Skipper (*Erynnis juvenalis*) is similar, but usually has a pair of whitish spots on the underside of the hindwing near the outer margin. Adults of Juvenal's Skipper are only present during the spring. Also carefully compare Horace's Dusky Wing with the Zarucco Dusky Wing. The dusky wing skippers are a challenging group to identify!

325. Horace's Dusky Wings (males left, females right; top row upper sides, bottom row undersides).

326. Juvenal's Dusky Wings (males; top = upper side, bottom = underside).

327. Dusky Wings usually hold the wings outstretched while perched.

328. The last-stage caterpillar.

329. The pupa.

330. Water Oak (*Quercus nigra*).

**Field Marks:** Somewhat small in size; brown with white spots on forewing; wings held open while perching.

**Larva:** The caterpillar is green with tiny white spots. The flattened head is brown with orange spots along the margin. Overwintering larvae are cream-colored.

**Pupa:** The pupa is green with a black stripe on the underside of the head, and a black knob over the thoracic spiracles. When viewed from the front, the pupa resembles the head of an animal with small black eyes.

**Host Plants:** Shrubs and trees in the Oak Family (Fagaceae). The caterpillar eats the leaves of Chapman's Oak (*Quercus chapmanii*), Sand Live Oak (*Quercus geminata*), Laurel Oak (*Quercus hemisphaerica*), *Quercus inopina*, Turkey Oak (*Quercus laevis*), Myrtle Oak (*Quercus myrtifolia*), Water Oak (*Quercus nigra*), Shumard Oak (*Quercus shumardii*), Small Post Oak (*Quercus stellata* var. *margaretta*), and Live Oak (*Quercus virginiana*).

**Natural History:** The eggs are pale yellow when first laid but soon change to orange. The females lay the eggs one at a time on the new growth of oaks. The young caterpillar eats two slits in the margin of a leaf and folds the flap over to make a shelter. Older larvae tie the margins of a single leaf together or use two or more leaves to make the nest. During the fall, the last stage larva overwinters in a cocoonlike leaf shelter on the ground, then pupates without further feeding in the spring. Several generations are produced each year. Adults of Horace's Dusky Wing occur from February through October. The flight is somewhat fast and erratic, near the ground. Males frequently perch on low vegetation and sometimes sip moisture from bare wet soil. Both males and females usually hold the wings open while perching.

**Distribution:** Horace's Dusky Wing is found in scrubs, sandhills, flatwoods, at the margins of hammocks, and in shrubby disturbed sites throughout Florida. Garden abundance may be moderate to high.

## Zarucco Dusky Wing

### *Erynnis zarucco*

**Adult:** The Zarucco Dusky Wing is a blackish butterfly with small white spots on the forewings. There is a distinctive pale patch beyond the middle the wing. Males have a narrow patch of androconial scales that is usually covered by a flap on the leading edge of the forewing. The upper wings usually have a faint purplish iridescence. The undersides of the wings are dark brown with a single row of small white spots on the hindwing. Wingspans range from 3.0 to 3.9 cm. Other dusky wing skippers are similar.

**Field Marks:** Somewhat small in size; pale patch present on the forewing; faint purplish iridescence to the upper wings; wings held open while perching.

**Larva:** The caterpillar is pale green with tiny yellowish spots. There is a narrow yellowish line on the sides. The head is dark brown with orange patches and spots.

**Pupa:** The pupa is green with a small black knob over the thoracic spiracles.

**Host Plants:** Herbs, vines, and shrubs in the Bean Family (Fabaceae). The caterpillars eat the leaves of milk peas (*Galactia elliottii, G. regularis, G. volubilis*), indigos (*Indigofera caroliniana, I. suffruticosa, I. spicata*), Orange Sesbania (*Sesbania punicea*), Bladderpod (*S. vesicaria*), and occasionally Wild Indigo (*Baptisia lactea*), Black Locust (*Robinia pseudo-acacia*), Hemp Sesbania (*Sesbania macrocarpa*), Florida Vetch (*Vicia floridana*), and American Wisteria (*Wisteria frutescens*).

**Natural History:** The yellowish eggs are laid singly on the leaves of the host. The young caterpillar eats two slits in the leaf margin and folds over the flap to make a shelter. Older caterpillars tie two or more leaves together to make a nest. The last-stage caterpillar overwinters, then pupates in the spring without further feeding. Several generations are produced each year. Adults of the Zarucco Dusky Wing occur from February through October. The flight is somewhat fast and erratic, near the ground. Males frequently perch on low vegetation and sometime drink from bare wet soil. Both males and females usually hold the wings open while perching.

**Distribution:** The Zarucco Dusky Wing is found in scrubs, sandhills, flatwoods, and disturbed sites such as roadsides, old fields, and utility corridors throughout Florida. Garden abundance is low.

## Hammock Skipper

### *Polygonus leo*

**Adult:** The Hammock Skipper is a blackish butterfly with three relatively large white spots on the forewings. There is also a group of small white spots near the tip of the wing. The wings above have a purplish luster near the base. The underside of the hindwing is pale purple with faint dark bands and a small dark spot near the base of the wing. Wingspans range from 4.3 to 4.9 cm.

**Field Marks:** Somewhat small in size; dark with three large white spots on forewing; the underside of the hindwing is pale purple with dark bands.

**Larva:** The caterpillar is green with tiny yellow spots and a yellow line on the sides. The head is white with a black stripe on the sides and two black spots on the upper face.

**Pupa:** The pupa is green with short points on the head and orange-brown markings.

**Host Plants:** Trees in the Bean Family (Fabaceae). The caterpillars eat the leaves of Jamaica Dogwood (*Piscidia piscipula*) and Pongam (*Pongamia pinnata*).

331. Zarucco Dusky Wings (males left, females right; top row upper sides, bottom row undersides).

332. The last-stage caterpillar.

333. The pupa.

334. Orange Sesbania (*Sesbania punicea*).

335. Hammock Skippers (males left, females right; top row upper sides, bottom row undersides).

336. The last-stage caterpillar.

337. Like most skippers, the larva lives in a silk-lined folded leaf.

338. The pupa.

339. Jamaica Dogwood (*Piscidia piscipula*).

**Natural History:** The green eggs are laid singly on the new growth of the host. The young caterpillar eats two slits in the leaf margin and folds the flap over to make a nest. Older larvae fold over entire leaflets or tie overlapping leaves together to make a nest. Many generations are produced each year. Adults of the Hammock Skipper occur all months of the year in south Florida. The flight is fast, from 1 to 2 meters above the ground. This butterfly often perches on the undersides of leaves.

**Distribution:** The Hammock Skipper is found at the edges of hammocks in southern Florida, but females will find and oviposit on host plants in nurseries, lawns, and parking lots. Garden abundance is low.

## Tropical Checkered Skipper

### *Pyrgus oileus*

**Adult:** The Tropical Checkered Skipper is a small white butterfly with black markings. Males have long bluish-white scales near the base of the wings above. Females are darker, especially near the base of the wings above. The underside of the hindwing is white with black lines. The fall and winter generations are mostly brownish below. Wingspans range from 2.5 to 3.0 cm.

The Common Checkered Skipper (*Pyrgus communis*) is a similar species. Males of the Common Checkered Skipper lack the long bluish-white scales on the upper wings. The underside of the hindwing has pale brown bands.

**Field Marks:** Small in size; wings white with black markings; the wings are usually held open while perching.

**Larva:** The caterpillar is green with faint white lines and rather long hairs on the body. The first thoracic segment is brown with pale spots. The head is black.

**Pupa:** The green pupa has small black spots and scattered hairs.

**Host Plants:** Herbs in the Hibiscus Family (Malvaceae). The caterpillars eat the leaves of Broomweed (*Sida acuta*), Indian Hemp (*Sida rhombifolia*), False Mallow (*Malvastrum corchorifolium*), and possibly Hollyhock (*Althea rosea*) and Poppy Mallow (*Callirhoe papaver*).

**Natural History:** The small greenish eggs are laid singly on the young leaves and flower buds of the host. The caterpillars fold and tie leaves together to make shelters. Several generations are produced each year. Adults of the Tropical Checkered Skipper are found all months of the year in south Florida. In the northern part of the state they are most often seen from August through December. The flight is somewhat fast and erratic, near the ground.

**Distribution:** The Tropical Checkered Skipper is found in weedy disturbed sites such as roadsides and weedlots in peninsular Florida. Garden abundance is usually low.

## Dorantes Skipper

### *Urbanus dorantes*

**Adult:** The Dorantes Skipper is a brown butterfly with yellowish spots on the forewings and long tails on the hindwings. Males have a small flap covering a band of androconial scales on the leading margin of the forewing. The underside of the hindwing is brown with dark spots and bands. Wingspans range from 3.8 to 4.3 cm. Compare this species with the Long-Tailed Skipper.

**Field Marks:** Somewhat small in size; brown with semi-transparent yellowish spots; tails present, unless broken off; the wings are held tightly closed while feeding at flowers.

**Larva:** The caterpillar is yellowish-green with a narrow dark line along the back and a chainlike band on the sides. The first thoracic segment is black on top and reddish below. The head is large, round, and black, with two small points at the top.

**Pupa:** The pupa is brown with dark markings and is thickest about the middle.

**Host Plants:** Herbs in the Bean Family (Fabaceae). The caterpillars feed on the leaves of Creeping Beggarweed (*Desmodium incanum*), Florida Beggarweed (*Desmodium tortuosum*), Garden Bean (*Phaseolus vulgaris*), and Cowpea (*Vigna luteola*).

**Natural History:** The greenish eggs are laid singly on the flower stalks and leaves of the host. The young caterpillar eats two slits in the margin of a leaf and folds the resulting flap over to make a shelter. The caterpillar sits upside-down on the domelike roof of the shelter. Older larvae tie the edges of an entire leaflet or several leaves together to make a nest. Many generations are produced each year. Adults of the Dorantes Skipper occur all months of the year in south Florida. In north Florida this species is most often seen from August through December. The flight is somewhat fast, up to 2 meters above the ground. Males frequently perch in forest clearings or along trails and make circular flights around the territory.

**Distribution:** The Dorantes Skipper is found in many habitats, especially in or near hammocks and disturbed sites such as roadsides and weedlots in peninsular Florida. Garden abundance may be moderate to high.

**Note:** The Dorantes Skipper is a recently established species in Florida. Although it is found in nearby Cuba, our population is the same as the Mexican and Central American race.

340. Tropical Checkered Skippers (left column males, top = upper side, bottom = underside; middle column females, top = upper side, bottom = underside; right column winter forms, top = underside male, bottom = underside female).

341. Common Checkered Skipper.

342. A mating pair of Tropical Checkered Skippers. The female is facing the top of the photo.

343. The last-stage caterpillar.

344. The pupa.

345. Broomweed (*Sida acuta*).

346. Dorantes Skippers (males left, females right; top row upper sides, bottom row undersides).

347. The last-stage caterpillar.

348. The pupa.

349. Florida Beggarweed (*Desmodium tortuosum*).

## Long-Tailed Skipper

### *Urbanus proteus*

**Adult:** The Long-Tailed Skipper is a dark brown butterfly with a bluish-green sheen on the wings above. The forewings have many semitransparent spots. There is a pair of long tails on the hindwings. The underside of the hindwing is brown with dark spots and bands. Males have a small flap covering a narrow patch of androconial scales along the leading edge of the forewings. Wingspans range from 3.9 to 4.8 cm.

**Field Marks:** Somewhat small in size; wings with a bluish-green sheen; tails present unless broken off; the wings are held partly open while feeding at flowers.

**Larva:** The caterpillar is yellowish-green with small black spots and a narrow dark line along the back. The sides have a yellow stripe that changes to orange on the last few segments. The first body segment is black on top and bright red below. Each proleg has an orange spot. The head is reddish-brown with a black face and two reddish eyespots near the mouth.

**Pupa:** The pupa is brown, covered by a white wax, and thickest about the middle.

**Host Plants:** Herbs and vines in the Bean Family (Fabaceae). The caterpillars eat the leaves of False Money-wort (*Alysicarpus vaginalis*), Hog Peanut (*Amphicarpa bracteata*), butterfly peas (*Centrosema floridanum, C. virginianum, Clitoria mariana, C. ternatea*), beggarweeds (*Desmodium floridanum, D. incanum, D. paniculatum, D. tortuosum, D. viridiflorum*), milk peas (*Galactia regularis, G. striata*), Lima Bean (*Phaseolus limensis*), Wild Bean (*P. polystachios*), Garden Bean (*P. vulgaris*), Kudzu (*Pueraria lobata*), Cowpea (*Vigna luteola*), and occasionally Soybean (*Glycine max*), Phasey Bean (*Macroptilium lathyroides*),

350. Long-Tailed Skippers (males left, females right; top row upper sides, bottom row undersides).

351. The wings seem to glow on this perching male.

352. Shelters of the young caterpillars.

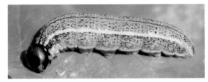

353. The last-stage caterpillar.

354. The pupa is covered with white wax.

355. Creeping Beggarweed (*Desmodium incanum*).

Garden Pea (*Pisum sativum*), Small Rhynchosia (*Rhynchosia minima*), American Wisteria (*Wisteria frutescens*), and Chinese Wisteria (*W. sinensis*). The Long-Tailed Skipper will also lay eggs on plants such as Cabbage (*Brassica oleracea*), Radish (*Raphanus sativus*), Rattlebox (*Crotalaria spectabilis*), and Large-Leaved Pipevine (*Aristolochia durior*). The young caterpillars will make shelters but cannot survive on these plants.

**Natural History:** The yellowish eggs are laid singly or in short stacks on the undersides of the leaves of the host. The young caterpillar eats two slits in the margin of a leaf and fold the resulting flap over to make a shelter. The caterpillar sits upside-down on the domelike roof of the shelter. Older larvae fold over an entire leaflet or several leaves to make a nest. Often the larger caterpillars make

their nest on broad-leaved herbs near the food plant. They crawl to the food plant, mostly at night, to eat. Many generations are produced each year. Adults of the Long-Tailed Skipper occur all months of the year in south Florida. This migratory butterfly is most common during late summer and fall (August through October) in the northern part of the state. The flight is somewhat fast, within a few meters of the ground. Males frequently perch in forest clearings or along trails and make circular flights around the territory. Adults sometimes squirt fluid from the rear end onto bird droppings, then suck up the nitrogen-rich solution.

**Distribution:** The Long-Tailed Skipper is found in many habitats, especially disturbed sites, throughout Florida. Garden abundance may be moderate to high.

## Giant Skippers (Family Hesperiidae: Subfamily Megathyminae)

### Yucca Giant Skipper

*Megathymus yuccae*

**Adult:** The Yucca Giant Skipper is a dark brown butterfly with yellow patches on the forewings. Females also have some yellow spots on the upper side of the hindwings. The underside of the hindwing is black and gray with a small white patch along the leading edge of the wing. Wingspans range from 5.3 to 7.2 cm.

**Field Marks:** Medium in size; thick body; wings dark brown with yellow patches; there is a small white patch midway along the leading edge of the hindwing below.

**Larva:** The caterpillar is very pale brown with a reddish-brown head. The first thoracic segment is black on the upper side. The rear end is blackish on top. The body is thickest at the thorax.

**Pupa:** The pupa is dark brown with a long abdomen.

**Host Plants:** Low herbs and shrubs in the Agave Family (Agavaceae). The caterpillars bore into the stems of yuccas such as Spanish Dagger (*Yucca aloifolia*), Stiff-Leaved Bear Grass (*Y. filamentosa*), Mound-Lily Yucca (*Y. gloriosa*), and Soft-Leaved Bear Grass (*Y. smalliana* [= *Y. flaccida*]).

**Natural History:** The relatively large brownish eggs are laid one at a time on the leaves of yuccas. The young caterpillar makes a nest of plant fragments and silk, often on the central leaves. Somewhat larger larvae tie several leaves together to make a nest but also start to bore into the center of the stem. As the larva grows larger, it tunnels deeper into the stem. A cigar-shaped tube, the "tent," of plant fragments and silk is constructed at the tunnel entrance. This tube allows the caterpillar room to turn around while still being concealed. The droppings are cast from the top of the tube. The last-stage larva produces quantities of flaky white wax from glands on the underside of the body, between the last two pairs of legs. The wax is used to line the tunnel. The caterpillar then overwinters within the burrow. In the spring, the larva pupates without further feeding, with the head oriented toward the tunnel entrance. The pupa is able to move up and down in the tunnel, which may extend several feet into the yucca

356. Yucca Giant Skippers (males left, females right; top row upper sides, bottom row undersides).

357. A newly emerged adult resting on the tent.

358. A hatched egg on Soft-Leaved Bear Grass.

359. The last-stage caterpillar.

360. A cut-away view of a small yucca showing the leaf nest and burrow of a young Yucca Giant Skipper caterpillar.

361. A Spanish Dagger stem showing the burrow of a large Yucca Giant Skipper caterpillar.

362. The top of a yucca shoot with a tent of the Yucca Giant Skipper.

363. A hatched pupa within the wax-lined larval burrow.

364. Spanish Dagger (*Yucca aloifolia*).

stem, by rotating the tip of the abdomen. Only one generation is produced each year. Adults of the Yucca Giant Skipper occur from early March until late April. The flight is fast and powerful, within 1.5 meters of the ground. Females are clumsy fliers and seem to bumble about, but nimbly dive toward even tiny host plants on which to lay eggs. Males perch on low vegetation or the ground at midday and make periodic flights around the territory. This butterfly does not visit flowers.

**Distribution:** The Yucca Giant Skipper is found in scrubs, sandhills, scrubby flatwoods, and at the margins of dry hammocks in north and central Florida. Garden abundance is low.

**Note:** Use caution when digging around yuccas. The sap from the roots causes a poison ivy–like dermatitis. The caterpillars kill the tip of the yucca shoot but do not kill the plant. The feeding damage causes the yucca to produce new shoots. The larvae of an exotic weevil (*Scyphophorus acupunctatus*) also bore into Spanish Dagger and often kill the plants.

# Moths in the Garden

About the time that the butterflies in your yard are going to sleep, other insects are just beginning to awaken. The many moths that have been hiding in the vegetation now seek out nectar, mates, or host plants. Caterpillars too, including those of butterflies, are especially active at night. Some caterpillars hide around the bases of their host plants during the day, march up to the leaves at dusk to feed, and return to their hiding spots before daybreak. Although your neighbors may scratch their heads, it's often rewarding to take a flashlight tour of the garden at night to look for moths or caterpillars.

Dusk is the best time to view moths at flowers. The sphinx or hawkmoths (Family Sphingidae) are especially noticeable. Some people mistake the larger species for hummingbirds. The proboscis of hawkmoths is as long or longer than the body. Like hummingbirds, they hover over flowers while feeding. A few day-flying species of hawkmoths resemble bees, and have somewhat clubbed antennae similar to the butterflies. The caterpillars (hornworms) usually have a spine on the rear end. When ready to pupate, the caterpillar changes color and begins to wander. Eventually it burrows in soft soil and pupates underground. If you're rearing hawkmoths indoors, provide the caterpillar with some sand or soil in which to burrow.

Silkmoths (Family Saturniidae) are among the largest insects in the world. There are over a dozen species in Florida. Although many spin a strong silk cocoon, some pupate in a cell underground, as do the hawkmoths. Adult silkmoths do not eat, and therefore do not visit flowers. All of their energy comes from fat stored by the larvae The adults frequently come to porch lights. Males have very feathery antennae. The female has a more slender antenna, and the abdomen may be very robust. It's fun to raise these moths to see the caterpillars and other stages. Eggs may be obtained by placing the female moth in a paper bag for a few days. Adding some sprigs of the food plant may help stimulate her to lay eggs. The eggs may be carefully picked or cut from the bag and transferred to rearing containers. The caterpillars are large and often spectacularly colored or ornamented. A few are occasionally abundant enough to defoliate trees. Caterpillars of the Io Moth and Buck Moth have stinging spines.

Owlet moths (Family Noctuidae) are a large and diverse group in Florida. They range in size from very small to very large. Some important crop pests, such as cutworms and armyworms, are in this group, but most are simply part of nature's web. Some species visit flowers at dusk. Others are attracted to porch lights. The Underwings (*Catocala* spp.) are spectacular moths that may occur in urban areas. The adults rest on tree trunks or buildings during the day. The forewings are colored like tree bark. The hindwings may be patterned with red, orange, yellow, or pure black. The caterpillars eat the leaves of oaks, hawthorns, hickories, blueberries, and other plants.

Tiger moths (Arctiidae) are relatives of the owlet moths. Sizes range from small to medium. The adults are protected by foul-tasting chemicals and are brightly colored to warn predators that they are not good to eat. Some species mimic wasps in their appearance. The caterpillars are hairy and eat many kinds of herbs and shrubs.

365. Tantalus Sphinx moth.

366. The last-stage caterpillar.

Inchworms (Geometridae), pyralids (Pyralidae), and many kinds of tiny moths are found in gardens. Moth identification can be quite challenging due to the lack of comprehensive guides, dull color patterns, or small size. Some good books to start with are the *Peterson Field Guide to the Moths of Eastern North America* by Charles V. Covell, Jr., and the *Golden Nature Guide to Butterflies and Moths* by Robert T. Mitchell and Herbert S. Zim.

Tent caterpillars (Lasiocampidae), clearwing moths (Sesiidae), prominents (Notodontidae), and bagworms (Psychidae) may defoliate or injure plants in the garden. Only a few moths have larvae with stinging or irritating hairs. These include the slug caterpillar moths (Limacodidae), flannel moths (Megalopygidae), and some kinds of tussock moths (Lymantriidae) and silkmoths.

Although moths will readily come to butterfly plants such as lantana and butterfly bush for nectar, they especially like white or yellow flowers with strong fragrances. Moth attracting plants for the Florida garden include Papaya (*Carica papaya*), Ganges Primrose (*Asystasia gangetica*), Wishbone Flower (*Torenia fournieri*), Petunia (*Petunia hybrida*), and Four-O-Clocks (*Mirabilis jalapa*). Some moths also visit fermenting fruit and sap flows.

## Hawkmoths (Family Sphingidae)

### Tantalus Sphinx

#### *Aellopus tantalus*

Wingspans range from 3.9 to 5.3 cm.
**Host Plants:** Inkberry (*Randia aculeata*) and Seven-Year Apple (*Casasia clusiifolia*) in the Madder Family (Rubiaceae), and occasionally Buttonwood (*Conocarpus erecta*, Combretaceae).
This interesting moth is most often seen hovering over flowers in the daytime. The adults like to perch on the underside of leaves.

### Nessus Sphinx

#### *Amphion floridensis*

Wingspans range from 4.6 to 5.0 cm.
**Host Plants:** Grape Family (Vitaceae): Pepper Vine (*Ampelopsis arborea*) and Wild Grape (*Vitis rotundifolia*).
The Nessus Sphinx is usually seen at flowers or laying eggs on host plants during the daytime. This moth also readily visits fermenting sap flows and fruit.

### Mournful Sphinx

#### *Enyo lugubris*

Wingspans range from 5.0 to 6.4 cm.

367. Nessus Sphinx moth.

368. The last-stage caterpillar.

369. Mournful Sphinx moth.

370. The last-stage caterpillar.

371. Hummingbird Clearwing moth.

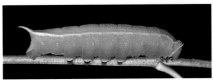

372. The last-stage caterpillar.

**Host Plants:** Grape Family (Vitaceae): Pepper Vine (*Ampelopsis arborea*) and Wild Grape (*Vitis rotundifolia*).

This small sphinx moth is usually seen visiting flowers at dusk.

## Hummingbird Clearwing

### *Hemaris thysbe*

Wingspans range from 5.1 to 5.8 cm.
**Host Plants:** Not known for Florida, but reported from hawthorn (*Crataegus* spp.), honeysuckle (*Lonicera* spp.), and cherry (*Prunus* spp.) elsewhere.

This beautiful moth is most often seen visiting flowers during the daytime.

## Carolina Sphinx

### *Manduca sexta*

Wingspans range from 10.5 to 12 cm.
**Host Plants:** Nightshade Family (Solanaceae): Tomato (*Lycopersicon esculentum*), Tobacco (*Nicotiana tabacum*), Flowering Tobacco (*Nicotiana alata*), Potato (*Solanum tuberosum*), and Climbing Nightshade (*Solanum seaforthianum*). The caterpillar is known as the Tobacco Hornworm.

The larvae are pests of tomatoes. The adults visit flowers at night.

373. Carolina Sphinx moth.

374. A Tobacco Hornworm.

## Tersa Sphinx

### *Xylophanes tersa*

Wingspans range from 5.7 to 7.6 cm.
**Host Plants:** Madder Family (Rubiaceae): *Richardia scabra*, *Spermacoce verticillata*, and especially *Pentas lanceolata*.

This lovely moth is often seen visiting flowers at dusk or perched near lights during the day.

375. Tersa Sphinx moth.

376. The caterpillar may be either green or brown.

377. A Luna Moth.

378. The last-stage caterpillar.

379. Polyphemus Moth.

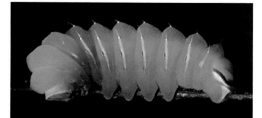

380. The last-stage caterpillar.

## Silk Moths (Family Saturniidae)

### Luna Moth

#### *Actias luna*

Wingspans range from 8.3 to 9.0 cm.
**Host Plants:** Sweet Gum (*Liquidambar styraciflua*), hickories (*Carya* spp.), and other trees.
The adults do not eat, but are easily attracted to light at night, or are sometimes found perching on trees during the day.

### Polyphemus Moth

#### *Antheraea polyphemus*

Wingspans range from 10.0 to 12.5 cm.
**Host Plants:** Oak Family (*Quercus* spp.).
The Polyphemus Moth is one of the largest species in Florida, and adults are commonly found flying around lights.

### Io Moth

#### *Automeris io*

Wingspans range from 5.5 to 7.9 cm.
**Host Plants:** Corn (*Zea mays*), willows (*Salix* spp.), Red Mangrove (*Rhizophora mangle*), Florida Trema (*Trema micranthum*), Wax Myrtle (*Myrica cerifera*), hibiscus

381. Io Moths (left = male, right = female).

382. Ouch! The caterpillar of the Io Moth bears stinging spines.

(*Hibiscus* spp.), Washingtonia Palm (*Washingtonia robusta*), and many other plants.

The adults are mostly seen at lights at night.

**Imperial Moth**

*Eacles imperialis*

Wingspans range from 8.8 to 10.1 cm.
**Host Plants:** Oaks (*Quercus* spp.), pines (*Pinus* spp.), and other trees.
This beautiful moth may be found at lights.

383. Imperial Moth.

384. The last-stage caterpillar.

## Tiger Moths (Family Arctiidae)

### Polka-Dot Moth

#### *Syntomeida epilais*

Wingspans range from 4.7 to 4.9 cm.
**Host Plants:** Oleander (*Nerium oleander*).
The adults are slow-flying wasp mimics that are active during the daytime. They readily come to flowers. A related species, the Scarlet Bodied Wasp Moth (*Cosmosoma myrodora*), which is beautiful bright red, also comes to flowers in gardens.

387. Ilia Underwing moth.

385. Polka-Dot Moth.

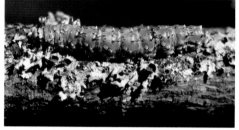

388. The lichen-like caterpillar.

## Owlet Moths (Family Noctuidae)

### Ilia Underwing

#### *Catocala ilia*

Wingspans range from 7.4 to 7.7 cm.
**Host Plants:** Oak Family (*Quercus* spp.).
The adults perch on tree trunks during the day. The color of the forewings blends in perfectly with the bark. The bright red hindwings may startle predators such as lizards or birds that discover the resting moths. Many other species with red, yellow, or black hindwings occur in Florida. Underwing moths readily visit fermenting fruit.

386. The last-stage caterpillar.

# Developing Your Butterfly Garden

A Tiger Swallowtail feeding on Lantana.

## Before You Dig

A butterfly garden can be as simple as a parsley plant on the back porch or as elaborate as any other formal garden. Gardening can be a creative and rewarding activity if you do only what you like doing and allow yourself opportunities to enjoy and share your accomplishments.

By following a few basic rules, anyone can develop a beautiful garden that will attract butterflies. Proper plant selection is one of the most important aspects of gardening. When selecting plants, be patient and seek out quality plants. Not just any garden section or corner plant shop will have all of the quality butterfly plants you may want. Some of the less usual but most important butterfly food and nectar plants can be obtained through your local chapter of the Florida Native Plant Society (FNPS). Local chapters usually have at least one annual native plant sale and often have plant raffles during meetings where you can choose native butterfly-attracting plants. FNPS chapters make a point

389. A border garden.

of inviting speakers to their meetings who will explain how to attract wildlife to gardens, and this includes butterflies in particular. See the resource guide in the back of this book for more information.

Planning is the other most important aspect of gardening. Even a very small garden will bring more enjoyment if you plan it out before you put it in. Take time to look over the yard before you start digging. Consider first any major changes to the yard. Should existing trees or shrubs be removed, walkways changed, fences or walls moved or installed? Should new buildings, decks, or patios be added? Always allow room for maintenance and fire protection of your home. The septic tank, well, and utility lines also may need maintenance from time to time. Check with your local utility companies. Technicians from the utilities will often locate water, sewer, electric, and gas lines on your property at no cost.

For an elaborate garden or landscape, you may want to make a sketch on a piece of graph paper showing the house and other buildings, property lines, sidewalks, driveway, septic tank, well, fences, slopes, wet areas, and existing vegetation such as trees, shrubs, and flower beds. For a garden of any size, you will want to consider the direction of the prevailing wind, lighting throughout the day, and possible seasonal changes in the yard, as these will affect the growth of plants. Also, consider your soil. Do any areas hold standing water after a heavy rain? The soil will also be wetter around buildings that lack gutters. You may want to use a shovel to check the soil at various sites. Soil samples can be analyzed for a nominal fee through your county extension agent. Check with the extension service for instructions on how to collect and submit samples. This will give you a solid understanding of your yard or garden site. Disregard any advice on soil amendment in favor of choosing a plant that is adapted to your particular soil type.

If you made a map of your present landscape, you can use a copy of it to sketch in the new garden design. If you have a computer, there are several landscape design programs available that may help with the planning. Trees and shrubs will help to shade your house, especially if planted on the east and west sides. The air conditioning compressor/condenser unit may also be screened or shaded with plants, so long as the airflow is not impeded. When young trees are planted under larger existing ones, they may be stunted or may bend toward the light and become one-sided. Shade adapted shrubs will usually grow well under existing trees. Lo-

390. Reduce the size of your lawn with mulched beds of butterfly attracting plants.

cate trees away from buildings and utility lines at least as far as the estimated mature canopy size. Tree roots grow amazingly fast and may invade and block septic tanks and drain fields if planted too close. Expect the roots of a tree to extend at least as far as the canopy.

For a complex garden, sketch in the location of the new flower beds, trellises, benches, gazebo, pond, or other items. If you are installing an irrigation system, add the water lines to your diagram. Most butterflies and their food plants are sun-loving, therefore the butterfly garden should be in an area that receives bright sunlight for at least half of the day during the growing season. The shape and location of the flower beds are important to the overall design of the landscape. Linear features such as property lines or most building foundations do well with border gardens. Giving the beds curvy edges adds interest. Other beds in open spaces will resemble islands in a sea of ground cover such as grass or mulch. These may be in the shape of polygons or have curvy edges, depending upon the style you wish to develop. One technique you can use is to sprinkle a line of powdered chalk or flour to mark where your beds or other garden features will lie directly on the ground.

One last thing before you dig: Some basic tools are necessary for installing and maintaining your butterfly garden. Your tool kit might include a pair of gloves,

a round-point shovel, a bow rake, a hoe, a leaf rake, pruning shears, a pruning saw, and one or more trowels. Get quality tools! Nothing is more frustrating than having the trowel you just bought snap in two, or the handle on the shovel break while you're moving a plant. Other items that you may find useful are a hose and nozzle, an edger, and a lawn mower. Rubber hoses are the most durable, and soaker hoses may save on water use. Environmentally friendly push mowers are making a comeback. It's a good way to get exercise while cutting the grass, it wastes no gasoline, and it never pollutes. It makes a pleasant whirring sound, not a nerve-wracking roar, and leaves a fragrance of fresh-cut grass with no stench of exhaust. Ours is made out of metal and wood, so is completely recyclable or biodegradable. Most tools will last for years if kept clean, oiled, and out of the weather.

## Breaking Ground

Now that you have a plan, it's time to start gardening! The landscape can be broken into sections such as the front, side, or back yard, and your plan implemented one part at a time. Knowledge gained on the installation of one section will help you avoid similar mistakes throughout the entire yard.

Begin by removing any unwanted trees and shrubs. Next, irrigation lines (if needed), walkways, decks, trellises, and other structures should be installed. Finally, the flower beds should be located and drawn on the ground. It's easier to plant the beds if the grass is removed first. We do not recommend the use of herbicides to kill the grass, as this may affect your plants, soil organisms, birds and other wildlife, or you. The grass can be smothered by a thick layer of mulch. We recommend at least five inches for best results.

With or without removal of the grass, apply a thick layer of mulch in the shape of the bed. Lay out the potted plants according to your design. Be careful of poisonous plants (such as Coontie) around small children or pets. Another important consideration is to group plants with similar water requirements together.

## Choosing What To Grow

Choose healthy plants to put into your garden. Avoid those that are potbound, weed infested, yellowed, or have obvious pest or disease problems.

You may like to use particular themes for individual beds. We've seen beds organized into groups such as all annuals, flowers of all one or two colors, collections of plants from one type of habitat (such as a scrub garden), collections of various species or varieties of one type of plant (such as *Lantana*, *Salvia*, *Buddleja*, or grasses), and herbs and vegetables attractive to butterflies (such as dill, parsley, collards, mustard, and mints). Mixed perennial beds are very popular too. Planting small groups of the same species will help you to keep track of the plants and, from a distance, produces a more effective display. Contrasts create a sense of excitement. Mixing species of different size, flower color, or leaf shape will create pleasing designs. Naturally, tall plants go toward the back or center of the beds, and low-growing plants toward the front or along edges. Allow enough space between perennial plants for future growth by imagining how big the plant will be next year, or for trees and shrubs, in five or ten years.

## Climate and Microclimate

Remember that plants not suited to the site due to shade, soil conditions, or climate will not thrive and will probably die. Many mail order companies list the hardiness zone ratings for the plants offered for sale in their catalogs. Plant hardiness zone maps were developed by the U.S. Department of Agriculture as a planting guide for farmers and gardeners. The zones are based on the average minimum temperature for a region. North Florida (from Ocala northward) is in Zone 8, where low temperatures may range between 10 and 20° F. Central Florida is in Zone 9, with minimum winter temperatures between 20 and 30° F. Most of south Florida (the area south of Lake Okeechobee) is in Zone 10, with lows between 30 and 40° F. Plants that are rated differently from your zone are not likely to survive, either because it does not get cold enough in the case of temperate species, or because it gets too cold for the more tropical kinds.

Local features such as urban areas, lakes, or the ocean cause warming effects. Sites near these features will be warmer in winter than other parts of a particular zone. Open, exposed sites on hilltops or in low-lying areas will be colder in winter than sheltered areas. Microclimate effects can be used to grow plants that normally would not survive in your area. The angle of the sun changes throughout the year, being most direct in summer and more southerly during winter. Therefore, minimum winter temperatures usually occur on the north side of a house. In contrast, maximum summer temperatures will occur on the unshaded western side. Although the southern exposure is relatively warm during the winter, this may stimulate new growth that will later be killed by late winter freezes. Fences, arbors, and buildings, as well as trees and shrubs, may be used to help shelter cold-sensitive plants.

The hole you dig for your new plants is very important. The planting hole should be two to three times the diameter of the root ball. The soil in the pot should be level with the ground surface. Do not pull plants from pots. First cut off any roots that are growing out of the drainage holes or cut the pot apart to release them. Turn the pot over and tap on the bottom until the root ball slides out. If the roots inside the pot are dense and tightly packed, cut them along the sides and loosen before planting. Do not allow the roots to dry out while planting. Spread the roots apart when placing them in the ground, carefully pack soil around them, and gently tamp down. Using compost or mild fertilizer will give the new plants a boost. Mounding the soil in a ring when you first put in a woody plant will help keep water around the roots. Mulch and water new plantings thoroughly.

391. An elegant container garden of butterfly and moth attracting plants for the patio.

## Keeping Track

It is nice to label the plants in your garden, especially woody species and perennial herbs. Most garden shops have plastic or metal labels available. The metal labels are durable and inexpensive. You may also want to keep a log book showing a map of the garden. Notes on the timing of flowering or of butterfly visitors will provide a record of garden events for future reference.

## Container Gardening

If space is extremely limited, container gardening may be the answer. Many butterfly nectar and host plants are easy to grow in pots on a sunny patio. A variety of plants can be grown together if large pots or tubs are used. Plastic and glazed ceramic pots will not need to be watered as often as unglazed terra cotta containers. The pots should have a hole at the bottom to allow excess water to flow out. Before adding soil to the pots, place a layer of small pebbles in the bottom to allow better drainage. Use a porous soil containing coarse sand, perlite or vermiculite, and peat. Poorly drained soils are likely to lead to root rot and other disease problems. After planting, keep the soil moist, but not wet. Watering is often easier for established plants by placing a deep dish under the pot. Capillary action will

wick the water from the dish to the soil in the pot. When the dish becomes dry, it's time to add more water. Use a mild fertilizer once a month, or a coated, slow release formulation.

## Salt Spray

Sites within a quarter of mile of the ocean will be affected by salt spray. Only certain kinds of plants are adapted to salty conditions. Soils and irrigation wells, even at inland sites, may also have salt or mineral concentrations too high for good plant growth. The solution is to plant salt-tolerant species, or to use containers or raised beds, where plants are protected from salt spray and water can be more easily controlled. Native vegetation found along the coasts may have already been "salt pruned" into dramatic forms which you can enjoy if you preserve the natural landscape. In fact, in many cases, preserving the natural vegetation ensures a built-in butterfly garden that requires very little maintenance.

## Maintaining the Garden

In spite of careful planning, as the garden grows, problems will develop. Some plants may languish or die, while others may become too big, spread excessively, or look out of place. Once installed, gardening is simply a matter of adding, subtracting, and experimenting. Heavily prune shrubs such as *Lantana* and *Buddleja* during the winter to keep them vigorous. January is a good time to mulch beds, trim branches, and prepare for the new growing season.

## Soil Fertility

Garden plants generally need fertilizer only two or three times per year during the growing season, if at all. Overfertilizing may lead to increased pest problems, excessive growth, or pollution of local water supplies. Some gardeners prefer coated chemical fertilizers because they are longer lasting. We recommend using compost, manure, and other natural fertilizers to enhance plant growth, because they are slower acting and improve the soil structure more than chemical types. Fertilizers high in nitrogen and micronutrients work well in Florida's sandy soils. The micronutrients are also important for plants grown on the alkaline soils that frequently occur in south Florida, coastal sites, and urban areas. The high pH renders many nutrients insoluble, leading to micronutrient deficiencies. For many of our best-known butterfly-attracting plants, growth is best if the soil pH is between 5.5 and 7. However, changing pH is difficult. Ask your local Florida Native Plant Society chapter if they can recommend native species adapted to your particular soil conditions before making any major changes.

Rainfall varies between 55 and 65 inches per year in Florida. That's about one inch per week. However, most rain occurs during the summer, from June through September. Droughty conditions are common during the winter and spring. Plants that are actively growing will need rain or artificial watering every three to five days. As Florida's population grows, clean water is becoming an expensive resource in many areas. Some urban areas have restrictions on irrigation since lawn and garden watering may account for up to 50 percent of home water use. You can save money on your water bill by watering only when the plants need it. Also, some cities are now offering reclaimed water (the clean discharge from treatment facilities) for irrigation. Reclaimed water has nutrients that benefit plants, and saves potable water. Maximize the benefits of watering by thoroughly soaking the soil. Usually a half to three-quarters of an inch is sufficient. Spot watering is useful in applying water only where it is needed. The amount applied by sprinklers may be checked by setting out open tin cans in the spray field. It is best to water early in the morning when wind and temperatures are low. Watering during the evening or at night may encourage diseases.

## Mulching

Using mulch in the garden helps to reduce evaporation, moderates temperatures, prevents erosion, and discourages weeds. Many different types of organic mulches are available commercially, including pine needles, cypress chips, and pine bark. Each has advantages and disadvantages. Pine needles are attractive and stable but are not dense enough to control some weeds. Shredded cypress is attractive and long lasting but is overly expensive and may float around during heavy rainstorms. We recommend you not buy it, because harvesting cypress trees damages Florida's wetlands. Pine bark looks good, is available in a variety of sizes,

and does not decompose very quickly, but it also floats during heavy rains. Often organic mulches may be available at no cost. Wood chips may be obtained from city tree-trimming operations and private tree-trimming companies. Tree trimmings may contain pine or hardwoods and are often coarse-textured. Dead leaves raked into piles in the fall will kill grass if bedded more than six inches deep, and they can be used to prepare beds for planting in the spring. All of the organic mulches gradually decay, enriching the soil.

A pitchfork, bow rake, and wheelbarrow are the best tools for applying mulch. A layer of mulch four inches thick usually lasts at least a year. Mulch may be used in flower beds as well as for walkways, driveways, and play areas. Keep highly flammable pine needles and leaves away from the base of buildings. Inorganic mulches such as gravel, pebbles, and crushed stone are more permanent, but they may be more expensive than some of the organic mulches. We do not recommend black polyethylene film or woven ground cloths because they do not biodegrade.

## Composting

Composting kitchen scraps, grass clippings, and yard wastes not only helps to reduce the trash buried at the local landfill, but provides a wonderfully enriched soil for your garden. Insectivorous birds such as wrens, Blue Jays, and Mockingbirds love to forage around composting bins. Let us warn you that meat, bones, fats, or dairy products attract scavenging mammals, including dogs, raccoons, and rats. Smaller pieces decompose faster, so chopping things up helps. Composting bins may be made from wire, concrete blocks, or purchased from garden supply companies. Some cities give away bins to help encourage composting. The bin should be at least three feet in diameter. Place the bin in a partly sunny spot, near a water supply, and away from view. For each six inches of vegetation, cover with two to four inches of mineral soil. Moisten the bin if it looks dry. When full, move the bin to a new spot. Allow the old compost to decompose for four to six weeks before using it in the garden.

## Pests

Gardens are a zone of intense interaction between plants and animals. Suppressing weeds and pests must be carried out if the garden is to flourish. Many insect pests can be controlled by hand-picking and destroying them, or by spot application of insecticidal soaps. Weeds can also be suppressed or eliminated without the use of herbicides by hand-pulling and mulching. Some of the worst yard weeds in Florida are Doveweed (*Murdannia nudiflora*), Globe Sedge (*Cyperus globulosus*), West Indian Chickweed (*Drymaria cordata*), Common Chickweed (*Stellaria media*), Asiatic Hawksbeard (*Youngia japonica*), spurges (*Chamaesyce* spp. and *Phyllanthus* spp.), Florida Betony (*Stachys floridana*), bedstraw (*Galium* spp.), pusley (*Richardia* spp.), Coinwort (*Centella asiatica*), and pennywort (*Hydrocotyle* spp.). The county extension office should be able to identify weed and pest species and offer control advice, but we do not recommend spraying herbicides, as they are toxic to other garden denizens and to you.

## Sources for Plants

Your local nursery or garden center will probably have some of the most common nectar plants used for attracting butterflies. Native plant nurseries and mail order catalogs offer additional plants. The resource guide at the back of this book lists numerous sources of plants. Another good way to build your butterfly garden is to trade plants with other gardeners, especially host plants which are usually hard to find offered for sale. You may even want to collect and propagate plants from the wild, and here are some tips. Never take plant materials from public parks and natural areas. Collecting seeds, cuttings, or plants from private lands can be undertaken with the owner's permission, providing the plants are not listed as endangered or threatened.

Transplanting mature plants usually does not work. Most will not survive the shock. Pawpaws, orchids, and lupines are notoriously difficult to transplant. The best way to propagate some plants is from seeds. Most wildflower seeds can be planted directly in the garden, but grass and competing plants should be removed first. Spreading seeds on top of thinly mulched beds often works well since the mulch suppresses weeds. Planting the seeds in pots requires more work, but allows more control over their growth. Small seeds can be sown on the surface of a pot partly filled with a starter mix. Larger seeds will need to be planted deeper. Some species have hard seed coats, especially *Cassia* and bean relatives, that need to be nicked by rubbing

the seeds on a file, sandpaper, or cement. The small cut allows a germination inhibiting chemical to leach from the seed. The seeds of some species may need a cold period before they will germinate. These can simply be sown and left out of doors during the fall or mixed with moist soil and kept in a plastic bag in a refrigerator for several months.

It's possible, even easy, to propagate both wild and ornamental plants from cuttings. Butterfly Bush, *Lantana, Pentas,* Blue Porterweed, *Salvia, Verbena,* and many others can be grown from cuttings. To make cuttings clip a branch having mature foliage. Cut the stem into sections having just a few leaves. Make the cut directly below the leaves. Dip the lower end of the stem into rooting hormone (available at most garden centers) and push into a pot of starter mix, perlite, or vermiculite. Four or five cuttings can be added to a six-inch pot. Water the pot thoroughly and loosely cover with a plastic bag. The pot can be set in a shallow dish of water to keep the growing medium moist. Place the cuttings in a bright, not sunny window. The roots will appear in three or four weeks if the cuttings are successful.

## Diversity

To attract a variety of butterflies to your yard, garden for diversity. Structural diversity (trees, shrubs, and herbs) creates habitat for woodland as well as meadow butterflies. Although some plants recommended in other gardening books are not very attractive to butterflies in Florida, they still have value by enriching and diversifying the garden, making it a more pleasing place. Flowers such as Black-Eyed Susans (*Rudbeckia hirta*), Purple Coneflower (*Echinacea purpurea*), Blanket Flower (*Gaillardia pulchella*), yarrow (*Achillea* spp.), tickseed (*Coreopsis* spp.), marigolds (*Tagetes erecta, T. patula*), goldenrod (*Solidago* spp.), sunflowers (*Helianthus* spp.), Stokes Aster (*Stokesia laevis*), Wild Petunia (*Ruellia caroliniensis*), Glossy Abelia (*Abelia x grandiflora*), azaleas (*Rhododendron* spp.), Elderberry (*Sambucus canadensis*), and roses (*Rosa* spp.) help add color and diversity to the garden.

Some exotic plants have escaped from cultivation in Florida and are taking over natural areas. Although they have some value to butterflies, we recommend that you remove any Mimosa (*Albizia julibrissin*), Brazilian Pepper (*Schinus terebinthifolius*), or Chinese Privet (*Ligustrum sinense*) from your property, because they are invading natural areas of Florida.

## Bought Butterflies and Other Gimmicks

When buying garden products for your yard, shop wisely. Do not buy live butterflies or moths to release in your garden. Plant the right plants and they will come. Providing resources, such as nectar and host plants, in one area acts to concentrate the butterflies that normally would be passing through the site. Butterfly gardening creates the conditions whereby the butterflies come to you. There is no need to buy butterflies. Releasing butterflies from other regions into your garden may be illegal, since the transportation of most live insects across state lines requires permits issued by the Florida Department of Agriculture and possibly other agencies. It is also unethical to release butterflies from other regions into your yard, since they may introduce new parasites or genetic material that could be detrimental to local butterflies.

Do not buy butterfly feeders or butterfly food. This is a gimmick designed to take advantage of naïve gardeners. Butterflies much prefer a bounty of beautiful flowers. They rarely visit artificial feeders. Nor do we know of anyone who has had a hibernating butterfly use a hibernation box (although they do make good conversation pieces or lawn ornaments). Lastly, many guides recommend creating puddling or watering areas for butterflies, but these are unlikely to work. Some butterflies may seek salts or nutrients from wet soil, but artificial puddles lack these components, and therefore usually do not attract butterflies. Most species get sufficient water from flower nectar and do not need to drink.

We highly recommend adding interesting items to the garden. Objects such as flat rocks or stepping stones, boulders, stumps, birdbaths, statuary, benches, trellises, arbors, gazebos, and low fences give plants support, create refuges for people, and make the garden a fun place to be. Fruiting trees and shrubs including Flowering Dogwood (*Cornus florida*), elms (*Ulmus* spp.), Gumbo Limbo (*Bursera simaruba*), Sea Grape (*Coccoloba uvifera*), Hackberry (*Celtis laevigata*), hollies (*Ilex* spp.), hawthorns (*Crataegus* spp.), blueberries (*Vaccinium* spp.), viburnums, and Wild Cherry (*Prunus serotina*) attract birds that do not eat butterflies. Birds and other animals need a source of water. A bird bath placed near shrubs will help to attract wildlife to your yard.

# The Basic Garden

The best way to begin the butterfly garden is to install one bed in the sunniest part of the yard. Later you may wish to expand the area or landscape the entire yard to attract butterflies. The following host plants are our recommended starter collection since they are commonly available from nurseries or other gardeners. They are guaranteed to attract lots of butterflies. Keep a list of the butterflies that you see in the yard. You may want to include other host plants to bring in the rarer species.

## Host Plants of Common Florida Butterflies

**Trees:**
Coconut Palm (*Coccos nucifera*) [South Florida]
Live Oak (*Quercus virginiana*)
Elm (*Ulmus americana*)
Redbay (*Persea borbonia*)
Hackberry (*Celtis laevigata*)
Sweet Bay (*Magnolia virginiana*)
Hercules Club (*Zanthoxylum clava-herculis*)
Sweet Orange (*Citrus sinensis*)
Jamaica Dogwood (*Piscidia piscipula*) [South Florida]
Wild Lime (*Zanthoxylum fagara*) [South and Central Florida]
**Shrubs:**
Christmas Senna (*Cassia bicapsularis*)
Saw Palmetto (*Serenoa repens*)
Leadwort (*Plumbago auriculata*)
Spanish Dagger (*Yucca aloifolia*)
**Herbs:**
Cabbage (*Brassica oleracea*)
Garden Bean (*Phaseolus vulgaris*)
Canna (*Canna* spp.)
Parsley (*Petroselinum crispum*)
Dill (*Anethum graveolens*)
Scarlet Milkweed (*Asclepias curassavicum*)
Fennel (*Foeniculum vulgare*)
**Grasses:**
Centipedegrass (*Eremochloa ophiuroides*)
St. Augustinegrass (*Stenotaphrum secundatum*)
Eastern Gamagrass (*Tripsacum dactyloides*)
Sugarcane (*Saccharum officinarum*)
Giant Reed (*Arundo donax*)
**Vines:**
Calico Flower (*Aristolochia elegans*)
Pelican Flower (*Aristolochia ringens*)
Maypop (*Passiflora incarnata*)

Providing flowering plants that are attractive to butterflies is what butterfly gardening is all about. The following herbs, shrubs, and vines are our recommended list of most attractive plants. Any one species or combination of plants will bring many butterflies to your yard.

392. Pentas (*Pentas lanceolata*).

## Nectar Plants to Attract Florida Butterflies

### Herbs

#### Pentas (*Pentas lanceolata*)

#### Madder Family (Rubiaceae)

Perennial erect herb to 3 feet tall. One plant may cover 3 square feet. Red, red with white center, blue, or white flowers. Dwarf and tall varieties. Propagated from cuttings. Full sun to partial shade. Moist soil. Blooms all year in south and central Florida. Very attractive to butterflies. Top-killed by freezing temperatures. Entire plant may be killed during especially cold winters in the northern part of the state. Sometimes susceptible to wilt diseases. The leaves are eaten by the Tersa Sphinx, which may defoliate the plants. Originally from Africa. Widely available.

#### Heliotrope (*Heliotropium amplexicaule*)
#### Borage Family (Boraginaceae)

Perennial trailing herb less than 1 foot tall. One plant may cover 6 to 8 square feet. Blue flowers. Propagated from seeds. Full sun to partial shade. Moist to dry soil. Very attractive to butterflies. Blooms from April to November. Top-killed by freezing temperatures. Originally from South America, but now naturalized in disturbed areas such as roadsides and weedy fields in north and central Florida. Limited availability.

Other species: *Heliotropium angiospermum* (native; white), *H. curassavicum* (native; white), and *H.*

393. Heliotrope (*Heliotropium amplexicaule*).

394. Tropical Sage (*Salvia coccinea*).

*polyphyllum* (native; yellow or white) are sometimes available from native plant nurseries. A relative, the garden herb Borage (*Borago officinalis*), also has blue flowers attractive to butterflies, and is available from seed catalogs.

#### Tropical Sage (*Salvia coccinea*)
#### Mint Family (Lamiaceae)

Annual, erect herb to 3 feet tall. One plant may cover 3 to 4 square feet. Red, pink, pink and white, or white flowers. Propagated from seeds. Full sun to partial shade. Somewhat attractive to butterflies and hummingbirds. Blooms all year in central and south Florida. Top-killed by freezing temperatures. Considered to be a native plant in south Florida. Available from native plant nurseries and seed catalogs. Other species: Hundreds of *Salvia* species exist, but only a few are cultivated in Florida. *Salvia farinacea* (Texas; blue), *S. greggii* (Texas and Mexico; hot pink, red, purple, white), *S. guarantica* (South America; sky-blue), *S. leucantha* (Mexico; blue), *S. miniata* (Central America, red), *S. patens* (Mexico; blue), and *S. vanhoutii* (South America; wine-red) are sometimes available at nurseries.

#### Zinnia (*Zinnia elegans*)
#### Aster Family (Asteraceae)

Annual erect herb to 3 feet tall. Use many plants together in beds. Red, pink, purple, yellow, white, or variegated flowers. Dwarf and tall varieties. Double-flow-

and *P. paniculata* (eastern U.S.; red, pink, white, blue, yellow, salmon) are frequently available from nurseries.

## Moss Verbena (*Glandularia pulchella*)
## Vervain Family (Verbenaceae)

Perennial trailing herb. One plant may cover 4 square feet. Purple, pink, or white flowers. Propagated from cuttings. Moist to dry soil. Full sun or partial shade. Very attractive to butterflies. Blooms from May through November. Originally from South America, but now naturalized along roads and in weedy fields in north and central Florida. Widely available. Other species: *G. tampensis* (native; purple) is available from native plant nurseries.

395. Zinnias (*Zinnia elegans*).

ered varieties are not attractive to butterflies. Propagated from seeds sown in pots or on tilled soil. Often reseeds. Full sun to partial shade. Attractive to butterflies. Blooms from May through November. Originally from Mexico. Widely available from nurseries, garden centers, and seed catalogs. Other species: *Zinnia haageana* (Mexico; orange or red and yellow) and *Z. linearis* (Mexico; orange) are also available.

## Phlox (*Phlox drummondii*)
## Phlox Family (Polemoniaceae)

Annual herb less than 1 foot tall. Use many plants together in beds. Pink, red, purple, white or variegated flowers. Propagated from seeds sown on tilled soil. Will reseed in dry, sandy areas. Full sun. Attractive to butterflies. Blooms from April through June. Originally from Texas, but now naturalized in disturbed areas such as roadsides and weedy fields in north and central Florida. Widely available. Other species: *Phlox floridana* (native; blue), *P. nivalis* (native; blue; trailing), *P. subulata* (eastern U.S.; pink, purple, white; matlike),

396. Phlox (*Phlox drummondii*).

397. Moss Verbena (*Glandularia pulchella*).

## Shrubs and Vines

Lantana (*Lantana camara*)
Vervain Family (Verbenaceae)

Perennial, erect or trailing, semi-woody shrub. One plant may cover up to 16 square feet. May be pruned into hedges or compact forms. Orange and yellow, yellow, pink and yellow, or white flowers. A form with yellow and green leaves is available. Propagated from seeds and cuttings. Moist to dry soil. Full sun to partial shade. Very attractive to butterflies. Blooms all year in south Florida. Top-killed by freezing temperatures. Originally from tropical America. Widely available. Other species: *Lantana involucrata* (native; white; shrub), *L. depressa* (native; an endangered species; yellow; trailing), and *L. montevidensis* (South America; purple; trailing) are also available from nurseries.

Blue or Nettleleaf Porterweed (*Stachytarpheta urticifolia*)
Vervain Family (Verbenaceae)

Perennial, erect, semi-woody shrub. One plant may cover 3 square feet. Dark blue flowers. Propagated from cuttings and seeds. Moist to dry soil. Full sun to partial shade. Very attractive to butterflies. Blooms all year in south Florida. Top-killed by freezing temperatures. Native to Asia. Available from nurseries and other gardeners. Other species: The exotic Nettleleaf Porterweed is often sold under the name Blue Porterweed. Our native Blue Porterweed, *S. jamaicensis,* is a low-growing or trailing species with pale blue flowers. It is seldom available for sale. The pink-flowered *S. mutabilis* is widely sold and is hardier than Nettleleaf Porterweed.

398. Lantana (*Lantana camara*).

400. Golden Dew Drop (*Duranta repens*).

399. Blue or Nettleleaf Porterweed (*Stachytarpheta urticifolia*).

December. Cold-tolerant. Does not survive well in central or south Florida. Widely available in north Florida. Some favorite cultivars are "Black Knight," "Burgundy," "Lavender Ice Cream," "Pink Delight," and "White Profusion." Other species: *Buddleja "weyeriana"* (yellow), *B. asiatica* (Asia; white), *B. globosa* (South America; orange), *B. japonica* (Japan; purple), *B. lindleyana* (China; purple), *B. macrostachya*, and *B. madagascariensis* (Madagascar; orange) are also sometimes grown.

### Golden Dew Drop (*Duranta repens*)
### Vervain Family (Verbenaceae)

Perennial shrub or small tree to 20 feet tall. One plant may cover up to 20 square feet or more. Blue or white flowers. Propagated from cuttings or seeds. Moist to dry soil. Full sun or partial shade. Very attractive to butterflies. Blooms nearly all year in south Florida. Top-killed by freezing temperatures. Probably not a native species, though frequently listed as such. Widely available.

### Butterfly Bush (*Buddleja davidii*)
### Logania Family (Loganiaceae)

Perennial shrub or small tree to 12 feet tall. One plant may cover 5 to 10 square feet. Blue, pink, purple, or white flowers. A few cultivars with green and white leaves are available. Propagated from cuttings. Moist to dry soil. Easy to grow in full sun or partial shade. Very attractive to butterflies. Blooms from April through

401. Butterfly Bush (*Buddleja davidii*).

402. Firebush (*Hamelia patens*).

### Firebush (*Hamelia patens*)
### Madder Family (Rubiaceae)

Perennial shrub or small tree up to 20 feet tall. One plant may cover from 15 to 20 square feet. Orange or red flowers. Propagated from cuttings and seeds. Moist soil. Partial shade to full sun. Attractive to butterflies and hummingbirds. Blooms all year in south Florida. Top-killed by freezing temperatures. Not recommended for northern Florida. Widely available. The leaves are eaten by the Pluto Sphinx (*Xylophanes pluto*).

### Hog Plum (*Prunus umbellata*)
### Rose Family (Rosaceae)

Perennial, small tree to 20 feet tall. One plant may cover 15 square feet or more. White flowers. Propagated from seeds. Moist to dry soil. Full sun to partial shade. Attractive to butterflies and other insects. Blooms from February through April. A common flowering tree of north and central Florida. Sometimes available at native plant nurseries. Other species: *Prunus angustifolia* or Chickasaw Plum is much less common in the wild, and is often confused with *P. umbellata*. Chickasaw Plum forms small thickets from root suckers and has a sweet fruit that is delightful to eat fresh or as preserves. *Prunus umbellata* usually has one or a few trunks and a very bitter fruit. *Prunus geniculata* is a low-growing endangered plant found only in central Florida scrubs. It is sometimes offered for sale by native plant nurseries.

403. Hog Plum (*Prunus umbellata*).

404. Mexican Sunflower (*Tithonia diversifolia*).

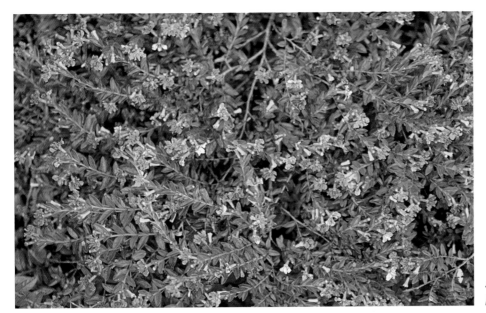

405. False Heather (*Cuphea hyssopifolia*).

**Mexican Sunflower (*Tithonia diversifolia*)**
**Aster Family (Asteraceae)**

Annual, erect herb to 12 feet tall. One plant may cover 4 to 6 square feet. Orange and yellow flowers. Propagated from seeds. Moist to dry soil. Full sun to partial shade. Very attractive to butterflies. Blooms from May through November. Originally from Mexico and Central America. Available from other gardeners, nurseries, and seed catalogs.

**False Heather (*Cuphea hyssopifolia*)**
**Loosestrife Family (Lythraceae)**

Perennial, erect semi-woody shrub to 1 foot tall. Use many plants together in beds or in rows for borders. May be pruned into hedges. Purple or white flowers. Propagated from cuttings. Moist soil. Full to partial sun. Somewhat attractive to butterflies and other insects. Blooms all year in south Florida. Originally from Mexico and Central America. Widely available.

**Flame Vine (*Senecio confusis*)**
**Aster Family (Asteraceae)**

Perennial vine to 15 feet or longer. Use a trellis or fence for support. Orange or orange-red flowers. Propagated from cuttings. Moist soil. Full sun. Attractive to butterflies. Blooms all year in south Florida. Top-killed by freezing temperatures. Not recommended for northern Florida. Originally from Mexico. Limited availability.

406. Flame Vine (*Senecio confusis*).

## Special Gardens

### Shady Sites

Few plants are able to grow under dense shade conditions. However, many understory plants in hammocks flourish with partial shade, and can be used to attract butterflies. The following list gives some shade tolerant nectar and host plants for Florida gardens.

**Nectar:**
Devil's Walkingstick (*Aralia spinosa*)
Sparkleberry (*Vaccinium arboreum*)
Firebush (*Hamelia patens*)
Wild Coffee (*Psychotria nervosa*)
*Impatiens* species

**Host Plants:**
Eastern Gamagrass (*Tripsacum dactyloides*)
Small-Fruited Pawpaw (*Asimina parviflora*)
Lance-Leaved Beggarweed (*Desmodium paniculatum*)
Snake Root (*Aristolochia serpentaria*)
Pellitory (*Parietaria floridana*)
Spikegrass (*Chasmanthium* species)
Redbay (*Persea borbonia*)
Yellow Passion-Flower (*Passiflora lutea*)

### Wet Sites (Water Gardens)

Plant roots need oxygen to live. However, under saturated conditions, microbes quickly consume most of the free oxygen in the soil. Wetland plants have special adaptations for living in these low-oxygen environments. Wetland plants are used both by adult and larval butterflies. The following species may be planted to attract butterflies to backyard pools, retention ponds, or to enhance natural wetlands on your property. It's also possible to grow many of these plants on upland sites, provided the bed is kept moist with a thick layer of mulch or frequent watering.

**Nectar:**
Buttonbush (*Cephalanthus occidentalis*)
Pickerelweed (*Pontederia cordata*)
Carolina Aster (*Aster carolinianus*)
Redroot (*Lachnanthes caroliniana*)

**Host Plants:**
Alligator Flag (*Thalia geniculata*)
Swampbay (*Persea palustris*)
Bastard Indigo (*Amorpha fruticosa*)
Sweet Bay (*Magnolia virginiana*)
Golden Canna (*Canna flaccida*)
Water Dropwort (*Oxypolis filiformis*)
Orange Sesbania (*Sesbania punicea*)
Water Hyssop (*Bacopa monnieri*)
Pink Swamp Milkweed (*Asclepias incarnata*)
White Swamp Milkweed (*Asclepias perennis*)
Sugarcane Plumegrass (*Erianthus giganteus*)

### Dry Sites (Scrub Gardens)

Much of Florida is covered by sandy soils. The soils are often poorly drained in flatlands and excessively drained on hills and ridges. Dry sites that normally support scrub and sandhill vegetation are also very infertile. Only plants adapted to these conditions will thrive. Luckily, there are many native nectar and host plants that grow on excessively drained soils. Some of these are among the most beautiful of Florida's wildflowers. If your yard includes very dry sandy areas, take advantage of this opportunity to create a sand garden. Plants can be purchased for the scrub garden from native plant nurseries. Do not attempt to transplant scrub species from the wild since they probably will not survive. You can add to your scrub garden by collecting and planting seeds.

**Nectar:**
Chickasaw Plum (*Prunus angustifolia*)
Saw Palmetto (*Serenoa repens*)
Garberia (*Garberia heterophylla*)
Scrub Palmetto (*Sabal etonia*)
Gopher Apple (*Licania michauxii*)
Shiny Blueberry (*Vaccinium myrsinites*)
Lantana (*Lantana camara*)
Summer Farewell (*Dalea pinnata*)
Paint Brush (*Carphephorus corymbosus*)
Velvet Leaf Milkweed (*Asclepias tomentosa*)
Sandhill Milkweed (*Asclepias humistrata*)
Yellow Buttons (*Balduina angustifolia*)

**Host Plants:**
Butterfly Weed (*Asclepias tuberosa*)
Pawpaws (*Asmina* species)
Butterfly Pea (*Clitoria mariana*)
Scrub oaks (*Quercus* species)
Climbing Butterfly Pea (*Centrosema virginianum*)
Silkbay (*Persea humilis*)
Hercules' Club (*Zanthoxylum clava-herculis*)
Velvet-Leaved Tick-Trefoil (*Desmodium viridiflorum*)
Partridge Pea (*Cassia fasciculata*)
Yuccas (*Yucca* species)
Passion-Flower (*Passiflora incarnata*)

### Tropical Gardens

Alas, even though most Floridians like to think that they are living in a tropical land, they are not. Think of the town of Frostproof in south-central Florida. It's not! In fact, very little of Florida is completely safe from winter freezes. Generally, our most cold-sensitive or tropical vegetation grows in a narrow band along the coast from Merritt Island on the Atlantic side to Tampa Bay on the Gulf. Much of Miami-Dade County, Collier County, and the Keys rarely experience freezing temperatures during the winter. Some spectacular butterfly nectar and host plants thrive in tropical gardens. Many of these can also be grown in central and north Florida with winter protection.

**Nectar:**
Bloodberry (*Cordia globosa*)
Golden Dewdrop (*Duranta repens*)
Bougainvillea (*Bougainvillea glabra*)
Lantana (*Lantana Camara*)
Clerodendrum (*Clerodendrum speciosissium*)
Papaya (*Carica papaya*)
Coco Plum (*Chrysobalanus icaco*)
Pentas (*Pentas lanceolata*)
Firebush (*Hamelia patens*)
Strongback (*Bourreria ovata*)
Firespike (*Odontonema stricta*)
Tropical Sage (*Salvia coccinea*)
Flame Vine (*Senecio confusis*)
Wild Coffee (*Psychotria nervosa*)

**Host Plants:**
Balloon Vine (*Cardiospermum halicacabum*)
Large-Flowered Dutchman's Pipe (*Aristolochia gigantea*)
Blackbead (*Pithecellobium keyense*)
Lead Plant (*Leucaena leucocephala*)
Broomweed (*Sida acuta*)
Leadwort (*Plumbago auriculata*)
Candle Plant (*Cassia alata*)
Mango (*Mangifera indica*)
Coconut Palm (*Cocos nucifera*)
Carpetweed (*Phyla nodiflora*)
Coontie (*Zamia pumila*)
Pelican Flower (*Aristolochia ringens*)

Corky-Stemmed Passion-Flower (*Passiflora suberosa*)
Scarlet Milkweed (*Asclepias curassavica*)
Golden Shower (*Cassia fistula*)
Sugarcane (*Saccharum officinarum*)
Green Shrimp Plant (*Blechum brownei*)
Tropical Pencilflower (*Stylosanthes hamata*)
Jamaica Dogwood (*Piscidia piscipula*)
Wild Lime (*Zanthoxylum fagara*)

## Vegetable and Herb Gardens

Some garden herbs and vegetables are relished by butterfly caterpillars. The Black Swallowtail, Cabbage White, and Long-Tailed Skipper are considered to be serious pests of crops. Farmers scorn the Parsleyworm, Cabbageworm, and Bean Leaf Roller. Butterfly gardeners find it possible to plant their plots of vegetables to attract the butterflies as well as furnish food for the table. There's usually plenty to go around. Here are some ideas for the kitchen garden.

**Nectar:**
Borage (*Borago officinalis*)
Thyme (*Thymus vulgaris*)

**Host Plants:**
Anise (*Pimpinella anisum*)
Nasturtium (*Tropaeolum majus*)
Cabbage (*Brassica oleracea*)
Parsley (*Petroselinum crispum*)
Carrot (*Daucus carota* var. *sativa*)
Rue (*Ruta graveolens*)
Corn (*Zea mays*)
Sugarcane (*Saccharum officinarum*)
Dill (*Anethum graveolens*)
Sweet Bay (*Laurus nobilis*)
Fennel (*Foeniculum vulgare*)
Turnip (*Brassica rapa*)
Green Bean (*Phaseolus vulgaris*)

# Recommended Host Plant Cultivation Guide

## Acanthaceae (Acanthus Family)

Brushfooted Butterfly Host Plants

### *Blechum brownei* (Green Shrimp Plant)

Malachite Butterfly host plant. Cultivated plant from tropical America, now naturalized in disturbed sites; herb less than 1.5 feet tall; perennial, evergreen; opposite leaves, white flowers with large green bracts; blooms from spring through fall; moist soil; partial shade; cold-sensitive; locally abundant in south Florida; limited availability from retailers; propagated from root divisions; matures quickly; spreads quickly by underground runners; easy to grow. This vigorous grower is best grown in containers so as not to become a weedy pest.

### *Dyschoriste oblongifolia* (Oblongleaf Twinflower)

Common Buckeye host plant. Native wildflower found in sandhills and dry flatwoods; herb less than 1 foot tall; perennial, deciduous; opposite leaves, small blue flowers; blooms from spring through fall; moist to dry, sandy soil; partial shade to full sun; cold-tolerant; locally abundant in north, central, and south Florida; available from some native plant nurseries; propagated from root divisions; matures quickly; easy to grow. Swamp Twinflower (*Dyschoriste humistrata*) is similar, but has smaller flowers and prefers moist to wet soil.

### *Ruellia caroliniensis* (Wild Petunia)

Malachite and Common Buckeye host plant. Native wildflower found in hammocks; herb to 1.5 feet tall; perennial, deciduous in north Florida; opposite leaves, large blue flowers; blooms from spring through fall; moist to dry soil; partial shade to full sun; cold-toler-ant; abundant in north, central, and south Florida; available from native plant nurseries; propagated from seeds and root divisions; matures quickly; spreads quickly; easy to grow.

## Agavaceae (Agave Family)

Yucca Giant Skipper Host Plants

### *Yucca aloifolia* (Spanish Dagger)

Cultivated plant from tropical America, naturalized in coastal areas; herb to 6 feet tall; perennial, evergreen; leaves long, narrow, stiff, and armed with a sharp spine at the tip, clusters of large white flowers; blooms during spring; moist to dry sandy soil; full sun to partial shade; cold-tolerant; grown throughout Florida; widely available from nurseries; propagated from stem cuttings; matures slowly; spreads slowly; easy to grow. Caution: The stiff leaves are tipped with sharp spines.

### *Yucca filamentosa* (Stiff-Leaved Bear Grass)

Native plant found in sandhills, scrubs, and dry pinelands; herb to 3 feet tall; perennial, evergreen; leaves long, narrow, stiff, and armed with a sharp spine at the tip; clusters of nice white flowers borne on a tall stalk; blooms during spring; dry, sandy soil; full sun to partial shade; cold-tolerant; locally abundant in north Florida; available from native plant nurseries, Wayside Gardens sells a handsome variegated form; propagated from suckers; matures slowly; easy to grow. Caution: Sap from the roots causes a poison ivy–like rash on exposed skin. Soft-Leaved Bear Grass (*Yucca smalliana* or *Yucca flaccida*) is a similar plant with wide, supple leaves that occurs in central and north Florida.

## Anacardiaceae (Cashew Family)

Red-Banded Hairstreak Host Plant

### *Mangifera indica* (**Mango**)

Cultivated tree from southern Asia more than 40 feet tall; evergreen; leaves dark green and pointed, to 15 inches long, clusters of small fragrant flowers, delicious fruit; blooms during spring; moist soil; full sun to partial shade; cold-sensitive; grown in south Florida; available from local nurseries; propagated from seeds and grafts; matures relatively quickly; easy to grow. Caution: The sap of this tree may cause a skin rash.

## Annonaceae (Custard Apple Family)

Zebra Swallowtail Host Plants

### *Asimina incarna* (**Flag Pawpaw**)

Native shrub found in sandhills and dry pinelands to 5 feet tall; deciduous; large white flowers appear before the leaves; leaves fuzzy when young and strongly scented when crushed; blooms during spring; dry, sandy soil; full sun; cold-tolerant; abundant in north and central Florida; limited availability; propagated by seeds; matures slowly; somewhat difficult to grow.

### *Asimina obovata* (**Scrub Pawpaw**)

Native shrub found in dry pinelands, sandhills, and scrubs to 12 feet tall; deciduous; large, white flowers appear with the leaves, strongly scented foliage; dry sandy soil; full sun; cold-tolerant; local in central Florida; limited availability; propagated by seeds; matures slowly; somewhat difficult to grow.

### *Asimina parviflora* (**Small-Fruited Pawpaw**)

Native shrub found in dry hammocks to 5 feet tall; deciduous; small maroon flowers, strongly scented foliage; blooms during spring; moist to dry soil; partial shade; cold-tolerant; locally abundant in north and central Florida; available from some native plant nurseries; propagated by seeds; matures slowly; one of the easiest pawpaws to grow.

### *Asimina reticulata* (**Flatwoods Pawpaw**)

Native shrub of dry pinelands and scrubs to 5 feet tall; deciduous; flowers white with a maroon center; leaves bluish-green, strongly scented; blooms during spring; dry sandy soil; full sun; cold-sensitive; locally abundant in south and central Florida; limited availability;

propagated by seeds; matures slowly; somewhat difficult to grow.

### *Asimina triboba* (**Dog Banana or Ornamental Pawpaw**)

Native tree found in hammocks to 20 feet tall; deciduous; flowers maroon, strongly scented foliage, fruit edible; blooms during spring; moist soil; partial shade; cold-tolerant; uncommon in the Florida panhandle; available from some mail-order nurseries; propagated by seeds; matures slowly; somewhat difficult to grow.

## Apiaceae (Carrot Family)

Black Swallowtail Host Plants

### *Anethum graveolens* (**Dill**)

Cultivated plant from southern Europe; herb to 4 feet tall; biennial, evergreen; finely divided, compound leaves, aromatic, flat heads of small yellow flowers; blooms during summer and fall; moist soil; full sun; cold-tolerant; can be grown throughout Florida; widely available; propagated from seeds; matures in two years; easy to grow.

### *Daucus carota* var. *sativa* (**Carrot**)

Cultivated plant from Europe to 1.5 feet tall; biennial, evergreen; finely divided, leaves, aromatic, flat heads of small white flowers; blooms during late summer and fall; moist soil; full sun; cold-tolerant; can be grown throughout Florida; widely available; propagated from seeds; matures in two years; easy to grow.

### *Foeniculum vulgare* (**Fennel**)

Cultivated herb from southern Europe and western Asia to 5 feet tall; biennial to weakly perennial, evergreen; finely divided leaves, aromatic, flat heads of small yellow flowers; blooms during late summer and fall; moist soil; full sun; cold-tolerant; can be grown throughout Florida; widely available; propagated from seeds; matures in two years; easy to grow; green and bronze foliage varieties available.

### *Oxypolis filiformis* (**Water Dropwort**)

Native wildflower found in ditches and marshes to 4 feet tall; perennial, deciduous; leaves round, hollow, slightly jointed near tip, aromatic, flat heads of small white flowers; blooms during fall; moist to wet soil; full sun; cold-tolerant; locally common throughout Florida; limited availability; propagated from seeds; matures somewhat slowly; easy to grow.

### *Petroselinum crispum* (Parsley)

Cultivated herb from Europe to 1.5 feet tall; biennial to weakly perennial, evergreen; somewhat broad, divided leaves, aromatic, flat heads of small white flowers; blooms during late summer and fall; moist soil; full sun; cold-tolerant; can be grown throughout Florida; widely available; propagated from seeds; matures in two years; easy to grow. Both curly leaf and Italian (flat leaf) varieties are available, but the butterflies seem to prefer the former.

### *Pimpinella anisum* (Anise)

Cultivated herb from the Mediterranean region to 5 feet tall; biennial, evergreen; finely divided leaves, aromatic, flat heads of small white flowers; blooms during late summer and fall; moist soil; full sun; cold-tolerant; can be grown throughout Florida; widely available; propagated from seeds; matures in two years; easy to grow.

## Arecaceae (Palm Family)
Monk Skipper Host Plants

### *Chrysalidocarpus lutescens* (Areca Palm)

Cultivated tree from Madagascar to 40 feet tall; evergreen; slender stems in clumps; pinnately compound leaves, short stalks of small white flowers; blooms during summer; moist soil; full sun; cold-sensitive; commonly grown in south Florida; available from local nurseries; propagated from seeds; matures slowly; easy to grow.

### *Coccothrinax argentata* (Silver Palm)

Native tree found in tropical pinelands and hammocks to 20 feet tall; evergreen; fan-shaped leaves with silvery undersides, long stalks of small white flowers; blooms during summer; moist to dry soil; full sun; cold-sensitive; south Florida, abundant in the lower Keys, also found in parts of Miami-Dade and Broward Counties; available from native plant nurseries; propagated from seeds; matures very slowly; somewhat difficult to grow.

### *Cocos nucifera* (Coconut Palm)

Cultivated tree from tropical Asia from 50 to 100 feet tall; evergreen; pinnately compound leaves, short stalks of small white flowers, huge edible fruit; blooms during summer; moist soil; full sun; cold-sensitive; commonly grown in south Florida; available from local nurseries; propagated from seeds; matures slowly; easy to grow;

lethal yellowing disease has killed many individuals, but resistant varieties are available.

### *Serenoa repens* (Saw Palmetto)

Native shrub or small tree found in flatwoods, scrubs, and sometimes hammocks to 15 feet tall; evergreen; leaves fan-shaped with small teeth along the petiole, long stalks of small white and fragrant flowers, trunk usually prostrate on ground; blooms during early summer; moist to dry sandy soil; partial shade to full sun; cold-tolerant; common throughout peninsular Florida, local in the Panhandle; available from native plant nurseries; matures slowly; easy to propagate from seeds, somewhat difficult to transplant; both green and silvery leaved forms available. Extracts of the fruits of this palm are now being used to treat prostate cancer.

### *Thrinax radiata* (Thatch Palm)

Native tree found in tropical hammocks and pinelands to 25 feet tall; evergreen; leaves fan-shaped, long stalks of small white flowers followed by small white fruit; blooms during summer; moist soil; partial shade to full sun; cold-sensitive; common in the lower Keys and parts of Miami-Dade County; available from native plant nurseries; propagated from seeds; matures very slowly; fairly easy to grow.

### *Veitchia merrillii* (Christmas Palm)

Cultivated tree from the Philippines to 15 feet tall; red fruit; evergreen; pinnately compound leaves, short stalks with small white flowers followed by nice red fruit; blooms during summer; moist soil; partial shade to full sun; cold-sensitive; commonly grown in south Florida; available from local nurseries; propagated from seeds; matures slowly; easy to grow.

## Aristolochiaceae (Dutchman's Pipe or Birthwort Family)
Pipevine Swallowtail and Tailless Swallowtail Host Plants

### *Aristolochia durior* (Large-Leaved Pipevine)

Cultivated vine from the southeastern U.S.; perennial, deciduous; leaves entire, hairy, strongly scented when crushed, small flowers; blooms during late summer and fall; moist soil; partial shade to full sun; cold-tolerant; can be grown in north and central Florida; limited availability; propagated from seeds, root divisions, and cuttings (with difficulty); matures quickly; spreads by underground runners, easy to grow.

### *Aristolochia elegans* (Calico Flower)

Cultivated vine from tropical America; perennial, deciduous in northern Florida; leaves entire, smooth, strongly scented when crushed, large handsome flowers; blooms during summer and fall; moist to dry soil; partial shade to full sun; cold-tolerant; can be grown throughout Florida; available at some nurseries; propagated from seeds, root divisions, and cuttings (with difficulty); matures quickly; spreads by underground runners, easy to grow. This is the most frequently grown Dutchman's Pipe in Florida.

### *Aristolochia gigantea* (Giant Pipevine)

Cultivated vine from tropical America; perennial, evergreen; entire leaves, strongly scented when crushed, very large flowers; blooms during summer and fall; moist soil; partial shade to full sun; cold-sensitive; can be grown in south and central Florida; limited availability; propagated from seeds, root divisions, and cuttings (with difficulty); matures quickly; easy to grow.

### *Aristolochia ringens* (Pelican Flower)

Cultivated vine from tropical America; perennial, evergreen; entire leaves and strongly scented when crushed, large pelican-shaped flowers; blooms during summer and fall; moist soil; partial shade to full sun; cold-sensitive; can be grown in south and central Florida; limited availability; propagated from seeds, root divisions, and cuttings (with difficulty); matures quickly; easy to grow.

### *Aristolochia serpentaria* (Snake Root)

Native herb to 1 foot tall; perennial, deciduous; lance-shaped leaves, tiny flowers produced at ground level; blooms during summer; moist to dry soil; partial shade to full sun; cold-tolerant; central and north Florida; widespread but local and inconspicuous; limited availability; propagated from seeds and root divisions; matures quickly; easy to grow.

## Asclepiadaceae (Milkweed Family)

### Queen, Monarch, and Soldier Host Plants

### *Asclepias curassavica* (Scarlet Milkweed)

Garden plant and a naturalized weed in pastures and disturbed areas of south and central Florida; from tropical America; herb to 4.5 feet tall; perennial and evergreen; clusters of orange flowers with red or yellow petals, a handsome all yellow variety is sometimes grown, milky sap; blooms from spring through fall; dry, moist, or wet soil; full sun to partial shade; cold-sensitive; can be grown in north Florida with protection; available from nurseries and other gardeners; propagated from seeds and cuttings; matures in a few months from cuttings; easy to grow. This milkweed is frequently attacked by a bright yellow insect, the Oleander Aphid (*Aphis nerii*). Honeydew produced by the aphids often coats the milkweed leaves. The honeydew is in turn colonized by a sooty fungus. The fungus does not hurt the plant, but milkweed butterfly caterpillars usually do not eat leaves coated by honeydew or the fungus. The aphids can be controlled by releasing ladybugs, or spraying with a mild detergent. If one waits and watches, predators and parasites often eventually arrive and decimate the aphid colony.

### *Asclepias incarnata* (Pink Swamp Milkweed)

Native wildflower found in marshes and at the edges of swamps; herb to 4.5 feet tall; perennial but deciduous; clusters of pink flowers, a white-flowered variety is also sold, milky sap; blooms from summer to fall; wet to moist soil; full sun to partial shade; cold-tolerant; uncommon throughout Florida; available from some mail-order nurseries; propagated by seeds and cuttings; matures quickly; easy to grow.

### *Asclepias perennis* (White Swamp Milkweed)

Native wildflower of swamps; herb to 1.5 feet tall; perennial, evergreen; clusters of white flowers with a pink tinge, milky sap; blooms from early summer to fall; moist to wet soil; full sun to partial shade; cold-tolerant; locally common in north and central Florida; limited availability; propagated by seeds and cuttings; matures quickly from cuttings; easy to grow.

### *Asclepias tuberosa* subsp. *rolfsii* (Southern Butterfly Weed)

Native wildflower of sandhills and dry pinelands; herb to 2 feet tall; perennial but deciduous; clusters of orange flowers, milky sap; blooms from early summer until fall; dry to moist sandy soil; full sun to partial shade; cold-tolerant; locally abundant throughout Florida except the Keys; available from nurseries; propagated from seeds and root divisions; matures somewhat quickly; easy to grow. Most often used as a nectar rather than a host plant.

### *Sarcostemma clausum* (White Vine)

Native vine of marshes, wet prairies, and disturbed sites; perennial, evergreen; clusters of white flowers, milky sap; blooms all year in south Florida; moist to wet soil; full sun; cold-sensitive; locally common in central and south Florida; limited availability; propagated from seeds and cuttings; matures quickly; grows rampantly on good sites.

## Asteraceae (Aster Family)
American Painted Lady Host Plants

### Gnaphalium obtusifolium (Sweet Everlasting)
Native wildflower of dry, open pinelands and fields; herb to 1.5 feet tall; annual; handsome dark green leaves, stems and undersides of leaves white, nice aromatic scent to dry leaves and flower heads; blooms during late summer and fall; moist to dry soil; full sun to partial shade; locally common throughout Florida; limited availability; propagated from seeds; matures quickly; easy to grow; an attractive bedding plant.

## Brassicaceae (Mustard Family)
Great Southern White and Cabbage White Host Plants

### Brassica campestris (Wild Mustard)
Exotic weed from Europe found in disturbed sites; herb to 2 feet tall; annual; small yellow flowers; blooms during spring and early summer; moist to dry soil; full sun; locally common in north and central Florida; often used in wild birdseed and volunteers around bird feeders or birdseed may be deliberately planted in a small patch; matures quickly; easy to grow.

### Brassica oleracea (Cabbage)
Cultivated vegetable plant from Europe; herb to 1.5 feet tall; annual; moist soil; full sun; numerous varieties are available from nurseries and seed suppliers; easy to grow with proper water and fertilizer applications.

## Cannaceae (Canna Family)
Canna Skipper Host Plants

### Canna Hybrids
Cultivated ornamentals from tropical America; herbs to 8 feet tall; perennial, deciduous; red, yellow, orange, pink, or salmon colored flowers, leaves green, red, or variegated; blooms all year in south Florida; moist soil; full sun to partial shade; cold-tolerant; widely available;

matures quickly; easy to grow. *Canna flaccida* is a native species with yellow flowers.

## Fabaceae (Bean Family)
Sulphur, Hairstreak, Blue, and Broadwinged Skipper Host Plants

### Aeschynomene americana (Joint Vetch or Shy-Leaf)
Barred Sulphur host plant. Native plant of disturbed sites; herb to 5 feet tall; annual, compound leaves 3–4 inches long with numerous small leaflets, small yellow flowers; blooms during late summer and fall; wet to dry soil; full sun; occurs throughout Florida; limited availability; propagated from seeds; matures quickly; has a tendency to spread; easy to grow.

### Amorpha fruticosa (Bastard Indigo)
Silver Spotted Skipper host plant. Native shrub found at the edges of swamps to 12 feet tall; deciduous; compound leaves to 18 inches long with numerous leaflets, short spikes of tiny purple flowers; blooms during summer; moist to dry soil; full sun to partial shade; cold-tolerant; occurs throughout Florida, except the Keys; limited availability; propagated from seeds; matures quickly; easy to grow.

### Amphicarpa bracteata (Hog Peanut)
Silver Spotted and Long-Tailed skipper host plant. Native vine of hammocks; perennial, deciduous; compound leaves of 3 leaflets, clusters of small white flowers; blooms during summer; moist soil; partial shade; cold-tolerant; locally common in north and central Florida; limited availability; propagated from seeds; matures quickly; easy to grow.

### Apios americana (Ground Nut)
Silver Spotted Skipper host plant. Native vine found at the edges of swamps; perennial, deciduous; compound leaves of 5–7 leaflets; small clusters of purplish flowers; blooms during summer; moist to wet soil; partial shade; cold-tolerant; locally common in north and central Florida; limited availability; propagated from seeds; matures quickly; easy to grow.

### Cassia alata (Candle Plant)
Orange-Barred Sulphur host plant. Cultivated shrub or small tree to 25 feet tall; evergreen; compound leaves to 3 feet long, with 20–22 leaflets, erect spikes of waxy, golden flowers; blooms all year in south Florida or late

summer/fall in north Florida; moist soil; full sun; cold-sensitive; available from nurseries; propagated from seeds; matures quickly; easy to grow.

### *Cassia bicapsularis* (Christmas Senna)

Sleepy Orange, Cloudless Sulphur, and Orange-Barred Sulphur host plant. Cultivated shrub from tropical America to 15 feet tall; evergreen; compound leaves to 5 inches long with 6–10 oval or somewhat pointed leaflets, clusters of yellow flowers; blooms during summer and fall; moist soil; more cold-tolerant than other shrubby Cassias, but top-killed by freezes in north Florida; can be grown throughout Florida; widely available; propagated from seeds; matures quickly; easy to grow.

### *Cassia chapmanii* (Bahama Senna)

Sleepy Orange, Cloudless Sulphur, and Orange-Barred Sulphur host plant. Native shrub found in tropical pinelands to 8 feet tall; evergreen; compound leaves to 6 inches long with 8–10 oval leaflets, clusters of yellow flowers; blooms during summer and fall; moist soil; full sun; cold-sensitive; can be grown in central and south Florida; available from native plant nurseries; propagated from seeds; matures quickly; easy to grow.

### *Cassia fasciculata* (Partridge Pea)

Little Sulphur, Cloudless Sulphur, Ceraunus Blue, and Gray Hairstreak host plant. Native wildflower of dry pinelands and the margins of hammocks; herb to 4 feet tall; annual; compound leaves to 3 inches long with numerous leaflets, nice yellow flowers; blooms in late summer; dry, sandy soil; full sun; abundant throughout Florida; limited availability; propagated from seeds; matures quickly; easy to grow. *Cassia nictitans* is similar, but has very small flowers, and grows on wetter sites.

### *Cassia fistula* (Golden Shower)

Orange-Barred Sulphur host plant. Cultivated tree from India to 40 feet tall; deciduous; compound leaves to 1 foot long with 8–16 leaflets, drooping clusters of yellow flowers produced before the new leaves appear in summer; moist soil; full sun; cold-sensitive; grown in south Florida; available from nurseries; propagated from seeds; matures quickly; easy to grow.

### *Cassia obtusifolia* (Sicklepod)

Sleepy Orange and Cloudless Sulphur host plant. Exotic weed from tropical America found in disturbed sites; herb to 5 feet tall; annual; compound leaves to 6 inches long with 6 oval leaflets; yellow flowers produced at the bases of the leaves; blooms in summer; dry to moist soil; full sun; common throughout Florida; limited availability; propagated from seeds; matures quickly; easy to grow. The native *Cassia occidentalis* (Coffee Senna) is similar, but its compound leaves have 10–12 pointed leaflets.

### *Cassia surattensis* (Glaucous Cassia)

Cloudless and Orange-Barred sulphur host plant. Cultivated tree from tropical America to 25 feet tall; evergreen; compound leaves dark green above, bluish-green below, with 8–12 leaflets, clusters of yellow flowers; blooms during late summer and fall; moist soil; full sun; cold-sensitive; grown in south Florida; available from nurseries; propagated from seeds; matures quickly; easy to grow.

### *Centrosema virginianum* (Climbing Butterfly Pea)

Long-Tailed Skipper host plant. Native vine found in dry pinelands and the margins of hammocks; perennial, deciduous; compound leaves with 3 leaflets, large purple flowers; blooms during summer; dry soil; full sun; cold-tolerant; common throughout Florida; limited availability; propagated from seeds; matures quickly; easy to grow.

### *Clitoria mariana* (Butterfly Pea)

Long-Tailed Skipper host plant. Native wildflower of dry pinelands; perennial, deciduous; compound leaves with 3 leaflets, dark green above, pale green below, stems trailing or weakly climbing, large purple flowers; blooms during summer; dry soil; full sun; cold-tolerant; uncommon throughout Florida; limited availability; propagated from seeds, matures quickly; easy to grow. The Asian vine *Clitoria ternatea* is similar. A handsome double-flowered variety is sometimes cultivated in Florida.

### *Desmodium tortuosum* (Florida Beggarweed)

Silver-Spotted Skipper, Dorantes Skipper, and Long-Tailed Skipper host plant. Native plant of roadsides and disturbed sites to 6 feet tall; annual; compound leaves with 3 leaflets, often with small red patches on the leaves, small pinkish flowers; blooms during summer and fall; moist to dry soil; full sun; common in central and northern Florida; limited availability; propagated from seeds; matures quickly; spreads easily; easy to grow. The seeds of beggarweeds stick easily to clothing.

### *Desmodium viridiflorum* (Velvet-Leaved Tick-Trefoil)

Gray Hairstreak and Long-Tailed Skipper host plant. Native plant of sandhills to 2 feet tall; perennial, deciduous; compound leaves with 3 rough textured leaflets, small pinkish flowers; blooms during summer and fall; dry sandy soil; full sun to partial shade; cold-tolerant; locally common in central and northern Florida; limited availability; propagated from seeds; matures somewhat slowly; easy to grow.

### *Galactia elliottii* (White Milk Pea)

Zarucco Dusky Wing host plant. Native vine/ground cover of dry pinelands; perennial, deciduous; compound leaves with 5–9 shiny, dark green leaflets, white flowers; blooms during summer; dry to moist sandy soil; full sun to partial shade; cold-tolerant; locally abundant throughout Florida; limited availability; propagated from seeds; matures quickly; easy to grow.

### *Galactia regularis* (Prostrate Milk Pea)

Ceraunus Blue, Gray Hairstreak, and Zarucco Dusky Wing host plant. Native vine and ground cover found in dry pinelands; perennial, deciduous; compound leaves with 3 leaflets, pink flowers produced on very short stalks; blooms during summer; dry to moist sandy soil; full sun to partial shade; cold-tolerant; locally abundant throughout Florida; limited availability; propagated from seeds; matures quickly; easy to grow. Twining Milk Pea (*Galactia volubilis*) is similar, but the flowers are borne on long stalks, and the stems twine vigorously. *Galactia striata* is a more robust, tropical species found along the beaches of south Florida and the Keys.

### *Leucaena leucocephala* (Lead Tree)

Tiny Hairstreak host plant. Cultivated and naturalized weedy shrub from tropical America to 20 feet tall found along roadsides; evergreen; twice-compound leaves with numerous leaflets, white flowers in round heads followed by dangling clusters of brown seed pods 6–8 inches long; blooms all year in south Florida; dry to moist soil; full sun; cold-sensitive; locally abundant in the Keys and south Florida; limited availability; propagated from seeds; matures quickly; easy to grow.

### *Lysiloma latisiliqua* (Wild Tamarind)

Large Orange Sulphur and Cassius Blue host plant. Native tree to 50 feet tall found in tropical hammocks; deciduous; twice-compound leaves with numerous leaflets, white flowers in small round heads followed by brown seed pods 3–6 inches long at tips of branches; blooms during spring and summer; moist to dry soil; full sun to partial shade; cold-sensitive; abundant in tropical south Florida; available from native plant nurseries; propagated from seeds; matures quickly; easy to grow. This is a handsome shade tree for the tropical garden.

### *Phaseolus vulgaris* (Garden Bean)

Gray Hairstreak and Long-Tailed Skipper host plant. Cultivated vine or bush; annual; compound leaves with 3 leaflets; moist soil; full sun; widely available; propagated from seeds; easy to grow if regularly watered and fertilized. Scarlet Runner Bean (*Phaseolus coccineus*) is a vigorous and handsome vine with red flowers attractive to hummingbirds.

### *Piscidia piscipula* (Jamaica Dogwood)

Hammock Skipper host plant. Native tree to 30 feet tall found in tropical hammocks; deciduous; compound leaves with 5–7 oval leaflets, clusters of purple pealike flowers followed by 3–4 inch brown pods with papery wings; blooms during early summer; moist to dry soil; full sun to partial shade; cold-sensitive; common in tropical south Florida; available from nurseries; propagated from seeds; matures quickly; easy to grow. Jamaica Dogwood is a beautiful and commonly used ornamental in south Florida.

### *Pithecellobium keyense* (Blackbead)

Large Orange Sulphur and Cassius Blue host plant. Native shrub or small tree to 20 feet tall found in tropical hammocks; evergreen; leaves with 4 oblong leaflets, white flowers in small round heads, brown twisted pods with black seeds enclosed by a fleshy, red aril; blooms during late spring/early summer; moist to dry soil; full sun to partial shade; cold-sensitive; abundant in tropical south Florida; available from native plant nurseries; propagated from seeds; matures quickly; easy to grow.

### *Pongamia pinnata* (Pongam)

Hammock Skipper host plant. Cultivated tree from tropical Asia to 40 feet tall; briefly deciduous to evergreen; leaves to about 8 inches long with 5–7 leaflets;

moist soil; full sun to partial shade; cold-sensitive; commonly grown in south Florida; propagated from seeds, matures quickly; easy to grow.

### *Robinia pseudo-acacia* (Black Locust)

Silver-Spotted Skipper host plant. Cultivated tree from the eastern U.S. to 40 feet tall; deciduous; compound leaves with numerous leaflets, drooping clusters of fragrant white flowers; blooms during spring; moist to dry soil; full sun to partial shade; cold-tolerant; grown in north Florida; available from nurseries; propagated from seeds; matures quickly; easy to grow.

### *Sesbania punicea* (Orange Sesbania)

Zarucco Skipper host plant. Native shrub to 15 feet tall found in old fields and roadside ditches; deciduous; compound leaves with numerous leaflets, clusters of orange flowers; blooms from spring to fall; wet to dry soil; full sun; cold-tolerant; abundant in north Florida; limited availability; propagated from seeds; matures quickly; easy to grow. Note: The seed coat should be nicked in order to germinate the seeds.

### *Stylosanthes hamata* (Tropical Pencilflower)

Barred Sulphur host plant. Native wildflower to 1 foot tall found in weedy places; perennial, evergreen; small compound leaves with 3 leaflets, small yellow flowers; blooms all year; moist to dry soil; full sun; cold-sensitive; common in south Florida and the Keys; limited availability; propagated from seeds; matures quickly; easy to grow. Pencilflower (*Stylosanthes biflora*) of north and central Florida sandhills is similar.

### *Vigna luteola* (Cowpea)

Gray Hairstreak and Long-Tailed Skipper host plant. Native vine found along rivers and in disturbed places; perennial, deciduous; compound leaves with 3 leaflets, yellow flowers on long stalks; blooms all year in south Florida; wet to moist soil; full sun; cold-tolerant; common throughout Florida; limited availability; propagated from seeds; matures quickly; easy to grow.

### *Wisteria sinensis* (Chinese Wisteria)

Silver-Spotted Skipper host plant. Cultivated vine from China; perennial, deciduous; compound leaves up to 16 inches long with 7–13 leaflets; clusters of purple or white flowers in spring; moist to dry soil; full sun; cold-tolerant; north and central Florida; widely available; propagated from seeds and suckers; matures quickly; easy to grow. This vine is rampant grower under favorable conditions and has a tendency to become weedy.

## Fagaceae (Oak Family)

Dusky Wing Skipper and White-M Hairstreak Host Plants

### *Quercus chapmanii* (Chapman's Oak)

Native tree found in sandhills and scrubs to 20 feet tall; briefly deciduous; small leaves with rounded lobes and fuzzy undersides, inconspicuous flowers; dry sandy soil; full sun to partial shade; cold-tolerant; locally abundant in north, central, and coastal south Florida; limited availability; propagated from seeds; matures slowly; easy to grow on the proper site.

### *Quercus hemisphaerica* (Laurel Oak)

Native tree found in hammocks and shrubby, disturbed sites to 60 feet tall; deciduous; leaves similar to Live Oak, but thin and flexible, inconspicuous flowers; moist to dry soil; full sun; cold-tolerant; locally abundant throughout Florida; widely available; propagated from seeds; matures relatively quickly; easy to grow.

### *Quercus laevis* (Turkey Oak)

Native tree found in sandhills to 40 feet tall; deciduous; large leaves with pointed lobes, inconspicuous flowers; dry sandy soil; full sun; cold-tolerant; locally abundant in north and central Florida; limited availability; propagated from seeds; matures slowly; easy to grow on dry sandy sites.

### *Quercus myrtifolia* (Myrtle Oak)

Native tree found in sandhills and scrubs to 20 feet tall; evergreen; small oblong leaves without lobes, inconspicuous flowers; dry sandy soil; full sun; cold-tolerant; locally abundant in north, central, and coastal south Florida; limited availability; propagated from seeds; matures slowly; easy to grow on the proper site.

### *Quercus nigra* (Water Oak)

Native tree found in hammocks to 50 feet tall; deciduous; young leaves with pointed lobes, typical mature leaves have a wide, rounded tip, inconspicuous flowers; moist soil; full sun; cold-tolerant; abundant in north and central Florida; limited availability; propagated from seeds; matures relatively quickly; easy to grow.

### *Quercus shumardii* (Shumard Oak)

Native tree found in hammocks to 60 feet tall; deciduous; large leaves with pointed lobes, inconspicuous flowers; moist soil; full sun; cold-tolerant; locally abundant in the Panhandle; available from nurseries; propagated from seeds; matures slowly; easy to grow.

### *Quercus stellata* var. *margaretta* (Small Post Oak)

Native tree found in sandhills to 20 feet tall; deciduous; smallish leaves with a wide, three lobed tip, inconspicuous flowers; dry, sandy soil; full sun; cold-tolerant; locally abundant in north and central Florida; limited availability; propagated from seeds; matures slowly; easy to grow on the right site.

### *Quercus virginiana* (Live Oak)

Native tree found in hammocks to 60 feet tall; deciduous for a short time in spring; young leaves with pointed lobes, mature foliage hard, no lobes, with curled margins, inconspicuous flowers; moist to dry soil; full sun; cold-tolerant; abundant throughout Florida; widely available; propagated from seeds; matures slowly; easy to grow.

## Lauraceae (Laurel Family)

### Palamedes and Spicebush Swallowtail Host Plants

### *Cinnamonum camphora* (Camphor Tree)

Cultivated tree from Asia to 60 feet tall; evergreen; shiny dark green leaves with whitish undersides, aromatic when crushed, inconspicuous yellow flowers; the small black fruit are eaten by birds; blooms during spring; moist to dry soil; full sun to partial shade; cold-sensitive; grown and naturalized in central and north Florida; available from nurseries; propagated from seeds; matures relatively quickly; easy to grow.

### *Persea borbonia* (Red Bay)

Native tree found in hammocks to 40 feet tall; evergreen; leaves dull green above and whitish below, aromatic when crushed, small yellow flowers; the small bluish fruit are eaten by birds; blooms during spring; moist to dry soil; full sun to partial shade; cold-tolerant; found throughout Florida, except the Keys; available from nurseries; propagated from seeds; matures relatively quickly; easy to grow. Silk Bay (*Persea humilis*) is similar, but the undersides of the leaves are covered with brown to golden hairs. This species is normally found in scrubs and grows best in well drained, sandy soils. The leaves of Swamp Bay (*Persea palustris*) are greenish with a few scattered, brownish hairs underneath. Although Swamp Bay grows mostly in swamps, it does well in the garden in moist soil. All of the bays are nice trees for the garden.

### *Sassafras albidum* (Sassafras)

Native tree found in sandhills and hammocks to 20 feet tall; deciduous; leaves entire or lobed, aromatic, small yellow flowers, the small bluish fruit are eaten by birds; blooms during spring; moist to dry soil; full sun to partial shade; cold-tolerant; found in north and central Florida; available from nurseries; propagated from seeds; matures relatively quickly; easy to grow.

## Magnoliaceae (Magnolia Family)

### Tiger Swallowtail Host Plants

### *Liriodendron tulipifera* (Tulip Tree)

Native tree found in hammocks to 60 feet tall; deciduous; leaves lobed, aromatic when crushed, large yellow and orange flowers in early summer; moist soil; full sun to partial shade; cold-tolerant; locally common in north and central Florida; available from nurseries; propagated from seeds; matures relatively quickly; easy to grow.

### *Magnolia virginiana* (Sweet Bay)

Native tree found in swamps and bayheads to 60 feet tall; evergreen to briefly deciduous; leaves entire with a white undersurface, aromatic when crushed, large white flowers in summer; moist to wet soil; full sun to partial shade; cold-tolerant; abundant throughout Florida, except the Keys; available from nurseries; propagated from seeds; matures relatively quickly; easy to grow.

## Malvaceae (Hibiscus Family)

### Checkered Skipper Host Plants

### *Althea rosea* (Hollyhock)

Cultivated flower; herb to 6 feet tall; biennial, evergreen; hibiscuslike flowers of various colors; blooms during summer and fall; moist soil; full sun to partial shade; cold-tolerant; can be grown in northern Florida; widely available; propagated from seeds; matures in two years; easy to grow.

### *Callirhoe papaver* (Poppy Mallow)

Native wildflower found in sandhills and dry hammocks to 1.5 feet tall; perennial, evergreen; large red flowers on slender stalks; blooms during late spring and early summer; moist to dry, well-drained soil; full sun to partial shade; cold-tolerant; rare in north

Florida; available from native plant nurseries; propagated from seeds and stem cuttings; matures quickly; easy to grow.

## Marantaceae (Arrow Root Family)

Canna Skipper Host Plants

### *Thalia geniculata* (**Alligator Flag**)

Native herb found in swamps and marshes to 12 feet; perennial, deciduous; large leaves, small purple flowers at tips of long stalks; wet to moist soil; full sun to partial shade; cold-tolerant; locally common throughout Florida, except the Keys; available at some nurseries; propagated from root divisions; easy to grow.

## Oleaceae (Olive Family)

Tiger Swallowtail Host Plants for North Florida

### *Fraxinus americana* (**White Ash**)

Native tree found in hammocks to 60 feet tall; deciduous; compound leaves with 7–9 oblong leaflets and inconspicuous flowers; moist soil; full sun to partial shade; cold-tolerant; occurs in north Florida, locally abundant; available at some nurseries; propagated from seeds; easy to grow. Pop Ash (*Fraxinus caroliniana*) is a smaller tree found in swamps that can be grown in moist soil in the garden.

## Passifloraceae (Passion-Flower Family)

Gulf Fritillary, Julia, Zebra Long Wing, and Variegated Fritillary Host Plants

### *Passiflora incarnata* (**Maypop**)

Native vine found in sandhills, old fields, and disturbed sites; perennial, deciduous; leaves with three lobes, large purplish flowers, filaments of flower somewhat bent, delicious fruit when brown and wrinkled; blooms during summer and fall; moist to dry soil; full sun; cold-tolerant; locally common in north and central Florida; available at some nurseries; propagated from runners and seeds; matures quickly; easy to grow. Suckers from the roots will pop up in unwanted places, but can be controlled simply by pulling the shoot. Or these shoots can be dug, potted, and given to friends. Feel underground for the cablelike root and cut about an inch on either side of a small shoot. Pot in good soil, water, and fertilize weekly.

### *Passiflora* x 'incense' (**Incense Passion-Flower**)

Cultivated flower; a hybrid between *P. incarnata* and *P. cincinnata;* perennial, deciduous to evergreen; leaves with five leaflets, large purplish flowers, filaments of flower very bent; moist to dry soil; full sun; cold-sensitive; can be grown throughout Florida, but needs winter protection in the northern part of the state; available at some nurseries; propagated from runners; matures quickly; easy to grow.

### *Passiflora multiflora* (**Many-Flowered Passion-Flower**)

Native vine found at the edges of tropical hammocks; perennial, evergreen; leaves without lobes and fuzzy, small greenish flowers; blooms during summer; moist to dry soil; full sun; cold-sensitive; found in coastal south Florida and the Keys; limited availability; propagated from runners and seeds; matures quickly; easy to grow.

### *Passiflora suberosa* (**Corky-Stemmed Passion-Flower**)

Native vine found in fields and disturbed sites; perennial, evergreen; leaves entire, small greenish flowers, small purple fruit; blooms during summer and fall; moist to dry soil; full sun; cold-sensitive; common in south and coastal central Florida; limited availability; propagated from runners and seeds; matures quickly; easy to grow.

## Plumbaginaceae (Leadwort Family)

Cassius Blue Host Plants

### *Plumbago auriculata* (**Leadwort**)

Cultivated shrub from southern Africa to 5 feet tall; perennial, evergreen; pale blue or white flowers; blooms all year in south Florida; moist soil; full sun to partial shade; cold-sensitive; can be grown throughout the state, but needs winter protection in the north; widely available; propagated from cuttings; matures quickly; easy to grow. The native leadwort (*Plumbago scandens*) is not as showy but is also eaten by the caterpillars.

## Poaceae (Grass Family)

Satyr and Branded Skipper Host Plants

### *Arundo donax* (**Giant Reed**)

Clouded Skipper host plant. Cultivated grass from the Mediterranean region to 12 feet tall; perennial, evergreen; clumping grass with large canes over 1 inch in diameter and leaves to 1–2 feet long regularly spaced along the stem, dense clusters of seeds at tips of canes in fall; dry to moist soil; full sun to partial shade; cold-tolerant; grown in north and central Florida; widely available; propagated from root divisions; matures quickly; easy to grow. The new growth of variety *versicolor* is striped with white. This large species needs a lot of room in the garden.

### Chasmanthium sessiliflorum (Longleaf Spikegrass)

Carolina Satyr host plant. Native grass found in moist hammocks to 15 inches tall; perennial, evergreen; clumping grass with leaves to 12–18 inches long, seeds on long spikes in fall; moist to dry soil; partial shade; cold-tolerant; abundant in north and central Florida; limited availability; propagated from root divisions; matures quickly; easy to grow.

### Cynodon dactylon (Bermudagrass)

Fiery Skipper, Whirlabout Skipper host plant. Cultivated grass from Africa less than 1 foot tall; perennial, evergreen; narrow leaves at intervals along a short stem, seeds produced on a number of short stalks attached like spokes of wheel to a single stalk; moist to dry soil; full sun; cold-tolerant; grown as a lawn grass throughout Florida and naturalized in weedy places; widely available; propagated from seeds, also sold as cut turf; matures quickly; easy to grow and maintain.

### Erianthus giganteus (Sugarcane Plumegrass)

Clouded Skipper host plant. Native grass found in marshes and roadside ditches to 8 feet tall; perennial, evergreen; clumping grass with silky hairs, leaves to 3 feet long, fuzzy pinkish seeds produced in clusters at the tips of leafy stalks; blooms during the fall; wet or moist soil; full sun to partial shade; cold-tolerant; locally abundant throughout Florida, except the Keys; limited availability; propagated from root divisions; matures quickly; easy to grow.

### Pennisetum setaceum var. rubrum (Red Fountain Grass)

Clouded Skipper host plant. Cultivated grass from Africa to 4 feet tall; perennial, evergreen; clumping grass with reddish leaves, 1–2 feet long, fuzzy pinkish seeds produced in clusters at the tips of leafy stalks; blooms during summer and fall; moist to dry soil; full sun to partial shade; cold-sensitive but will re-sprout from the roots if mulched during the fall; grown throughout Florida; widely available; propagated from root divisions; matures quickly; easy to grow. This species has a tendency to spread and become weedy in south Florida.

### Saccharum officinarum (Sugarcane)

Clouded Skipper host plant. Cultivated grass from India to 12 feet tall; perennial, evergreen; clumping grass with large canes over 1 inch in diameter and leaves 3 feet long regularly spaced along the stem, dense clusters of seeds at tips of canes in fall; dry to moist soil; full sun to partial shade; cold-sensitive, but will re-sprout from the roots if mulched during the fall; grown throughout Florida; widely available; propagated from root divisions or by burying cut sections of the canes with at least two nodes; matures quickly; easy to grow. Green or red foliage forms are available. This large species needs a lot of space. Trim this grass with care. Tiny teeth on the margins of the leaves can cause razorlike cuts to the skin.

### Stenotaphrum secundatum (St. Augustinegrass)

Carolina Satyr, Fiery Skipper, Clouded Skipper, and Whirlabout Skipper host plant. Cultivated grass probably from South America less than 1 foot tall; perennial, evergreen; leaves in clusters at regular intervals along runners, seeds produced on one side of a thick stalk; moist to dry soil; full sun to partial shade; cold-tolerant; grown as a lawn grass throughout Florida and naturalized in moist forests; widely available; sold mostly as cut turf; matures quickly; easy to grow and maintain. This grass is susceptible to some insect pests such as chinch bugs and sod webworms as well as fungal pathogens, but is one of the most commonly used turf grasses.

### Tripsacum dactyloides (Eastern Gamagrass)

Clouded Skipper and Three-Spotted Skipper host plant. Native grass found at the edges of hammocks and roadside ditches to 8 feet tall; perennial, evergreen; clumping grass with leaves 3 feet long, seeds produced in chains at the tips of stalks during the fall; moist to dry soil; full sun to partial shade; cold-tolerant; locally abundant throughout Florida, except the Keys; available at native plant nurseries; propagated from root divisions; matures quickly; easy to grow. As with Sugarcane, trim this grass with care due to the tiny teeth on the margins of the leaves.

## Rosaceae (Rose Family)

Tiger Swallowtail and Red-Spotted Purple Host Plant

### *Prunus serotina* (Wild Cherry)

Native tree found along fence lines, hammock edges, and shrubby, disturbed sites to 40 feet tall; deciduous; shiny, lance-shaped leaves with finely toothed margins, clusters of white flowers, small black fruit; blooms during spring; moist to dry soil; full sun; cold-tolerant; abundant in central and north Florida; limited availability; propagated from seeds; matures quickly; easy to grow.

## Rutaceae (Citrus Family)

Giant Swallowtail Host Plants

### *Amyris elemifera* (Torchwood)

Native shrub or small tree found in tropical hammocks to 25 feet tall; evergreen; compound leaves with three lance-shaped leaflets that are aromatic when crushed, clusters of white flowers, sweet, fleshy, bluish-black fruit; blooms in early summer; moist to dry well-drained soil; full sun to partial shade; cold-sensitive; locally abundant in the Keys; available from some native plant nurseries; propagated from seeds; matures slowly; somewhat difficult to grow.

### *Citrus sinensis* (Sweet Orange)

Cultivated tree from Asia to 25 feet tall; evergreen; glossy lance-shaped leaves, aromatic when crushed, fruit ripens by fall, juveniles and wild types with stout spines on the branches; blooms during spring and early summer; moist to dry soil; full sun to partial shade; cold-sensitive; grown mostly in south and central Florida, may be grown in north Florida with winter protection; widely available; propagated by grafting buds onto Sour Orange or other root stock; matures quickly; easy to grow. Other citrus species are similar in their cultivation requirements, with Tangerine, Grapefruit, and Honey Tangerine among the most cold-tolerant and Key Lime the most cold-sensitive.

### *Ptelea trifoliata* (Wafer Ash, Common Hoptree)

Native shrub or small tree found at the edges of hammocks to 25 feet tall; deciduous; compound leaves with three lance-shaped leaflets, aromatic when crushed, small foul-smelling, whitish flowers, clusters of flat, papery fruits in the fall; blooms in spring and early summer; moist to dry soil; full sun to partial shade; cold-tolerant; uncommon in north and central Florida; limited availability; propagated from seeds; matures slowly; easy to grow.

### *Severinia buxifolia* (Box Thorn)

Cultivated shrub from Asia to 10 feet tall; evergreen; small, shiny leaves, aromatic when crushed, white flowers, stout thorns on stems, small, juicy black fruit; blooms during early summer; moist to dry soil; full sun to partial shade; cold-tolerant; can grown throughout Florida; available at many nurseries; propagated from seeds; matures quickly; easy to grow, usually planted and trimmed for hedges.

### *Zanthoxylum clava-herculis* (Hercules Club, Toothache Tree)

Native tree found along fence lines and at the margins of coastal hammocks and sandhills to 25 feet tall; deciduous; compound leaves with seven to nine glossy leaflets, aromatic when crushed, clusters of white flowers, interesting spines on trunk, branches, and leaves; blooms during early summer; dry, sandy soil; full sun; cold-tolerant; locally abundant throughout Florida; available from native plant nurseries; propagated from seeds; matures slowly; easy to grow. The leaves contain a chemical that when chewed causes numbing and tingling of the mouth.

### *Zanthoxylum fagara* (Wild Lime)

Native shrub or small tree found in tropical hammocks to 30 feet tall; evergreen; compound leaves with 9–13 bright green leaflets, aromatic when crushed, small white flowers, small clusters of dry capsules containing one or two shiny, black seeds, cat clawlike spines on trunk, branches, and leaves; blooms during early summer; dry to moist soil; full sun to partial shade; cold-sensitive; locally abundant in the Keys and coastal areas of south Florida; available from native plant nurseries; propagated from seeds; matures quickly; easy to grow.

## Salicaceae (Willow Family)

Viceroy and Red-Spotted Purple Host Plants

### *Salix babylonica* (Weeping Willow)

Cultivated tree from China to 60 feet tall; deciduous; long, narrow leaves on pendulous branches, clusters of small yellow flowers; blooms during spring; wet to moist soil; full sun; cold-tolerant; grown in north and central Florida; available from nurseries; propagated from stem cuttings; matures quickly; easy to grow.

### *Salix caroliniana* (Carolina or Coastal Plain Willow)

Native shrub or small tree found in marshes, swamps, roadside ditches, and along the margins of ponds and lakes to 40 feet tall; deciduous; long, narrow leaves that are whitish underneath, clusters of small yellow flowers; blooms during spring; wet to moist soil; full sun; cold-tolerant; abundant throughout Florida; available from native plant nurseries; propagated from stem cuttings; matures quickly; easy to grow. Black Willow (*Salix nigra*) is similar, but taller and the undersides of the leaves are green. This willow occurs only in the northern part of the state.

## Sapindaceae (Soapberry Family)

Gray Hairstreak and St. Christopher Hairstreak Host Plant

### *Cardiospermum halicacabum* (Balloon Vine, Heart-Seed)

Native vine found at the margins of tropical hammocks; perennial, evergreen; small yellow flowers, fruit an inflated green pod that turns brown and dry when mature, each pod contains three black seeds with a white, heart-shaped scar; blooms throughout the year; moist to dry soil; full sun; cold-sensitive; found in the Keys and Miami-Dade County; limited availability; propagated from seeds; matures quickly; easy to grow. *Cardiospermum corindum*, which has a semicircular scar on the seed, also grows in southern Florida. The Small-Fruited Balloon-Vine (*Cardiospermum microcarpum*) has very small pods and occurs in Miami-Dade and Broward counties.

## Scrophulariaceae (Snapdragon Family)

Common Buckeye and White Peacock Host Plant

### *Agalinis fasciculata* (Cluster-Leaf Gerardia or False Foxglove)

Common Buckeye host plant. Native wildflower found in disturbed pine flatwoods and sandhills to 5 feet tall; annual; leaves short and narrow, deep-throated purple flowers; blooms during the fall; moist to dry soil; full sun; found throughout Florida, except the Keys; limited availability; propagated from seeds; matures quickly; somewhat difficult to establish.

### *Bacopa monnieri* (Water Hyssop)

White Peacock host plant. Native wildflower found in open wet areas, less than 6 inches tall; perennial, evergreen; fleshy light green leaves, small purplish flowers, trailing stems; blooms spring through fall; moist to wet soil; full sun; cold-sensitive; found throughout the state, but most abundant in central and south Florida; limited availability; propagated from cuttings; matures quickly; easy to grow.

## Tropaeolaceae (Nasturtium Family)

Great Southern White Host Plant

### *Tropaeolum majus* (Nasturtium)

Cultivated plant from South America to 1.5 feet tall; annual; round leaves with the petiole attached in the middle, smells of mustard when crushed, edible as a vegetable in salads, yellow or orange flowers, trailing stems; blooms from summer to fall; moist soil; full sun; may be planted throughout Florida; widely available; propagated from seeds; matures quickly; easy to grow.

## Ulmaceae (Elm Family)

Snout Butterfly, Question Mark, Hackberry Butterfly, and Tawny Emperor Host Plants

### *Celtis laevigata* (Hackberry or Sugarberry)

Native tree found in hammocks to 50 feet tall; deciduous; lance-shaped leaves with fine teeth on the margins, small drab flowers, the reddish-brown fruits are highly favored by birds, bark with corky growths; moist soil; full sun to partial shade; cold-tolerant; found throughout Florida, except the Keys; available from nurseries; propagated from seeds; matures quickly; easy to grow.

### *Ulmus americana* (American Elm)

Native tree found in hammocks to 50 feet tall; deciduous; lance-shaped leaves with doubly toothed margins; small drab flowers, flat papery seeds; blooms during very early spring; moist to wet soil; full sun to partial shade; cold-tolerant; found in north and central Florida; available from nurseries; propagated from seeds or root suckers; matures quickly; easy to grow. Winged Elm (*Ulmus alata*) is similar, but has corky growths on the branches and is a smaller tree. This species is also found in north Florida.

## Urticaceae (Nettle Family)

Red Admiral Host Plant

### *Boehmeria cylindrica* (False Nettle)

Native plant found in marshes, swamps, and margins of streams and ponds to 4 feet tall; perennial, deciduous; four-angled stem, lance-shaped leaves with teeth along the margins, greenish flowers in clusters; blooms during summer and fall; moist to wet soil; full sun to partial shade; cold-tolerant; common throughout Florida except the Keys; limited availability; propagated from root divisions; matures quickly; easy to grow.

## Verbenaceae (Vervain Family)

Common Buckeye and Phaon Crescent Host Plant

### *Phyla nodiflora* (Carpetweed, Cape Weed, Matchheads, Creeping Charlie, or Lippia)

Native wildflower found in pastures and weedy areas less than 1 foot tall; perennial, evergreen; trailing stems with small dark green or reddish leaves, pale purple flowers borne in a cluster at the tip of short stalk; blooms from summer through fall; wet to dry soil; full sun to partial shade; cold-tolerant; abundant throughout Florida; limited availability; propagated from stem cuttings; matures quickly; easy to grow.

## Zamiaceae (Arrow Root Family)

Florida Atala Host Plant

### *Zamia pumila* (Coontie)

Native plant found in sandhills, coastal hammocks, and tropical pinelands to 2 feet tall; perennial, evergreen; fernlike leaves arise from a swollen basal stem, flowers produced in fleshy cones at the base of the plant, individual plants are all male or all female, orange fruit produced by female plants; blooms during summer; moist to dry soil; full sun to partial shade; cold-tolerant; local and uncommon in peninsular Florida; widely available from nurseries; propagated from seeds; matures slowly; easy to grow. This plant may be fatal to pets and children if eaten.

## Common Host Plants of Weedy Sites

*Alysicarpus vaginalis* (False Moneywort or Alyce-Clover): Long-Tailed Skipper host plant.

*Aster dumosus* (Bushy Aster): Pearl Crescent host plant.

*Bidens alba* var. *radiata* (Spanish Needles): Dainty Sulphur host plant.

*Buchnera americana* (Blueheart): Common Buckeye host plant.

*Desmodium incanum* (Creeping Beggarweed): Gray Hairstreak, Dorantes Skipper, and Long-Tailed Skipper host plant.

*Digitaria sanguinalis* (Crabgrass): Whirlabout Skipper host plant.

*Gnaphalium falcatum* (Narrow-Leaved Cudweed), *Gnaphalium pensylvanicum* (Pennsylvania Cudweed), *Gnaphalium purpureum* (Purple Cudweed): American Painted Lady host plants.

*Herissantia crispa* (Bladder Mallow): Gray Hairstreak host plant.

*Indigofera spicata*: Ceraunus Blue and Zarucco Skipper host plant.

*Lepidium virginicum* (Pepper Grass): Great Southern White, European Cabbage White, and Checkered White host plant.

*Linaria canadensis* (Toad Flax): Common Buckeye host plant.

*Parietaria floridana* (Pellitory): Red Admiral host plant.

*Plantago lanceolata* (English Plantain), *Plantago virginica* (Southern Plantain): Common Buckeye host plants.

*Ptilimnium capillaceum* (Mock Bishop's Weed): Black Swallowtail host plant.

*Sida acuta* (Broomweed), *Sida rhombifolia* (Indian Hemp): Gray Hairstreak, Columella Hairstreak, and Checkered Skipper host plants.

# Activities with Butterflies

Many people who try butterfly gardening find that it draws them into increasingly closer contact with nature. People who normally recoil when they see an insect may find themselves nurturing tiny caterpillars through their instars (larval stages) to the pupal stage in order to reap the reward of watching the perfect butterfly emerge from the chrysalis. Part of this contact is exploration and investigation into what caterpillars and plants, butterflies and their predators, are all about. These descriptions of investigative activities are included for students as well as those of you who are curious and enraptured enough with butterflies to go beyond the rest. In fact, there is plenty of room within the study of Lepidoptera, including butterflies and their behaviors, life histories, and interactions with other plants and animals, for pioneering research, even in your own backyard. Not so much is known already that you cannot make new discoveries of your own. All of these suggested experiments have the potential to unearth new discoveries for you, as well as for science. Teachers and parents can use these investigations to introduce their students to the fun side of science, and get them started in the right direction. We hope that you will share your discoveries with us, and use these activities as a springboard into your own line of investigation.

## Activity 1: Butterfly Metamorphosis

Level of Difficulty: Easy.

Background Information: Most butterfly eggs hatch in three to five days. Be sure to have fresh leaves available for the hungry caterpillars. When ready to molt, the larva stops eating for a few days, and rests on a mat of silk, often on the side or lid of the rearing container. Large caterpillars may pupate on a Popsicle stick, dead twig, or similar object placed in the rearing container. Rearing time from egg to adult usually takes a minimum of five weeks.

Materials: Rearing containers, notebooks, pencils, rulers, butterfly eggs or caterpillars, host plant, and an emergence cage. Suitable rearing containers include plastic deli tubs, petri dishes, glass jars, or plastic shoeboxes. We prefer pint-sized deli tubs with a hole cut in the top of the lid and a piece of screen glued over the hole. An inexpensive emergence cage can be made from a medium-sized cardboard box. Cut large panels from three of the sides and glue netting over the holes. Use a knife to make three cuts in the remaining side for a door. The uncut portion acts as a hinge. A drawer pull can be purchased from a hardware store and installed as a door knob.

How To Do It: Look for butterfly eggs on a host plant such as Cassia, Fennel, or Passion-Flower. You may even be able to observe a female laying eggs in the garden. If eggs are not available, use small caterpillars. Cut some stems with fresh growth from the host plant to feed the caterpillars. Clean out the frass (droppings) and wash the rearing containers with detergent and warm water at least twice a week. Be careful not to disturb molting or pupating caterpillars. Replace wilted or excessively chewed host plant with fresh leaves. Transfer the chrysalides from the rearing containers to the emergence cage after the pupa has hardened. Record the date and time of egg hatch, larval molts, pupation, and adult emergence. Measure the length of the caterpillar's body every few days. Retrieve the shed head capsules and glue them to a card. Measure the size of the head capsules with a millimeter ruler. Make drawings or diagrams of the caterpillar's color pattern at each stage.

407. Students examining caterpillars and other insects shaken from a tree branch onto a white sheet.

**Questions To Ponder:** How long does each stage last? How does the caterpillar move? How is the pupa formed? How much larger does a caterpillar become at each molt? How much does head size change at each stage. Does the color of the caterpillar change at each stage or stay the same? Do bigger caterpillars make bigger butterflies? Are the biggest caterpillars males or females? What do the larvae and pupae look like to you? Crumpled leaves? Bird droppings? Scary snakes? Monster faces? What might they look like to potential predators such as birds or lizards? Which sex is the first to emerge, males or females?

## Activity 2: Caterpillar Chemistry

**Level of Difficulty:** Easy.
**Background Information:** Swallowtails have an eversible defensive gland behind the head. The color and odor of the gland amazes students of all ages. Some of the chemicals produced by the gland, or their precursors, are also found in the aromatic host plants. This activity can be accomplished with a single visit to a garden with swallowtail host plants and caterpillars. The instructor may want to scout out the garden beforehand, or bring the caterpillars and plants indoors for the class to compare.
**Materials:** Caterpillars of the Giant Swallowtail, Black Swallowtail, and/or Spicebush Swallowtail, Q-tips, notebooks, pencils.
**How To Do It:** Find a swallowtail caterpillar and gently prod or squeeze the rear end until the osmeterium is everted. Then rub a Q-tip on the gland, and pass it around for the students to sniff. The Q-tip may be kept in a vial or plastic film container for later reference.

Next sniff a crushed leaf of the host plant. Try to compare a few species of swallowtails and their hosts. Describe the color and odor of the osmeterium as well as the aroma of the host plant.
**Questions To Ponder:** What does the osmeterium smell like? Does the fragrance resemble that of the host plant? What might this indicate about the metabolism (breakdown) of the chemicals in the plant in the caterpillar's body? Is the smell stronger in the plant or in the animal? How does the osmeterial smell differ from that of the host plant? What might be the source of these other components?

## Activity 3: Butterfly Perfume

**Level of Difficulty:** Easy.
**Background Information:** Adult butterflies have a variety of scents that can be detected by the human nose. Some have a flowery or perfume type of aroma, while others are acrid or unpleasant to smell. This activity can be accomplished with a single visit to the garden.
**Materials:** Butterfly nets, field guide, medium- to large-sized butterflies (swallowtails, Gulf Fritillary, Cloudless Sulphur, Monarch, etc.), host plants, notebooks, and pencils.
**How To Do It:** Have the students collect and identify live butterflies. Sweep the butterfly into the net and fold the netting over the rim. Close the wings over the back of the butterfly and gently remove it from the net. Carefully handle the butterfly by the wings. To test each butterfly species, the students should hold the butterfly close to their noses and sniff. Release the butterfly when the class is finished testing it. Collect a sample of the host plant and sniff a crushed leaf. The students should

record the species of butterfly, host plant, and describe the scents. Especially try to test swallowtails, butterflies with warning colors (Gulf Fritillary, Zebra Longwing, Gold Rim Swallowtail, Monarch), and plainly marked species.

**Questions To Ponder:** Do the adult butterflies tested smell like their host plants? Do all swallowtails have a sweet perfume? Do butterflies with warning colors smell differently from those that do not? Do males of the Gold Rim Swallowtail smell differently from the females?

## Activity 4: Butterfly Migration

**Level of Difficulty:** Easy.

**Background Information:** Monarch Watch is an outreach program that the promotes conservation of Monarch butterflies. The program is a collaborative network of students, teachers, volunteers and researchers investigating Monarch migration. During the fall of 1995, at least 30,000 students in 30 states participated in the program. For a $10.00 annual fee to cover the cost of supplies and postage, Monarch Watch members receive a tagging kit containing 20 tags, glue, and instructions, plus a summary of the season's research and a newsletter. Tagging kits are mailed in August before the migration begins. To order kits write to Monarch Watch, c/o O. R. "Chip" Taylor, Department of Entomology, University of Kansas, Haworth Hall, Lawrence, KS 66045-2106. This activity can be accomplished with single or multiple visits to the garden.

**Materials:** Monarchs in the garden, butterfly nets, tags, glue, and data sheets.

**How To Do It:** Teams of students catch live Monarchs and glue a small tag bearing a unique number and the Monarch Watch address to the underside of the hindwing. Data such as the location and sex of the individual are also recorded before the butterfly is released unharmed. The data sheets are mailed to Monarch Watch for processing. Anyone finding a tagged specimen reports the number and location to Monarch Watch, where researchers track the butterflies' movements.

**Questions To Ponder:** Did the Monarchs stay in the garden or disperse? If some of the tagged Monarchs were later recovered, how far did they travel? In what direction from the release point did the butterflies move? How many days passed from release to recapture? What happened to all of the butterflies that were marked, but were not found again?

## Activity 5: Butterfly Guide

**Level of Difficulty:** Moderate.

**Background Information:** This activity develops the students ability to observe and describe the natural world and allows for a high degree of creativity. The guide can be expanded with each succeeding class. Bound copies may be kept in the school library for future reference. Plan the format for the booklet with the class. The focus may be on the butterflies, host plants, or nectar sources. The students may want to concentrate only on the butterflies, or include other subjects as well. The format may vary from scientific and descriptive to literary, poetic, or humorous, depending upon the class. This activity can be accomplished with one or more trips to the garden as well as classroom time to write and illustrate the final entries.

**Materials:** Notebooks, sketching or painting paper (clipboards or cardboard may be needed for a backing), pencils, erasers, field guide, a butterfly garden or natural area for study, and a camera with film, paints, or colored pencils for illustrating butterflies and host plants.

**How To Do It:** Have the students bring pencils and paper, camera and/or paints, into the butterfly garden. Each student should choose a particular species that is present in the garden to study. Students should observe the butterflies closely, making sketches and taking notes on behavior, flowers visited, egg laying, etc. The students may want to collect and raise eggs or caterpillars to describe the life cycle. Back in the classroom, and at the library, students can find out more about the species they observed. Each entry should include both a written and an illustrated element. You may want to include the following information: common and scientific name; family; a photo, drawing, or painting of the butterfly and the caterpillar, egg, and pupa; descriptions of the life stages; the host plant(s); the butterfly's behavior; and interactions with other animals and plants. The entries can be punched and put into a binder.

**Questions To Ponder:** How many species were found by the class? Which ones had not previously been found? How many, would you predict, might be found in future years through subsequent observation? Did the students observe any new or unusual behaviors or feeding preferences?

## Activity 6: Butterfly Flight Patterns

**Level of Difficulty:** Moderate.

**Background Information:** The various groups of butterflies each have distinctive styles of flying. Some are fast and darting, while others are slow and gliding. Butterflies also fly at different levels from the ground. Those that live primarily in the tree tops may be brightly colored, while those near the ground have dull patterns. This activity can be accomplished with a single visit to the garden. Also allow time in the classroom to summarize and discuss the results.

**Materials:** Field guides, notebooks, pencils, and a sunny day in a butterfly garden.

**How To Do It:** Have the students closely observe as many species of butterflies as possible. For each individual butterfly, record the species, family, behavioral activity (mate locating, egg laying, dispersing), flight pattern, and height above the ground.

**Questions To Ponder:** What color of butterflies fly near the ground versus those that occur in the trees? Do large butterflies fly higher than small ones? Were the butterflies seeking nectar or host plants? Is it safer (because of fewer predators) to be at a particular level? How does the flight of skippers compare to swallowtails? Which species use perching versus patrolling mate-locating behavior?

## Activity 7: The Ideal Butterfly Flower

**Level of Difficulty:** Moderate.

**Background Information:** Some butterflies have longer "tongues" than others, and may tend to favor colors in the red and yellow range. Particular flowers may be favored by bees or other insects rather than butterflies.

**Materials:** Butterfly garden, pencils, notebooks, and field guides.

**How To Do It:** In the garden, the students should note which kinds of butterflies and other insects are visiting particular flowers. Record the species of butterfly or type of visitor (bee, fly, beetle, etc.) and the flower characteristics. The students may note the following characteristics: flowers few or many; flowers single or in heads; flowers small, medium, or large; flower shape open and flat or tubular; petals hairy or smooth; flower color uniform or with spots or stripes; color red, blue, yellow, white, etc.; fragrance sweet or musty; amount of nectar present; and amount of pollen present. The nectar and pollen can be observed by carefully tearing open a flower.

**Questions To Ponder:** Do some flowers attract more visitors than others? Do certain types of visitors appear to prefer certain types of flowers? Which characteristics seem to attract the most butterflies? How about bees? Were any of the butterflies carrying pollen?

## Activity 8: Butterflies at Bait

**Level of Difficulty:** Moderate.

**Background Information:** Some species of butterflies and moths are strongly attracted to fermenting fruit. A simple bait trap can be made from a hanging flower pot and netting. The butterflies enter the trap through a narrow gap, get drunk on the bait, then fly up into the cone of netting. Not only butterflies, but moths, beetles, flies, and wasps will be attracted to the bait. Raccoons and flying squirrels may raid the traps if they are able to reach them. The bait will be attractive for only about five days. This activity requires at least two visits to the garden and time in the classroom to summarize and discuss the results.

**Materials:** Fruit (apples, pears, bananas, etc.), molasses, deli containers, hanging baskets, netting, paper clips, field guides, notebooks, and pencils.

**How To Do It:** First cut the fruit into chunks. Old fruit from the grocery or home works fine. Mix one cup of molasses with four cups of warm water, and add to the fruit. The liquid should cover the fruit. Spoon the bait into the deli containers and loosely cover with the lids. After a few days, the bait should begin to ferment. Remove the lids and place each container into a hanging basket purchased from a garden shop. Wrap the netting tightly around the wires supporting the basket, leaving a three-fourth-inch gap between the bottom of the netting and the top of the pot. This will give the butterflies and other insects a way to enter the trap. Use paper clips or staples to hold the netting in place. Hang the completed traps in shrubs, tree branches, or other supports at least five feet above the ground. Choose a variety of locations such as a wooded area, butterfly garden, or open field. Leave the traps for a few days, then record the butterfly species and other types of insects in the traps. Open the netting, release the insects, and clean up. Other experiments can be designed to test which kind of fruit or which height above the ground is most attractive.

**Questions To Ponder:** What types of butterflies are attracted to fermenting fruit? Are they colorful or cryptic? What other animals are attracted? Are shady places as good as sunny ones in attracting butterflies to the bait? Do more butterflies come to bait near the ground or high in the trees?

## Activity 9: Butterfly Habitat

Level of Difficulty: Advanced.

Background Information: While some places are butterfly hotspots, others just aren't, even in peak season. Finding out what factors affect butterfly abundance will help the students to learn about spatial patterns of diversity. This activity can be accomplished with a single out-of-doors sampling period.

Materials: Butterfly nets, field guides, notebooks, pencils, and watches.

How To Do It: Divide the students into small groups. Each team should record the species and number of butterflies seen in a particular habitat, such as a butterfly garden, lawn, weedlot, wooded or shady area, etc. Unknown butterflies should be caught and identified. Butterfly resources such as the presence or absence of flowers for nectar or host plants should also be recorded. Sampling time should be kept short, from 15 to 30 minutes.

Questions To Ponder: Do butterflies prefer sunny or shady areas? Which habitat had the greatest abundance of butterflies? Which had the most species? Are brightly colored butterflies more likely to be found in sunny or shady habitats? Were more butterflies found near host plants or flowers?

## Activity 10: Bumbling Butterflies?

Level of Difficulty: Advanced.

Background Information: What is going on in the minds of butterflies busy at flowers? Are they thinking about what they are doing, or just doing some rote mechanical series of movements, bumbling through, with no consideration for variations in flowers or nectar?

Materials: If your school has some orange or pink Lantana (*Lantana camara*) growing in the garden or on the school grounds, the students can try this experiment. Also needed are some small paper bags, notebooks, pencils, and tweezers.

How To Do It: Early one morning, or during the previous day, the instructor should choose several Lantana flower heads and cover each with small paper bags. The next afternoon, have the students check the uncovered Lantana flowers for butterflies. They should carefully watch the behavior of butterflies at the flowers. There are usually two colors of flowers in each head. Brighter or lighter flowers are in the center, surrounded by darker flowers at the edges. The students should tally how many edge flowers versus central flowers are probed for nectar. Next, students can pluck flowers

from a Lantana flower head and place the base of the flower on their tongues to see if they can detect a difference between inner and outer flowers. They couldn't tell the difference between the flowers? Now have the students try this—take the paper bags off the covered flowers, pluck one of each type, and place the flower base on their tongues. Now can they tell the difference?

Questions To Ponder: Does the butterfly probe mostly dark outer flowers, or does it prefer the lighter center flowers? Why might this be? Which kind of flower seems to have more nectar? What does this show about our ability to perceive nectar compared to the butterfly's ability? If the outer flowers aren't producing nectar, and so aren't attracting pollinators anymore, why might they remain in the flower head, instead of wilting and dropping off? What advantage would keeping spent flowers be to a plant? Might they serve as a landing platform or a target marker to augment the attractiveness of the flower head?

Further Research: Once you have taken the paper bags off the Lantana flowers, compare how long the butterflies stay. Do previously bagged flowers detain butterflies significantly longer than unbagged flowers? Does keeping a butterfly in one place provide an advantage for a flower that wants to exchange pollen *via* butterflies?

## Activity 11: Population Studies (Mark and Release)

Level of Difficulty: Advanced.

Background Information: Ecologists can estimate the size of a population of a particular species using a mark-recapture technique. With this investigative activity, the students can use indelible-ink pens to mark butterfly wings and discover how many individuals of a chosen species occur in an area. Large butterflies such as swallowtails, Gulf Fritillaries, and Cloudless Sulphurs are easier to mark than smaller species. This activity requires at least two sample periods, but best results occur if you sample every day for a week. The lifespans and movements of the butterflies can also be tracked using this technique. The recapture rate of marked individuals will be very low for migratory or highly dispersive species. The class's data can be compared with population estimates from previous years. The instructor may also want to sample every two or three weeks to track an adult population's dynamics through a single generation or season. The number of individuals in the population can be estimated by applying the Lincoln Index. This simple formula is calculated by multiplying the total number of individuals marked by the total number of individuals in the second sample, and then dividing by the total number of recaptures in the second sample.

**Materials:** Butterfly nets, indelible pens, notebooks, field guide, pencils, and a calculator.

**How To Do It:** Students should be grouped into teams and assigned a particular species. Each team will gently use a net to capture butterflies. While a butterfly is in the net, fold the wings closed over the back, and remove it with the fingers. Carefully write a unique number near the middle of the hindwing on the underside with an indelible pen. Record date, time of capture, location, number, sex of the specimen, and wing condition (freshly emerged, moderately worn wings, or wings tattered and faded), then release the specimen. Resample the garden at a later date. The following day is best, but every few days or the following week may also work. During the next sampling period, record the date, time of capture, location, and number written on the recaptured butterflies. If the experiment is ongoing, mark any new butterflies with unique numbers, then release the specimens.

**Questions To Ponder:** How many butterflies are estimated to be in the local population? Was the sex ratio of the butterflies in the sample 50:50 male to female, or skewed toward one of the sexes? Why might there be more males than females in the sample? How long did the butterflies live? What may have happened to individuals that were marked, but not found again?

## Activity 12: Caterpillar Diet

**Level of Difficulty:** Advanced.

**Background Information:** Butterfly caterpillars are picky eaters. They usually prefer only a few plants that are closely related. In this series of experiments the students will find out about plant chemistry and butterfly growth. This activity may take five to eight weeks to complete, although some parts can be accomplished over a few days.

**Materials:** Rearing containers (see Activity 1 above), marking pen, caterpillars, host plant, weight scale, notebooks, and pencils. Gulf Fritillaries, Cloudless Sulphurs, Monarchs, Giant Swallowtails, and Black Swallowtails are good species with which to experiment.

**How To Do It:** Collect at least ten butterfly eggs from the garden. Raise the caterpillars in individual containers. The containers can be numbered to keep better track of the individual caterpillars. Give half of the caterpillars tender young leaves of the host plant to eat, and the other half only mature leaves. Record the date of egg hatch, duration of the larval stage in days, and weight of the pupa. Average the pupal weights for each group, and compare.

**Another Way To Do It:** Collect ten butterfly caterpillars of similar size, and place them in individual containers. Put both young tender leaves and an old mature leaf into each container with the caterpillar. The next day record which type of food was eaten and how much.

**Questions To Ponder:** Which type of leaf produced larger pupae or was eaten by the caterpillars? What might this say about the ideal time for caterpillars to be growing up? What might plants do to keep caterpillars from eating their leaves? Do species that feed on trees such as the Giant Swallowtail show a much greater effect than those that feed on herbs or vines?

**Still Another Experiment:** Collect some host plant foliage and some leaves of a closely related species. You might try to use your nose to find a match. Often plants with similar fragrance will have similar chemistry, and will be closely related. Some examples to try are different species of *Cassia* for the sulphurs; mustard, collards, cabbage, and broccoli for the Cabbage White; various species of *Aristolochia* for the Gold Rim Swallowtail; different species of passion-flower for any of the Heliconiids; parsley, dill, anise, or other carrot relatives for the Black Swallowtail; various citrus species for the Giant Swallowtail, and so forth. Put both the genuine host plant and the test plant into the container with the caterpillar and leave it over night. Then record which plant was eaten, and how much.

**More Questions:** After one kind of plant is all eaten, does the caterpillar switch over to the other? Why might a caterpillar refuse to eat a different plant? If it ran out of food plant in the wild, how might it find more? Is the brightness of the butterfly's larval or adult coloration related to its host plant specificity? Why might this be? How might you devise a test for this question?

**Still More To Do:** Collect some fresh, tasty-looking host plant and some equally delicious-looking leaves of a nearby plant and place them in the rearing container with a caterpillar. The next day record which plant was eaten and how much.

**Even More Questions:** Did the caterpillar eat any of the other plant? What does this tell you about the needs of this caterpillar? What might be keeping the caterpillar from switching food plants?

# Checklist of Florida Butterflies

*Note:* This list excludes stray or nonresident species.

## Family Papilionidae (Swallowtails)

___ *Battus philenor* (Pipevine Swallowtail)
___ *Battus polydamas lucayus* (Tailless or Gold Rim Swallowtail)
___ *Eurytides marcellus floridensis* (Florida Zebra Swallowtail)
___ *Heraclides andraemon bonhotei* (Bahama Swallowtail)
___ *Heraclides aristodemus ponceanus* (Schaus' Swallowtail)
___ *Heraclides cresphontes* (Giant Swallowtail)
___ *Papilio polyxenes asterius* (Eastern Black Swallowtail)
___ *Pterourus glaucus australis* (Southern Tiger Swallowtail)
___ *Pterourus glaucus glaucus* (Eastern Tiger Swallowtail)
___ *Pterourus palamedes* (Palamedes Swallowtail)
___ *Pterourus troilus ilioneus* (Southern Spicebush Swallowtail)
___ *Pterourus troilus troilus* (Spicebush Swallowtail)

## Family Pieridae (Whites and Sulphurs)

### Subfamily Pierinae (Whites)

___ *Appias drusilla neumoegenii* (Florida White)
___ *Ascia monuste phileta* (Great Southern White)
___ *Pieris rapae* (European Cabbage White)
___ *Pontia protodice* (Checkered White)

### Subfamily Coliadinae (Sulphurs)

___ *Aphrissa statira floridensis* (Florida Statira Sulphur)
___ *Colias eurytheme* (Alfalfa Butterfly)
___ *Eurema daira daira* (Barred Sulphur)
___ *Eurema daira palmira* (Caribbean Barred Sulphur)
___ *Eurema dina helios* (Bush Sulphur)
___ *Eurema lisa* (Little Sulphur)
___ *Eurema nicippe* (Sleepy Orange)
___ *Eurema nise* (Jamaican Sulphur)
___ *Kricogonia lyside* (Guayacan Sulphur)
___ *Nathalis iole* (Dainty Sulphur)
___ *Phoebis agarithe maxima* (Large Orange Sulphur)
___ *Phoebis philea philea* (Orange-Barred Sulphur)
___ *Phoebis sennae eubule* (Cloudless Sulphur)
___ *Zerene cesonia* (Eastern Dogface)

## Family Lycaenidae (Blues and Hairstreaks)

### Subfamily Miletinae

___ *Feniseca tarquinius tarquinius* (Harvester)

### Subfamily Polyommatinae (Blues)

___ *Brephidium isophthalma pseudofea* (Eastern Pigmy Blue)
___ *Celastrina ladon* (Spring Azure)
___ *Everes comyntas* (Eastern Tailed Blue)
___ *Hemiargus ceraunus antibubastus* (Ceraunus Blue)
___ *Hemiargus thomasi bethunebakeri* (Miami Blue)
___ *Leptotes cassius theonus* (Cassius Blue)

## Subfamily Theclinae (Hairstreaks)

__ *Atlides halesus halesus* (Great Purple Hairstreak)
__ *Calycopis cecrops* (Red-Banded Hairstreak)
__ *Chlorostrymon maesites* (Verde Azul Hairstreak)
__ *Chlorostrymon simaethis simaethis* (St. Christopher's Hairstreak)
__ *Electrostrymon angelia* (Fulvous Hairstreak)
__ *Eumaeus atala florida* (Florida Atala)
__ *Fixsenia favonius* (Southern Oak Hairstreak)
__ *Harkenclenus titus mopus* (Southern Coral Hairstreak)
__ *Incisalia henrici henrici* (Henry's Elfin)
__ *Incisalia henrici margaretae* (Margaret's Elfin)
__ *Incisalia irus* (Frosted Elfin)
__ *Incisalia niphon niphon* (Eastern Pine Elfin)
__ *Mitoura gryneus gryneus* (Olive Hairstreak)
__ *Mitoura gryneus sweadneri* (Sweadner's Hairstreak)
__ *Mitoura hesseli* (Hessel's Hairstreak)
__ *Parrhasius m-album* (White-M Hairstreak)
__ *Satyrium calanus* (Banded Hairstreak)
__ *Satyrium kingi* (King's Hairstreak)
__ *Satyrium liparops liparops* (Florida Striped Hairstreak)
__ *Satyrium liparops strigosus* (Striped Hairstreak)
__ *Strymon acis bartrami* (Bartram's Hairstreak)
__ *Strymon columella modesta* (Dotted Hairstreak)
__ *Strymon martialis* (Martialis Hairstreak)
__ *Strymon melinus melinus* (Gray Hairstreak)
__ *Tmolus azia* (Tiny Hairstreak)

# Family Nymphalidae (Brushfooted Butterflies)

## Subfamily Apaturinae (Hackberry Butterflies)

__ *Asterocampa celtis celtis* (Hackberry Butterfly)
__ *Asterocampa celtis reinthali* (Reinthal's Hackberry Butterfly)
__ *Asterocampa clyton clyton* (Tawny Emperor)
__ *Asterocampa clyton flora* (Florida Tawny Emperor)

## Subfamily Charaxinae (Leafwing Butterflies)

__ *Anaea andria* (Goatweed Butterfly)
__ *Anaea troglodyta floridalis* (Florida Leafwing)

## Subfamily Danainae (Milkweed Butterflies)

__ *Danaus eresimus tethys* (Soldier)

__ *Danaus gilippus berenice* (Queen)
__ *Danaus plexippus* (Monarch)

## Subfamily Heliconiinae (Longwing Butterflies)

__ *Agraulis vanillae nigrior* (Gulf Fritillary)
__ *Dryas iulia largo* (Julia Butterfly)
__ *Heliconius charitonius tuckeri* (Zebra Longwing)

## Subfamily Nymphalinae (Brushfooted Butterflies)

__ *Anartia jatrophae guantanamo* (White Peacock)
__ *Anthanassa texana seminole* (Seminole Crescent)
__ *Basilarchia archippus floridensis* (Florida Viceroy)
__ *Basilarchia arthemis astyanax* (Red-Spotted Purple)
__ *Charidryas nycteis nycteis* (Silvery Checkerspot)
__ *Eresia frisia* (Cuban Crescent)
__ *Eunica monima* (Dingy Purple Wing)
__ *Eunica tatila tatilista* (Florida Purple Wing)
__ *Euptoieta claudia* (Variegated Fritillary)
__ *Junonia coenia* (Common Buckeye)
__ *Junonia evarete* (Black Mangrove Buckeye)
__ *Junonia genoveva* (Caribbean Buckeye)
__ *Marpesia petreus* (Ruddy Dagger Wing)
__ *Nymphalis antiopa* (Mourning Cloak)
__ *Phyciodes phaon* (Phaon Crescent)
__ *Phyciodes tharos tharos* (Pearl Crescent)
__ *Polygonia comma* (Comma Anglewing)
__ *Polygonia interrogationis* (Question Mark)
__ *Siproeta stelenes* (Malachite Butterfly)
__ *Vanessa atalanta rubria* (American Red Admiral)
__ *Vanessa cardui* (Painted Lady)
__ *Vanessa virginiensis* (American Painted Lady)

## Subfamily Satyrinae (Satyrs and Wood Nymphs)

__ *Cercyonis pegala abbotti* (Abbott's Wood Nymph)
__ *Cyllopsis gemma* (Gemmed Satyr)
__ *Enodia portlandia floralae* (Florida Pearly Eye)
__ *Enodia portlandia portlandia* (Southern Pearly Eye)
__ *Hermeuptychia hermes sosybius* (Carolina Satyr)
__ *Megisto cymela cymela* (Little Wood Satyr)
__ *Megisto cymela viola* (Viola's Wood Satyr)
__ *Neonympha areolata areolata* (Georgia Satyr)
__ *Satyrodes appalachia* (Appalachian Eyed-Brown)

## Family Libytheidae (Snout Butterflies)

__ *Libytheana bachmanii* (Bachman's Snout Butterfly)

## Family Hesperiidae (Skipper Butterflies)

### Subfamily Hesperiinae (Branded Skippers)

__ *Amblyscirtes aesculapius* (Cobweb Little Skipper)
__ *Amblyscirtes alternata* (Florida Little Skipper)
__ *Amblyscirtes belli* (Bell's Little Skipper)
__ *Anatrytone logan* (Delaware Skipper)
__ *Ancyloxypha numitor* (Least Skipperling)
__ *Asbolis capucinus* (Cuban Palm Skipper)
__ *Atalopedes campestris* (Field Skipper or Sachem)
__ *Atrytone arogos arogos* (Arogos or Brown Rim Skipper)
__ *Atrytonopsis hianna loammi* (Loamm's Skipper)
__ *Calpodes ethlius* (Canna Skipper)
__ *Copaeodes minima* (Tiny Skipper)
__ *Cymaenes tripunctus* (Three-Spotted Skipper)
__ *Euphyes arpa* (Palmetto Skipper)
__ *Euphyes berryi* (Berry's Skipper)
__ *Euphyes dion* (Dion Skipper)
__ *Euphyes dukesi calhouni* (Calhoun's Skipper)
__ *Euphyes pilatka klotsi* (Klots' Sawgrass Skipper)
__ *Euphyes pilatka pilatka* (Palatka or Sawgrass Skipper)
__ *Euphyes ruricola metacomet* (Eastern Dun Skipper)
__ *Hesperia attalus slossonae* (Slosson's Dotted Skipper)
__ *Hesperia meskei straton* (Gulf Coast Skipper)
__ *Hesperia meskei* subspecies (Rimrock Grass Skipper)
__ *Hylephila phyleus* (Fiery Skipper)
__ *Lerema accius* (Clouded Skipper)
__ *Lerodea eufala* (Gray Skipper)
__ *Nastra lherminier* (Swarthy Skipper)
__ *Nastra neamathla* (Southern Swarthy Skipper)
__ *Oligoria maculata* (Twin Spot Skipper)
__ *Panoquina ocola* (Ocola Skipper)
__ *Panoquina panoquin* (Salt Marsh Skipper)
__ *Panoquina panoquinoides* (Beach Skipper)
__ *Poanes aaroni howardi* (Howard's Marsh Skipper)
__ *Poanes viator zizaniae* (Wild Rice Skipper)
__ *Poanes yehl* (Southern Swamp Skipper)
__ *Poanes zabulon* (Zabulon Skipper)
__ *Polites baracoa* (Baracoa Skipper)
__ *Polites origenes* (Cross Line Skipper)
__ *Polites themistocles* (Tawny Edged Skipper)
__ *Polites vibex* (Whirlabout Skipper)
__ *Pompeius verna* (Little Glassy Wing)
__ *Problema byssus* (Byssus Skipper)
__ *Wallengrenia egeremet* (Broken Dash)
__ *Wallengrenia otho* (Red Broken Dash)

### Subfamily Pyrginae (Broadwinged Skippers)

__ *Achalarus lyciades* (Hoary Edge)
__ *Autochton cellus* (Golden Banded Skipper)
__ *Epargyreus clarus clarus* (Silver Spotted Skipper)
__ *Ephyriades brunneus floridensis* (Florida Dusky Wing)
__ *Erynnis baptisiae* (Indigo Dusky Wing)
__ *Erynnis brizo brizo* (Banded Oak Dusky Wing)
__ *Erynnis brizo somnus* (Somber Dusky Wing)
__ *Erynnis horatius* (Horace's Dusky Wing)
__ *Erynnis juvenalis juvenalis* (Juvenal's Dusky Wing)
__ *Erynnis martialis* (Mottled Dusky Wing)
__ *Erynnis zarucco zarucco* (Zarucco Dusky Wing)
__ *Erynnis zarucco* subspecies (Caribbean Dusky Wing)
__ *Phocides pigmalion okeechobee* (Florida Mangrove Skipper)
__ *Pholisora catullus* (Common Sooty Wing)
__ *Polygonus leo* (Hammock Skipper)
__ *Pyrgus albescens* (Western Checkered Skipper)
__ *Pyrgus communis* (Common Checkered Skipper)
__ *Pyrgus oileus oileus* (Tropical Checkered Skipper)
__ *Staphylus hayhurstii* (Southern Sooty Wing)
__ *Thorybes bathyllus* (Southern Cloudy Wing)
__ *Thorybes confusis* (Confused Cloudy Wing)
__ *Thorybes pylades* (Northern Cloudy Wing)
__ *Urbanus dorantes dorantes* (Dorantes or Brown Tailed Skipper)
__ *Urbanus proteus* (Long-Tailed Skipper)

### Subfamily Megathyminae (Giant Skippers)

__ *Megathymus cofaqui cofaqui* (Cofaqui Giant Skipper)
__ *Megathymus yuccae bucholzi* (Yucca Giant Skipper)

# Butterfly Gardening Resource Guide

Palamedes Swallowtails on Pickerelweed flowers.

## Butterfly Organizations

**Association for Tropical Lepidoptera, Inc.**
John Heppner, Director
c/o Florida State Collection of Arthropods
P.O. Box 141210
Gainesville, FL 32614-1210
(352) 372-3505

**Carolina Butterfly Society**
4209 Bramlet Place
Greensboro, NC 27407
(910) 294-9697

**The Lepidoptera Research Foundation, Inc.**
9620 Heather Road
Beverly Hills, CA 90210-1757
(310) 274-1052

**The Lepidopterists' Society**
Julian P. Donahue, Assistant Secretary
Natural History Museum of Los Angeles County
900 Exposition Boulevard
Los Angeles, CA 90007-4057
(213) 744-3364

**North American Butterfly Association, Inc.**
Jeffrey Glassberg, Director
4 Delaware Road
Morristown, NJ 07960
(201) 285-0907

**Southern Lepidopterists' Society**
Jeffrey R. Slotten, Secretary/Treasurer
5421 NW 69th Lane
Gainesville, FL 32653

**Xerces Society**
10 Southwest Ash Street
Portland, OR 97204
(503) 222-2788

## Entomological Supplies

**BioQuip Products**
17803 LaSalle Avenue
Gardena, CA 90248-3602
(310) 324-0620

**Carolina Biological Supply Co.**
2700 York Road
Burlington, NC 27215
(800) 334-5551

**Ward's Natural Science Establishment**
5100 West Henrietta Road
P.O. Box 92912
Rochester, NY 14692

## Gardening Groups

**Association of Florida Native Nurseries**
P.O. Box 434
Melrose, FL 32666

**Children's Haven & Adult Center, Inc.**
4405 DeSoto Road
Sarasota, FL 32235

**Florida Chapter of the American Horticultural
Therapy Association**
Kathy Teal, Director
4215 NW 69th Street
Gainesville, FL 32606

**Florida Federation of Garden Clubs**
1400 S. Denning Drive
Winter Park, FL 32789-5662

**Florida Native Plant Society**
P.O. Box 6116
Spring Hill, FL 34606
(407) 856-2366

**Florida Nurserymen & Growers Association**
5401 Kirkman Road, Suite 650
Orlando, FL 32819
(407) 345-8137

**National Council of State Garden Clubs, Inc.**
4401 Magnolia Ave.
St. Louis, MO 63110

## Gardening Magazines

**American Horticulturist**
7931 East Blvd. Drive
Alexandria, VA 22308

**Birds & Blooms**
P.O. Box 5359
Harlan, IA 51593-2859

**Fine Gardening**
The Taunton Press
P.O. Box 5506
Newtown, CT 06470-9955

**Florida Gardening**
P.O. Box 500678
Malabar, FL 32950

**Flower & Garden**
4251 Pennsylvania Avenue
Kansas City, MO 64111

**Horticulture**
P.O. Box 51455
Boulder, CO 80323-1455

**Southern Living**
Box 523
Birmingham, AL 35201

## Seeds, Plants, and Garden Supplies: Florida

**Apalachee Native Nursery**
Route 3 Box 156
Monticello, FL 32344

**American Native Products**
P.O. Box 2703
Titusville, FL 32781

**Alexander's Landscaping and Plant Farm**
910 S. Flamingo Road
Davie, FL 33325

**Association of Florida Native Nurseries**
Plant and Service Directory
P.O. Box 434
Melrose, FL 32666-0434

**Breezy Oaks Nursery**
23602 SE Hawthorne Road
Hawthorne, FL 32640

**Chiappini Farm Native Nursery**
P.O. Box 436
Melrose, FL 32666

**Green Images**
1333 Taylor Creek Road
Christmas, FL 32709

**Horticultural Systems, Inc.**
P.O. Box 70
Parrish, FL 34219

**Mandarin Native Plants**
13500 Mandarin Road
Jacksonville, FL 32223

**Maple Street Natives**
2395 Maple Street
West Melbourne, FL 32904
(407) 729-6857

**Mesozoic Landscapes, Inc.**
7667 Park Lane Road
Lake Worth, FL 33467

**Native Nurseries of Tallahassee, Inc.**
1661 Centerville Road
Tallahassee, FL 32308

**The Natives, Inc.**
2929 J. B. Carter Road
Davenport, FL 33837

**The Palmetto Patch**
12959 SR 54
Odessa, FL 33556
(813) 926-9954

**Runway Growers, Inc.**
2911 SW 36th Street
Fort Lauderdale, FL 33312

**The Wetlands Company, Inc.**
1785 South Wood Street
Sarasota, FL 34231
(941) 921-6609

## Seeds, Plants, and Garden Supplies: Other Sources

**W. Altee Burpee & Co.**
300 Park Avenue
Warminster, PA 18974

**Gardener's Supply Co.**
128 Intervale Road
Burlington, VT 05401

**Henry Field's Seed & Nursery Co.**
415 North Burnett
Shenandoah, IA 51602

**Gardens Alive!**
5100 Schenley Place
Lawrenceburg, IN 47025

**Gurney Seed & Nursery**
Page Street
Yankton, SD 57079

**Harris Seeds**
P.O. Box 22960
Rochester, NY 14692

**H. G. Hastings Co.**
P.O. Box 4274M
Atlanta, GA 30302

**Izard Ozark Natives**
P.O. Box 106
Eureka Springs, AR 72632

**Jackson & Perkins**
P.O. Box 1028
Medford, OR 97501

**Johnny's Selected Seeds**
Foss Hill Road
Albion, ME 04910

**J. W. Jung Seed Co.**
335 South High Street
Randolph, WI 53957

**Mellinger's Inc.**
2310 West South Range Road
North Lima, OH 44452

**Park Seed Co.**
Cokesbury Road
Greenwood, SC 29647

**Southern Perennials & Herbs**
98 Bridges Road
Tylertown, MS 39667

**R. H. Shumway's**
P.O. Box 1
Graniteville, SC 29829

**Stokes Seeds, Inc.**
Box 548
Buffalo, NY 14240

**Thompson & Morgan, Inc.**
P.O. Box 1308
Jackson, NJ 08527

**Virginia Natives**
P.O. Box D
Hume, VA 22639

**Wayside Gardens**
1 Garden Lane
Hodges, SC 29695

## Major Gardens and Live Butterfly Displays

**Alfred B. Maclay State Gardens**
3540 Thomasville Road
Tallahassee, FL 32308
(850) 487-4556

**Bok Tower Gardens**
1151 Tower Blvd.
Lake Wales, FL 33853-3412
(863) 676-1408

**Butterflies in Flight**
1100 Hooygate Land
Naples, FL 33940
(941) 262-6895

**Butterfly World**
3600 West Sample Road
Coconut Creek, FL 33073
(954) 977-4400

**Cecil B. Day Butterfly Center**
Callaway Gardens
Pine Mountain, GA 31822-200
(706) 663-2281

**Dreher Park Zoo**
1301 Summit Boulevard
West Palm Beach, FL 33405
(561) 533-0887

**Fairchild Tropical Garden**
10901 Old Cutler Road
Coral Gables, FL 33156
(305) 667-1651

**Harry P. Leu Gardens**
1920 North Forest Avenue
Orlando, FL 32803-1291
(407) 246-2620

**Kanapaha Botanical Gardens**
4700 SW 58th Drive
Gainesville, FL 32608
(352) 372-4981

**Marie Selby Botanical Gardens**
811 South Palm Avenue
Sarasota, FL 34236
(813) 366-5731

**Mead Botanical Gardens**
South Denning Drive
Winter Park, FL 32789

**Mounts Botanical Garden**
531 North Military Trail
West Palm Beach, FL 33415
(561) 233-1749

**Museum of Science and Industry**
4801 East Fowler Avenue
Tampa, FL 33617
(813) 987-6300

**Nature Walk and Butterfly House**
Jct. U.S. 98 and State Road 399
Navarre, FL

**Sarasota Garden Club**
1131 Boulevard of the Arts
Sarasota, FL 34236
(813) 955-0875

**Wings of Wonder Butterfly Conservatory**
Cypress Gardens
P.O. Box 1
Cypress Gardens, FL 33884
(813) 324-2111

## Butterfly Gardening Books

Ajilvsgi, G. 1990. *Butterfly Gardening for the South.* Dallas: Taylor Publishing Co. 348 pp. ISBN 0-87833-738-5.

Dennis, J. V., and M. Tekulsky. 1991. *How to Attract Hummingbirds and Butterflies.* San Ramon, Calif.: Ortho Books. 112 pp. ISBN 0-89721-232-0.

Emmel, T. C. 1997. *Butterfly Gardening: Creating a Butterfly Haven in Your Garden.* New York: Friedman/Fairfax. 112 pp. ISBN 1-56799-525-X.

Huegel, C. 1991. *Butterfly Gardening with Florida's Native Plants.* Orlando: Florida Native Plant Society. 35 pp.

Kilmer, A. N.d. *Gardening for Butterflies and Children in South Florida.* West Palm Beach: Published by the author. 40 pp.

Lewis, A. 1990. *Butterfly Gardens: Luring Nature's Loveliest Pollinators to Your Yard.* Brooklyn: Brooklyn Botanic Garden. ISBN 0-94535-288-3.

Ruffin, J. 1994. *Where Are the Butterfly Gardens?* Lawrence, Kan.: Lepidopterists' Society/Allen Press. 40 pp.

Schneck, M. 1993. *Creating a Butterfly Garden: A Guide to Attracting and Identifying Butterfly Visitors.* New York: Simon and Schuster. 80 pp. ISBN 0-671-89246-0.

Sedenko, J. 1991. *The Butterfly Garden: Creating Beautiful Gardens to Attract Butterflies.* New York: Villard. 144 pp. ISBN 0-394-58982-3.

Stokes, D., L. Stokes, and E. Williams. *The Butterfly Book: An Easy Guide to Butterfly Gardening, Identification, and Behavior.* Boston: Little, Brown. 96 pp. ISBN 0-316-81780-5.

Tekulsky, M. 1985. *The Butterfly Garden: Turning Your Garden, Window Box, or Backyard into a Beautiful Home for Butterflies.* Boston: Harvard Common Press. 144 pp. ISBN 0-916782-69-7.

Warren, E. J. M. 1988. *The Country Diary Book of Creating a Butterfly Garden.* New York: Holt. 144 pp. ISBN 0-8050-0814-4.

Xerces Society. 1990. *Butterfly Gardening: Creating Summer Magic in Your Garden.* San Francisco: Sierra Club. 192 pp. ISBN 0-87156-615-X.

## Butterfly Gardening Brochures

Allyn Museum of Entomology. 1989. Butterfly gardening. Sarasota, Fla. 3 pp.

Hannahs, E. 1987. Butterfly gardening. Florida Game and Fresh Water Fish Commission, Nongame Wildlife Section, Tallahassee, Fla. 2 pp.

Huegel, C. N.d. Butterfly gardening in central Florida. Publication SS-WIS-903, Pinellas County Cooperative Extension Service, Largo, Fla. 4 pp.

Lenberger, S. 1987. Butterfly gardening in Broward County. Broward County Parks and Recreation Division, Fort Lauderdale, Fla. 2 pp.

Schaefer, J., C. N. Huegel, F. J. Mazzotti. N.d. Butterfly gardening in Florida. Publication SS-WIS-22, Pinellas County Cooperative Extension Service, Largo, Fla. 14 pp.

## Butterfly Identification Guides

Castner, J. L. 1994. Florida butterflies sheet 2. University of Florida, Institute of Food and Agricultural Sciences Insect Identification Sheet SP 151. 2 pp.

Castner, J. L., F. A. Johnson, and D. E. Short. 1992. University of Florida, Institute of Food and Agricultural Sciences Insect Identification Sheet SP 108. 2 pp.

Emmel, T. C. 1997. *Florida's Fabulous Butterflies.* Tampa: World Publications. 96 pp. ISBN 0-911977-15-5.

Gerberg, E. J., and R. H. Arnett, Jr. 1989. *Florida Butterflies.* Baltimore: Natural Science Publications. 90 pp. ISBN 0-89140-031-1.

Harris, L., Jr. 1972. *Butterflies of Georgia.* Norman: University of Oklahoma Press. 326 pp. ISBN 0-8061-0965-3.

Kimball, C. P. 1965. *The Lepidoptera of Florida: An Annotated Checklist.* Gainesville: Florida Department of Agriculture, Division of Plant Industry. 363 pp.

Minno, M. C., and T. C. Emmel. 1993. *Butterflies of the Florida Keys.* Gainesville: Scientific Publishers. 168 pp. ISBN 0-945417-88-8.

Mitchell, R. T., and H. S. Zim. 1964. *Butterflies and Moths: A Guide to the More Common American Species.* New York: Golden Press. 160 pp. ISBN 0-3072-4052-5.

Opler, P. A., and G. O. Krizek. 1984. *Butterflies East of the Great Plains: An Illustrated Natural History.* Baltimore: Johns Hopkins University Press. 294 pp. ISBN 0-8018-2938-0.

Opler, P. A., and V. Malikul. 1992. *A Field Guide to Eastern Butterflies.* Boston: Houghton Mifflin. 396 pp. ISBN 0-395-63279-X.

Pyle, R. M. 1984. *The Audubon Society Handbook for Butterfly Watchers.* New York: Scribners. 274 pp. ISBN 0-684-18151-7.

Scott, J. A. 1986. *The Butterflies of North America.* Stanford: Stanford University Press. 583 pp. ISBN 0-8047-1205-0.

Stiling, P. D. 1989. *Florida's Butterflies and Other Insects.* Sarasota: Pineapple Press. 95 pp. ISBN 0-910923-54-X.

## Butterfly Videos

*Audubon Society's Butterflies for Beginners.*
Audubon Society's Butterfly Gardening.
MasterVision
969 Park Avenue
New York City, NY 10028

## Plant Identification Guides

Bell, C. R., and B. J. Taylor. 1982. *Florida Wild Flowers and Roadside Plants.* Chapel Hill: Laurel Hill Press. 308 pp. ISBN 0-9608688-0-1.

Burch, D., D. B. Ward, and D. W. Hall. 1988. *Checklist of the Woody Cultivated Plants of Florida.* Gainesville: Florida Cooperative Extension Service, Institute of Food and Agricultural Sciences, University of Florida. 80 pp.

Clewell, A. F. 1985. *Guide to the Vascular Plants of the Florida Panhandle.* Gainesville: University Presses of Florida. 605 pp. ISBN 0-8130-0779-8.

Hall, D. W. 1993. *Illustrated Plants of Florida and the Coastal Plain.* Gainesville: Maupin House. 431 pp. ISBN 0-929895-40-1.

Miller, J. F., A. D. Worsham, L. L. McCormick, D. E. Davis, R. Cofer, and J. A. Smith. N.d. *Weeds of the Southern United States.* U.S. Department of Agriculture. 45 pp.

Murphy, T. R., D. L. Colvin, R. Dickens, J. W. Everest, D. Hall, and L. B. McCarty. N.d. *Weeds of Southern Turfgrasses.* Gainesville: Florida Cooperative Extension Service, Institute of Food and Agricultural Sciences, University of Florida. 208 pp.

Nelsen, G. 1994. *The Trees of Florida: A Reference and Field Guide.* Sarasota: Pineapple Press. 338 pp. ISBN 1-56164-055-7.

———. 1996. *The Shrubs and Woody Vines of Florida: A Reference and Field Guide.* Sarasota: Pineapple Press. 391 pp. ISBN 1-56164-110-3.

Orsenigo, J. R., D. S. Burgis, W. L. Currey, D. W. Hall, W. T. Scudder, T. J. Stelter, and D. B. Ward. 1977. *Florida Weeds,*

*Part II: A Supplement to Weeds of the Southern United States.* Gainesville: Florida Cooperative Extension Service, Institute of Food and Agricultural Sciences, University of Florida. 19 pp.

Scurlock, J. P. 1987. *Native Trees and Shrubs of the Florida Keys: A Field Guide.* Bethel Park, Penn.: Laurel Press. 220 pp. ISBN 0-9619155-2-8.

Taylor, W. K. 1992. *The Guide to Florida Wildflowers.* Dallas: Taylor Publishing Co. 320 pp. ISBN 0-87833-747-4.

———. 1998. *Florida Wildflowers in Their Natural Communities.* Gainesville: University Press of Florida. 384 pp. ISBN 0-8130-1616-9.

Wunderlin, R. P. 1982. *Guide to the Vascular Plants of Central Florida.* Gainesville: University Presses of Florida. 472 pp. ISBN 0-8130-0748-8.

———. 1998. *Guide to the Vascular Plants of Florida.* Gainesville: University Press of Florida. 806 pp. ISBN 0-8130-1556-1.

## Landscaping Guides

Association of Florida Native Nurseries. 1991. *Xeric Landscaping with Florida Native Plants.* San Antonio, Fla. 67 pp.

Beriault, J. G. 1990. *Planning and Planting a Native Plant Yard.* Third edition. Spring Hill: Florida Native Plant Society. 20 pp.

Betrock Information Systems, Inc. *Plant Finder: Wholesale Guide to Foliage and Ornamental Plants.* 7770 Davie Road Ext., Hollywood, Fla., 33024.

Black, R. J., and K. C. Ruppert. 1995. *Your Florida Landscape: A Complete Guide to Planting and Maintenance.* Gainesville: University of Florida, Institute of Food and Agricultural Sciences, Publication SP 135. 234 pp.

Broschat, T. K., and A. W. Meerow. 1991. *Betrock's Reference Guide to Florida Landscape Plants.* Hollywood, Fla.: Betrock Information Systems. 428 pp. ISBN 0-9629761-0-5.

Bush, C. S., and J. F. Morton. 1978. *Native Trees and Plants for Florida Landscaping.* Tallahassee: Florida Department of Agriculture and Consumer Services. 144 pp.

Cerulean, S., C. Botha, and D. Legare. 1986. *Planting a Refuge for Wildlife: How to Create a Backyard Habitat for Florida's Birds and Beasts.* Tallahassee: Florida Game and Fresh Water Fish Commission, Nongame Wildlife Program. 33 pp.

DeFreitas, S. 1987. *Complete Guide to Florida Gardening.* Revised edition. Dallas: Taylor Publishing Co. 352 pp. ISBN 0-87833-572-2.

Florida Department of Agriculture and Consumer Services. 1979. *Urban Trees for Florida.* Tallahassee: Division of Forestry. 92 pp.

———. N.d. *Florida Aquatic Plant Locator.* Tallahassee: Aquaculture Program.

Huegel, C. 1995. *Florida Plants for Wildlife.* Orlando: Florida Native Plant Society. 118 pp.

————. N.d. Native plants that attract wildlife: Central Florida. Publication SS-WIS-09, Pinellas County Cooperative Extension Service, Largo, Fla. 8 pp.

MacCubbin, T., and G. B. Tasker. 1997. *Florida Gardener's Guide: The What, When, How, and Why of Gardening in Florida.* Franklin, Tenn.: Cool Springs Press. 464 pp. ISBN 1-888608-31-5.

Maxwell, L. S., and B. M. Maxwell. 1960. *Florida Lawns and Gardens.* Tampa: Lewis S. Maxwell. 120 pp.

————. 1961. *Florida Plant Selector: A Guide to Choice and Use of Over 100 Landscape Plants.* Tampa: Lewis S. Maxwell. 114 pp.

McCarty, L. B., R. J. Black, and K. C. Ruppert, eds. 1990. *Florida Lawn Handbook: Selection, Establishment, and Maintenance of Florida Lawngrasses.* Gainesville: University of Florida, Institute of Food and Agricultural Sciences, Publication SP 45. 208 pp.

Morton, J. F. 1981. *500 Plants of South Florida.* Second edition. Coral Gables: Fairchild Tropical Garden.

————. 1990. *Trees, Shrubs, and Flowers for Florida Landscaping: Native and Exotic.* Tallahassee: Florida Department of Agriculture and Consumer Services. 232 pp.

Schaefer, J., and G. Tanner. 1998. *Landscaping for Florida's Wildlife: Re-creating Native Ecosystems in Your Yard.* Gainesville: University Press of Florida, in cooperation with the University of Florida, Institute of Food and Agricultural Sciences. 92 pp. ISBN 0-8130-1571-5.

Smith, H., M. Hoppe, A. Garner, T. Floyd, and J. Stevely. 1994. *Florida Yards and Neighborhoods: The Bay's First Line of Defense.* Gainesville: University of Florida, Institute of Food and Agricultural Sciences, Bulletin 295. 56 pp.

Stein, Sara. 1977. *Planting Noah's Garden: Further Adventures in Backyard Ecology.* Boston: Houghton Mifflin. 448 pp. ISBN 0-395-70960-1.

Stresau, F. B. 1986. *Florida, My Eden: Exotic and Native Plants for Use in Tropic and Subtropic Landscape.* Port Salerno, Fla.: Florida Classics Library. 299 pp. ISBN 0-912451-19-X.

Vanderplank, John. 1991. *Passion Flowers and Passion Fruit.* Cambridge, Mass.: MIT Press. 176 pp. ISBN 0-262-22043-1.

Watkins, J. V., and T. J. Sheehan. 1975. *Florida Landscape Plants: Native and Exotic.* Revised Edition. Gainesville: University Presses of Florida. 420 pp. ISBN 0-8130-0861-1.

Watkins, J. V., and H. S. Wolfe. 1986. *Your Florida Garden.* Fifth edition. Gainesville: University Presses of Florida. 356 pp. ISBN 0-8130-0862-X.

Workman, R. 1980. *Growing Native: Native Plants for Landscape Use in Coastal South Florida.* Sanibel, Fla.: Sanibel-Captiva Conservation Foundation. 137 pp.

# References

Crosswhite, F. S., and C. D. Crosswhite. 1985. The southwestern pipevine (*Aristolochia watsonii*) in relation to snakeroot oil, swallowtail butterflies, and ceratopogonid flies. *Desert Plants* 6(4):203–7.

Feinsinger, P., and M. Minno. 1990. *Handbook to Schoolyard Plants and Animals of North Central Florida.* Tallahassee: Nongame Wildlife Program, Florida Game and Fresh Water Fish Commission. iv + 128 pp.

Hammer, R. L. 1995. The coontie and the Atala Hairstreak: The story of two historically abundant Florida natives. *Palmetto* 15(4):3–5.

———. 1996. New food plants for *Eumaeus atala* in Florida. *News of the Lepidopterists' Society* 38(1):10.

Jenkins, V. S. 1994. *The Lawn: A History of an American Obsession.* Washington, D.C.: Smithsonian Institution Press. 246 pp. ISBN 1-56098-406-6.

Lippincott, C. 1996. Current estimates of cultivated, native, naturalized, and weedy plant species in Florida. *Resource Management Notes* 8(2):40–41.

Miller, J. Y. 1992. *The Common Names of North American Butterflies.* Washington, D.C.: Smithsonian Institution Press. 177 pp. ISBN 1-56098-122-9.

Morris, J., and C. Herzog. 1995. Butterfly gardening for education, recreation, and therapy. *Proceedings of the Florida State Horticulture Society* 108:391–93.

Myers, R. L., and J. J. Ewel, eds. 1990. *Ecosystems of Florida.* Gainesville: University Presses of Florida. 765 pp. ISBN 0-8139-1022-5.

# *Index*